MW00989334

The Santillana Codes

The Santillana Codes

The Civil Codes of Tunisia, Morocco, and Mauritania

Dan E. Stigall

LEXINGTON BOOKS

Lanham • Boulder • New York • London

Published by Lexington Books
An imprint of The Rowman & Littlefield Publishing Group, Inc.
4501 Forbes Boulevard, Suite 200, Lanham, Maryland 20706
www.rowman.com

Unit A, Whitacre Mews, 26-34 Stannary Street, London SE11 4AB

British Library Cataloguing-in-Publication Information Available

Library of Congress Cataloging-in-Publication Data

ISBN 978-1-4985-6175-4 (cloth : alk. paper)
ISBN 978-1-4985-6176-1 (electronic)

∞™ The paper used in this publication meets the minimum requirements of American
National Standard for Information Sciences—Permanence of Paper for Printed Library
Materials, ANSI/NISO Z39.48-1992.

Printed in the United States of America

For Liz and Madeleine, my muses and fellow adventurers.

And for Jack and Norma, who, on a drive back from New Orleans, unwittingly inspired their son's infatuation with unearthed arcana.

Contents

List of Figures and Tables

FIGURES

TABLES

Acknowledgments

This book would not have been possible without the assistance of many friends and colleagues across the globe and from various disciplines. I must specifically thank Professor Olivier Moréteau of the Louisiana State University (LSU) Paul M. Hebert Law Center and the Center for Civil Law Studies (CCLS), at which I maintain status as a Contributing Fellow. This book began as an article written for the Journal of Civil Law Studies—a publication that exists under the aegis of LSU and the CCLS—and it is only with the permission and encouragement of Professor Moréteau and the CCLS that I endeavored to write it.

I must also expressly thank Professor Chibli Mallat, a learned author, international lawyer, and former candidate for the presidency in Lebanon. As a noted scholar, Professor Mallat has illuminated the field of Middle Eastern legal systems for a new generation of scholars. On a more personal level, he has—for many years—provided me with insight and guidance on complex issues relating to Middle Eastern legal systems and has freely lent his amazing intellect to elevate more than one of my comparative law projects. His willingness to review this manuscript and provide insight greatly enhanced its depth and quality. He made this a better book.

I must also thank many other close friends and colleagues who (either directly or indirectly) contributed to this book, including Ms. Sannou Sana Bhar, a most remarkable Tunisian lawyer and international practitioner; Dr. Sean Foley, Middle Tennessee State University, a Middle East expert and dear friend who generally reads my drafts and makes me look smarter than I am; Professor Haider Ala Hamoudi, University of Pittsburgh School of Law, who enriched this work by providing me insight on Islamic Law—and for sitting with me in New Jersey as we were screamed at by a Congressman; Professor Alain Levasseur, LSU Law, for always imbuing the subject of civil law with such excitement and romance; Professor Christopher Blakesley, UNLV Law, for taking the time to mentor me as a comparativist from the very outset and igniting my interest in Middle Eastern legal systems; Professor Symeon Symeonides, Willamette Law, for always being available for guidance and advice; and to Clark and the crew at Highland Coffees in Baton Rouge, which has always been something of an intellectual laboratory. I must equally thank Professor Ignazio Castellucci, Università di Trento (Italy); Professor Gian Maria Piccinelli, Università di Napoli (Italy); Professor John Randall Trahan, LSU Law (Geaux Tigers); Ms. Emily Carr, Senior Legal Reference Librarian at the Law Library of Congress; Ms. Talesa Bradley and Ms. Maria Walls, Library Technicians at the U.S. Department of Justice Law Library; Mr. Ibrahim Ba, a valuable and noteworthy Mauritanian lawyer; all my colleagues at Juris Diversitas; and the helpful staff at both the Harvard and Stanford Law Libraries.

I must further thank the faculty and students at The Judge Advocate General's Legal Center and School (TJAGLCS), a U.S. Army institution where I have regularly lectured on comparative law and international law for several years. The amazing leadership at that institution—as with every Army unit with which I have served—consistently encouraged my comparative law scholarship. Of equal value has been the intense discussion with the formidable students at TJAGLCS—military officers from across every U.S. armed force as well as from diverse militaries around the globe. Those fascinating discussions helped sharpen the focus of my comparative law work and pushed me to think deeply on the nexus between comparative law and global security. I must similarly thank my leadership at the U.S. Department of Justice, which has given me the opportunity to work with legal cultures across the world for many years and, with benign grace, has endured my scholarly pursuits. And many thanks to Oscar for serving so many years as my loyal research assistant and best friend. I owe all of you a sincere debt of gratitude and multiple cappuccinos.

Any opinion expressed in this book is purely my own. Any error is attributable to my misspent youth.

Works of comparativists and others from diverse systems may reshape our prism, providing a chance to see different refractions, a fuller spectrum of possibilities, producing a deeper appreciation of one's own law and that of other systems. The heightened refraction is magical and, frankly, ought to be extremely helpful in solving legal problems facing students, scholars, judges, and practitioners[.]

—Christopher L. Blakesley,
Law, Language, Crime, and Culture: The Value and Risks of Comparative Law, 49 Crim. L. Bull. 438, 459 (2013).

Introduction

At the close of the nineteenth century, in the small North African country of Tunisia, as newly erected colonial architecture cast its shadow over Carthaginian ruins and the flag of the Ottoman Empire, a small group of jurists gathered to accomplish something extraordinary. Tunisia had recently become a French protectorate and, though the Ottoman Bey was still in office and Tunisia maintained nominal independence, there was no denying the force of French political will. A colonial government with deep reverence for the *Code Napoléon* sought to impose its vision of law in the land of the Qur'an. In this frothing crosscurrent of European and North African cultural forces, learned men convened to create a remarkable legal document—a civil code—which could appease the colonial government as well as the people and local leaders on which it would be imposed. Their effort would last years and would involve French lawyers and judges, Tunisian magistrates and religious scholars, and would be led by a Jewish man of Tunisian origin. His name was David Santillana.

Over a century later, in 2014, beneath the frayed but vibrant red and white flag of an independent Tunisia, a new government was still reeling from the shock of the Jasmine Revolution. The newly formed Tunisian Constituent Assembly had voted on the provisions of its new post-revolution constitution and, in the raucous aftermath of that vote, international media reports—noting that the new constitution contained no express reference to Islamic law—ebulliently declared that Tunisia had rejected Islamic law and embraced secular civil law.[1] Shortly thereafter, on the same day the rhapsodic headlines were printed, the deliberation on the Tunisian constitution was suspended "after a deputy claimed he had received death threats because a colleague had accused him of being an 'enemy of Islam.'"[2] The issue of whether or not the Tunisian constitution would reference Islamic law had, throughout

the preceding year, been the focus of intense and acrimonious debate within
Tunisia and among international actors with an interest in Tunisia's post-
revolution transition to democracy.[3] Therefore, when the new constitution
omitted mention of Islamic law, it was viewed in certain circles as a triumph
of progressive liberalism and, in others, a defeat of Islamic legal principles.[4]

Though debate over the role of Islamic law in a domestic legal system had
long gained international attention, in the context of Tunisia it had focused
almost exclusively on the allure of a new post-revolution constitution, ignor-
ing aspects of Tunisian law that quietly and gracefully persisted outside the
view of the commentariat. Among the many things overlooked was the code
crafted by Santillana and his team of jurists so many years prior, and which
has governed Tunisia's law of obligations and contracts for well over a century. In fact, this code has been so admired that it has been replicated in both
the Kingdom of Morocco and the Islamic Republic of Mauritania. These
codes, referenced collectively in this book as "the Santillana Codes," are the
subject of this book.

A family of civil codes of this nature is a complex object of study—one
that is, to invoke geometric metaphors, both prismatic and kaleidoscopic.
A prism is "a timeless device" while "the turning of a kaleidoscope adds a
dimension of development over time."[5] The subject of this book, similarly,
has some fixed qualities and others which exhibit flux. It is a topic with many
facets or aspects that must be observed in order to appreciate the subject as
a whole: their sources and influences (both ancient and contemporary); their
author and the team of jurists who aided in his pursuit; the countries where
those codes were received and implemented; and the sociopolitical forces that
defined the epochs of their creation. Such subjects are difficult and intrigu-
ing due to a certain darkness in the literature surrounding the law and legal
history of Maghrebian and Sahelian states—a veil of obscurity which has
served to undervalue African, Islamic, and Jewish contributions to global
legal development. This book seeks to dispel this obscurity by illuminating
the work of David Santillana, an influential jurist and lawyer who worked
in North Africa and Europe during the late nineteenth and early twentieth
centuries. This book also seeks to cast light on his innovative approach to
codification which still thrives in the Maghreb and the Sahel.

Despite his importance as a legal figure, Santillana remains among the least
studied civil law innovators. This has been a rather sinful omission as Santillana's work represents a significant legal milestone in the history of civil
law, notably the earliest attempt at a comprehensive fusion of modern civil
law (based on European law) with Islamic law—"*une tentative de conciliation unique en son genre entre droits civils de pays européens et droit civil
musulman.*"[6] The result of his efforts—and that of the jurists who assisted
him—was the creation of a "mixed" civil law system which incorporates

elements of continental civil law, Islamic law, and local custom into a single code.[7] This unique approach to legal codification has since influenced subsequent codifications in North Africa and the Sahel, specifically in Morocco and Mauritania,[8] and still thrives as the product of a nineteenth-century *aggiornamento* of Islamic law that occurred throughout the wider Middle East and North African region.

A discussion of Santillana and his work seems particularly timely due to world events that have drawn the collective gaze of the national security and international affairs establishments to places on the map which are sometimes consigned to the oblivion of secondary concerns, such as the countries of the Maghreb and Sahel. Such places, throughout history, have garnered relatively little attention from the West, scholarly or otherwise. Recent years, however, have witnessed especially dramatic political and social upheaval as the reverberations of the Arab Spring[9] have made countries in the region more prone to "destabilizing ethnic and sectarian rivalries"[10] and "created opportunities for extremist groups to find ungoverned space from which to destabilize the new governments[.]"[11] Extremist groups, benefitting from the years of turmoil in the region, have thrived and metastasized.[12] Developing and fragile states in Africa are especially vulnerable to myriad terrorist groups and transnational criminal organizations that seek to exploit the inability of poorer countries to contain them. Additionally, non-state armed groups operating in the region are increasingly recognized as a source of global—not merely local—insecurity. As a result, international policymakers must consider engagement with the institutions of these countries to address these concerns.

Central to the transition of Arab Spring countries from autocracy to democracy is the question of what law will apply and the sources from which that law is to be derived.[13] Many of the ongoing post-revolution debates have revolved around the role of Islamic law in contemporary society, basic challenges of institution-building, and methods of addressing state fragility in the region. Although the major focus of analysis and debate in this regard is frequently on new constitutions,[14] civil codes in developing countries and fragile states are equally important and frequently function as stable institutions that can provide institutional stability during political changes. A better understanding of the unique civil codes in force in such areas, therefore, can be important for those seeking to understand how durable institutions can be fostered in fragile states. Thus, once relegated to the dusty, umbral reaches of the back shelves, knowledge of the vital legal institutions of developing countries and their institutions is now increasingly important.

The pages that follow, therefore, tell the story of David Santillana and his legacy of codification in Tunisia, Morocco, and Mauritania. The book demonstrates that the advent of Santillana's codal design was an inflection point in the history of comparative law as a discipline—the first synthesis of

Islamic law and modern continental civil law. The code Santillana drafted, together with those codes that replicate its content, represents a separate and unique codal category which stretches across the Maghreb and touches the Sahel. This family of codes is marked by a spirit of eclecticism, innovativeness, pluralism, and syncretism—attributes which are an expression of both a deep-rooted tradition of pluralism in Islamic law and, likewise, values shaped by Santillana's life in Tunisia, his international education, and his experiences as a Sephardic Jew in Ottoman territory. The substance of those codes was also shaped by input from Islamic legal scholars in Tunisia and their efforts to ensure the desideratum of Islamic legal compatibility. Through an analysis of the history, sources, and operation of the Santillana Codes, this book demonstrates how Santillana's model is remarkably well-suited to the task of accommodating a diverse society, parts of which might insist on (or desire) the application of certain Islamic legal norms.[15]

A NOTE ON THE COMPARATIVE ANALYSIS

Santillana's approach to codification was remarkably complex. To succeed at the first major attempt in synthesizing Islamic law with continental civil law to create a modern civil code compatible with both, Santillana had to adopt a multiplex approach to codification in which he sought to distill rules from sometimes amorphous areas of Islamic law, find analogies between Islamic and continental civil law, and give expression to rules that could best accommodate both systems—all without running afoul of the intransgressible principles of Islamic law. This sometimes resulted in concessions that departed from the standard civil law model. In other cases, however, careful analysis reveals that Santillana reached deeply into the wealth of existing civil codes of that era and found a civil law model that permitted the maintenance of the essential Islamic concept within a recognized civil law structure. The result was not a disjointed melange but, rather, a complete fusion of Islamic law and continental civil law—like a body and soul. On occasion, this resulted in the adoption of concepts that were at the avant-garde of civil law during that era and imbued the Tunisian code with legal concepts and structures that European codes would not adopt for decades.

The principal resource to facilitate an understanding of Santillana's approach is the *Avant-Projet du Code Civil et Commercial Tunisien*, which was published in 1899. In this report, Santillana explained the philosophy undergirding his approach to codification and arrayed many of the sources from which the Tunisian code was derived. In his *Avant-Projet*, Santillana cited numerous Islamic legal sources for his codal prototype, including Zein el-dyn Ibn Nadjim al Misry (Ibn Nadjim), a jurist who wrote a treatise on Hanafite legal principles;[16] Abu Bakr Al-Kaffal as-Shashi (El Kaffal), a Shafi'i jurist who was also a renown philosopher and poet;[17] Tassouli, a Moroccan jurist of great acclaim;[18] Ibn 'Abidin and his influential nineteenth-century Hanafite work entitled *Radd al-Muhtar* (sometimes transliterated as *Radd-el-Mohtar*);[19] El Hamaoui, a Hanafite jurist;[20] and Abd Al Baqi Az-Zarqani, a respected Malikite jurist.[21] He also cited to civil codes from across Europe and the Middle East. Among those codes are the French Code Civil and the Italian *Codice Civile* that was enacted in 1865.

A reading of the *Avant-Projet*, however, indicates an emphasis on demonstrating the Islamic bona fides of the many articles proposed rather than a full explication of their various sources. This imbues the *Avant-Projet* with a certain opacity that is only dispelled upon a careful analysis of the text of the Tunisian code and a comparison of that text with other codes in force at that time. In that regard, an 1868 French translation of the Italian *Codice Civile* by Professor J.B. Gandolfi, Secretary to the Italian Consulate in Geneva, has proved a remarkably enlightening point of comparison. Throughout this book, the original French text of the Tunisian code is compared with the French text of that work (and other such codes) to demonstrate similarities in phraseology and linguistic structure as evidence of Santillana's reliance on—and occasional appropriation of—the substance of other codes.

Similarly, throughout this book, references are made to other civil codes to demonstrate the presence or prevalence of certain civil law rules. Frequently, reference is made to the Louisiana Civil Code. While Louisiana is far from Tunisia, this North American code is important as a paragon of civil law during the time Santillana was drafting the Tunisian code. This is because, in contrast to the French code which was somewhat static in terms of substance in the latter part of the nineteenth century, the Louisiana code had gone several dramatic revisions—promulgated first in 1808 as a Digest of the Civil Laws now in Force in the Territory of Orleans[22]; then revised as the Louisiana Civil Code of 1825 with redactors drawing heavily from French doctrine and jurisprudence[23]; and then again in 1875. It has been described by civil law jurist A.N. Yiannopoulos as "perhaps, the most Romanist civil code ever enacted anywhere."[24] Its cultural and geographic distance from Tunisia notwithstanding, it was an influential legal work during the nineteenth century and serves as a worthy focus of comparison.

Through an analysis of these and other codes in force at the end of the nineteenth century, one may peer beyond what is known from the *Avant-Projet*, understand Santillana's approach to codification, and divine the major sources of the codes that are derived from his work. The chapters that follow will analyze the way Santillana synthesized Islamic law and continental civil law, observing key features of both systems and demonstrating the parallels that exist in both Islamic and continental civil law—analogues that Santillana honed and shaped to complete his codification. To conduct such an analysis effectively, the first few chapters of this book are devoted to more general topics that provide needed context. Thereafter, the book delves more deeply into substantive law and, finally, concludes by reviewing what can be gleaned from a comparative analysis of Santillana's work and its utility in the contemporary world order.

A NOTE ON THE CONCEPT OF "THE SANTILLANA CODES"

This book is the first to consider the Tunisian, Moroccan, and Mauritanian codes together as a unique class of civil code—and the first to refer to them as "the Santillana Codes," a designation that is used in the succeeding chapters to reference all three of these codes collectively. As this book will detail, David Santillana did not write all of these codes alone. In fact, he was only involved in the creation of the Tunisian prototype on which the others are based. Likewise, Santillana was not the sole author of the Tunisian code, though he was the dominant intellectual force responsible for its creation. In addition, the Santillana Codes are not facsimiles of one another. As the succeeding chapters will demonstrate more fully, the countries of Morocco and Mauritania adopted codes based on the Tunisian prototype, but altered the model to suit the needs and demands of their own countries. Otherwise stated, each code is different in terms of authorship, circumstances, and substance. Each successive code lost something in its substance from the original and changed its provisions to fit the new legal landscape into which it was imported. For instance, Morocco adopted a truncated version of the Tunisian code and, thereafter, Mauritania adopted a modified version of the Moroccan variant. The Mauritanian code, therefore, resembles the Moroccan code more closely than its Tunisian progenitor—and its provisions were further modified to make certain Islamic legal prohibitions applicable as a general matter. Nonetheless, for each code the basic framework and style of the Santillana approach to codification remains intact: the same substantive rules (drawn from a plurality of legal sources) governing obligations in general; the same rules for vices of consent, including Santillana's innovative approach to error; the same hybrid concept of lesion; the same basic substance for the nominate contracts of sale, exchange, deposit, and mandate; etc. Their differences notwithstanding, the major substance of all three codes are based on the paradigm created by Santillana and his fellow scholars—and it is proper to refer to this family of codes collectively as the Santillana Codes.

CHAPTER OVERVIEW

Chapter 1 introduces the concepts of civil law and civil codes and provides basic conceptual background—including the historical context for continental civil law, tracing its history from ancient Rome to nineteenth-century France. The chapter details the key features of a civil law system, explains the concept of a civil code, and discusses the various "families" of civil codes that exist in civil law jurisdictions around the globe.

Chapter 2 provides basic background on the concept of Islamic law, its history, its sources, and its methodology. The chapter explores the way in which Islamic law facilitates legal pluralism, permitting minority religious groups to be governed—to an extent—by their own laws and institutions. Finally, the chapter briefly addresses the way in which Islamic law regulates contracts.

Chapter 3 provides historical context for the creation of the Santillana Codes, including a discussion of each country's history, culture, and religion. The chapter includes a discussion of each country's history, culture, and religion. It also gives an introduction to David Santillana, the author of the Tunisian code that inspired the other codes that are the subject of this book. The chapter also briefly details the history of the Jewish community in which Santillana lived, and how David Santillana's family came to Tunisia. It then discusses Santillana's education and early life and how Santillana grew to become a comparative law scholar, a practitioner, and an expert in Islamic law. Finally, the chapter explains how each of the codes developed and entered into force.

Chapter 4 discusses the sources of law in the Santillana Codes. It provides background on the sources of law in civil law systems generally and demonstrates that Santillana's work was extremely innovative in its manner of approaching the sources of law, giving a defined role to custom in the legal hierarchy, recognizing that legal solutions were to be sometimes found beyond the codal text, and providing guidance to judges in that regard. The chapter also details the provisions regarding sources of law in each of the Santillana Codes and discusses the role of Islamic law as a subsidiary source of law.

Chapter 5 provides an overview of the law of obligations (contracts) in the Santillana Codes. The chapter reviews the law's substance and highlights the areas in which Santillana's work, at the time of his codification, was at the cutting edge of civil law theory. The chapter also highlights the uniquely pluralistic approach adopted in the Tunisian code—an approach which, under a unified legal framework, provides a degree of individuation to accommodate religious prohibitions that exist for Muslim citizens.

Chapter 6 details various nominate contracts in the Santillana Codes, such as the contracts of sale, exchange, deposit and sequestration, and mandate.

The chapter reviews how the Santillana Codes regulate these specific nominate contracts. It also discusses how these provisions align with civil law, Islamic law, and the uniquely pluralistic approach woven into the codes.

Chapter 7 is the conclusion and provides final thoughts on Santillana's work and its importance in the aftermath of the Arab Spring. The concluding chapter reviews notable aspects of the Santillana Codes, accentuating how Islamic law was fused with continental civil law—and how that synthesis resulted in codes that were durable, effective, and progressive. The chapter also highlights the importance of civil codes to post-conflict stability and reconstruction and underscores their innate stability-promoting qualities that are of such critical importance in the contemporary Maghreb and Sahel.

NOTES

1. See *Tunisia Opts for Civil, not Sharia Law as Assembly Votes on New Constitution,* Reuters (Jan. 5, 2014), http://rt.com/news/tunisia-rejects-islam-law-196/. ("Tunisia's Islamist-dominated constituent assembly has compromised in rejecting Islam as the main source of law as it voted on a new constitution for the country that spawned the Arab spring.")

2. *Id.*

3. Aziz El Yaakoubi, *Death Threats Disrupt Tunisia Constitution Debate*, Reuters (Jan. 5, 2014). ("Since the 2011 uprising, tensions over the role of Islam in Tunisia and the assassination of two secular politicians by hardline Islamist militants last year have widened divisions between Islamists and secular parties.")

4. *Id.*

5. *See* CHRISTOPH MENKE, THE SOVEREIGNTY OF ART 117 (1999).

6. *See* FAOUZI BELKNANI, *Code des Obligations et des Contrats et la Codification*, in LIVRE DU CENTENAIRE DU CODE DES OBLIGATIONS ET DES CONTRATS 1906–2006 17 (2006).

7. There are numerous schools of Islamic law (or *madhabs*). Although the Maliki madhab prevails in Tunisia (*see* HALIM RANE, ISLAM AND CONTEMPORARY CIVILISATION: EVOLVING IDEAS, TRANSFORMING RELATIONS 83 [2010]), the Hanafi madhab is also significant. Other minority madhabs, such as the Ibadi madhab, can also be found in Tunisia. *See, generally,* J.H. van Riel, *The Ibāḍī Traders of Bilād al-Sūdān* (2012) (unpublished M.A. thesis, The American University in Cairo, School of Humanities and Social Sciences).

8. *See id.*

9. *See* MARC LYNCH, THE ARAB UPRISING: THE UNFINISHED REVOLUTIONS OF THE NEW MIDDLE EAST 7 (2012) ("The uprisings that have profoundly shaped the Middle East began in a remote outpost of southern Tunisia on December 17, 2010, with the self-immolation of an unknown young man named Mohammed Bouazizi in protest against abusive and corrupt police."). *See also* Ayodeji K. Perrin, *Introduction to the Special Issue on the Arab Spring*, 34 U. PA. J. INT'L L. i, i–iv (2013). ("What

quickly became known as the 'Arab Spring' is a series of protest movements, reform movements, and revolutions.") *But see* CHIBLI MALLAT, PHILOSOPHY OF NONVIOLENCE: REVOLUTION, CONSTITUTIONALISM, AND JUSTICE BEYOND THE MIDDLE EAST 3 (2015). (Disfavoring the label "Arab Spring" as being "as inchoate as it is poetical," and preferring the label of "the Middle East nonviolent revolution.")

10. *U.S. Intelligence: Arab Spring Generated Threats* (Woodrow Wilson ctr., Mar. 15, 2013), http://www.wilsoncenter.org/islamists/article/us-intelligence-arab-spring-generated-threats.

11. *Id.*

12. *See The Islamic State of Iraq and Greater Syria: Two Arab Countries Fall Apart*, Economist (June 14, 2014) (hereinafter *Two Arab Countries Fall Apart*), http://www.economist.com/news/middle-east-and-africa/21604230-extreme-islamist-group-seeks-create-caliphate-and-spread-jihad-across

13. *See* Asma Ghribi, *Role of Islamic Law in Tunisian Constitution Provokes Debate, Tunisialive* (Mar. 4, 2017, 3:42 PM), www.tunisia-live.net/2012/03/22/role-of-islamic-law-in-tunisian-constitution-provokes-debate/#sthash.mgLeAjgP.dpuf

14. *See* El Yaakoubi, *supra* note 3.

15. *See* Haider Ala Hamoudi, *The Death of Islamic Law*, 38 Ga. J. Int'l Comp. L. 293, 295 (2009–2010). ("That the Muslim world is replete with political institutions and leaders [described herein, in their multitudinous varieties and approaches, as 'Islamist'] who seek a greater role than this for the shari'a in the affairs of the state is obvious to anyone even faintly familiar with the region.")

16. *See* JEAN JOSEPH LÉANDRE BARGÈS, COMPLEMENT DE L'HISTOIRE DES BENI-ZEIYAN: ROIS DE TLEMCEN 331, n. 5 (1887).

17. ABŪ AL-ʿABBĀS AḤMAD ET AL., IBN KHALLIKAN'S BIOGRAPHICAL DICTIONARY 605 (1843).

18. A. SABATERY, ÉLÉMENTS DE DROIT MUSULMAN, COMPRENANT L'EXPOSÉ DE L'ORGANISATION DE LA JUSTICE DANS LE PACHALIK D'ALGER AVANT 1830, LES PRINCIPES DE DROIT CONTENUS DANS LE KORAN, CLASSÉS DANS L'ORDRE DU CODE NAPOLÉON, LA JURISPRUDENCE EN DROIT MUSULMAN DU TRIBUNAL SUPÉRIEUR ET DE LA COUR IMPÉRIALE D'ALGER DEPUIS LEUR CRÉATION 24 (1866).

19. FARHAD DAFTARY, INTELLECTUAL TRADITIONS IN ISLAM 82 (2001).

20. 22 ROBERT ESTOUBLON, REVUE ALGÉRIENNE, TUNISIENNE ET MAROCAINE DE LÉGISLATION ET DE JURISPRUDENCE 16 (1907).

21. *See Mission scientifique du Maroc,* 13 REV. MONDE MUSULMAN 227 (1974).

22. *See, generally,* John T. Hood, Jr., *The History and Development of the Louisiana Civil Code*, 19 LA. L. REV. (1958), http://digitalcommons.law.lsu.edu/lalrev/vol19/iss1/14

23. A.N. Yiannopoulos, *The Civil Codes of Louisiana*, 1 CIV. L. COMMENT. 1, 1, 15 (2008), http://www.civil-law.org/v01i01-Yiannopoulos.pdf.

24. *Id.* at 17.

Chapter 1

Civil Law and Civil Codes

This book is, in essence, about a certain family of civil codes. But what do we mean when we talk about *civil codes*? What does it mean to refer to *civil law*? What makes this system of law different? Such questions must necessarily be addressed at the outset this work. This initial chapter, therefore, provides basic background on the concept of continental civil law and civil codes. It briefly describes the historical context for continental civil law, tracing its history from ancient Rome to nineteenth-century France. The chapter also explains the concept of a civil code and provides an explanation of the various "families" of civil codes in force across in various countries (and in various cultures) around the globe.

CIVIL LAW AND ITS HISTORICAL CONTEXT

As a general rule, all stories must start in the beginning. The story of civil codes, to the extent such an arcane and highly specific legal topic can constitute a story, is an ancient one. It is the story of a system of laws that has germinated since the time of the Roman Empire[2] and which lives on luminously in countries across the globe today. As Judge John Minor Wisdom, a famed civil law jurist in Louisiana (a North American civil law enclave) once said, "When the Angles and Saxons were howling savages, painted blue and eking out an existence in the fens of England, we had a civilized system of law based on the Code Justinian. And [today] ... I am indeed gratified that we have a loyal civilian learned in the civil law ... to support the position that the Angles and the Saxons would still be in the fens of England, but for the benefits they have derived from exposure to the civil law."[3] That civil law

1

system referenced by Judge Wisdom prevails today across Europe, Africa, Asia, South America, Central America, North America, and the Middle East.

Civil law, therefore, as that term is used in this book, refers to a genre of highly systematized and structured legal systems (also called continental, Romanist, or Romano-Germanic legal systems) which are, based on legal concepts, categories, and rules, derived from Roman law.[4] Such systems generally are distinguished from other legal systems, such as "common law" systems, by their unique history; a tradition of deeply rooted attitudes about the role of law in society and the polity; and a belief in the proper organization of a legal system.[5] For instance, most jurisdictions of this sort undertake codifications of civil law that rely on declarations of broad, general principles.[6] The jurists who are a part of that civil law tradition are called *civilians*.

The Roman law lineage stressed in the quote above from Judge Wisdom is essential to the identity of continental civil law and, in fact, it is difficult to find descriptions of civil law that are not entwined with references to its history. One commentator, for instance, has defined the civil law tradition as:

> that legal tradition which has its origin in Roman law, as codified in the Corpus Juris Civilis of Justinian, and as subsequently developed in Continental Europe and around the world. Civil law eventually divided into two streams: the codified Roman law (as seen in the French Civil Code of 1804 and its progeny and imitators-Continental Europe, Quebec and Louisiana being examples); and uncodified Roman law (as seen in Scotland and South Africa).[7]

Looking back to those Roman origins, in roughly 462 BC, the patricians in Rome consented to the creation of a compilation of customary law into what would eventually become twelve panels or "tables."[8] This salient moment in legal history marked the point at which legislation became a source of law for the citizens of Rome.[9] It also marked the beginning of centuries of Roman legal development and accomplishment. As with all things, however, the Western Empire began to decline and, in the fifth century, it began to fall to Germanic tribes in the north.[10] As the Western Empire declined, however, the Eastern Empire saw a renaissance of legal development under the Emperor Justinian. "A year after he had become Emperor in 527, Justinian ordered that a Codex containing the still relevant constitutions of his predecessors be put together."[11] Within a year, this effort produced the *Codex Jutinianus*.[12] Justinian would then order a compilation of all the writings of the classic jurists of Rome.[13] The result of this effort would be known as the Digest or Encyclopedia.[14]

After the fall of the Rome, Justinian's work was largely forgotten until, in the eleventh century, Roman law experienced a revival that began at the University of Bologna, Italy. During that efflorescent era, the study of Roman law spread throughout Europe and surviving manuscript copies of Justinian's compilation were rediscovered, studied, and reproduced.[15] "These new editions of the compilation, which were given the name *Corpus Juris Civilis* ('body of civil law'), became the foundational source for Roman law in the Western tradition."[16] Two groups particularly prominent scholars which studied Roman law during that era, the Glossators and the Commentators, "produced an immense literature, which itself became the object of study and discussion and came to carry great authority."[17] Roman law, therefore, became the *jus commune* in Europe—"a common legal language, and a common method of teaching and scholarship."[18]

In addition, as Rome declined and Germanic tribes took control, Roman law continued to be used by those Germanic tribes in their administration of conquered territory.[19] For instance, both the Edict of Theodoric and the code complied by King Aleric II of the Visigoths were based on Roman law and were intended to permit conquered Roman subjects to continue to live under the laws they had known.[20] Thus, with the fall of Rome, Roman authority ended, but the normative force of Roman law—to a degree—persisted.

Centuries after the rule of the Emperor Justinian, another prominent leader would bring about a similarly dramatic legal advancement. In early modern France, the proliferation of different *coutumes* (customs) served to create legal uncertainty for common citizens and, for kings attempting to consolidate their power, divisions that inhibited the goals of political centralization.[21] Civil law in France, at that time, was divided into the country of written law in the north (*pays de coutume*) and the country of written law in the south (*pays de droit écrit*).[22] The disjointed nature of French law during that period inspired Voltaire's famous remark: "Is it not an absurd and terrible thing that what is true in one village is false in another? What kind of barbarism is it that citizens must live under different laws? . . . When you travel in this kingdom you change legal systems as often as you change horses."[23]

Disunity in law, like fractionalization of any sort, can pose a threat to a sovereign seeking to project political power throughout a unified territory. It is no wonder, therefore, that the unification of French law had been a concern of the French Monarchy long before Napoleon's ascent to power.[24] It was, however, Napoleon who would, in 1800, finally accomplish the unification of French civil law—and in a way that would leave his mark on legal orders across the globe for centuries to come.

It is then that a single man stood, ambitious and conquering, against the destructive forces of the dying Revolution, to revive the spirit and the glow of the first days. Proclaiming the Constitution of the Consulate, on the 15th day of December, 1799, the First Consul told the Nation: "the Constitution is based on the sacred rights of property, equality and liberty ... . Citizens, the Revolution is stabilized according to the principles that started it. It is finished." Napoleon's genius was that he interpreted the feeling of the greatest majority of the French people and his glory was that, having made a promise, he fulfilled it completely.[25]

To accomplish this momentous task, Napoleon selected four jurists to create a civil code for France:[26] Tronchet, Maleville, Bigot de Prémeneu, and Portalis.[27] Drawing on Roman law, canon law, customary law, and other sources of French law (such as the Law of the Revolution), these jurists compiled what would eventually become the *Code Civil des Français* or, as it would later be called, the *Code Napoléon*.[28] This code became "not only the heart of the private law in France but also the great model for the codes of private law of the whole Romanistic legal family."[29]

It merits highlighting the fact that the drafters of the French civil code were not making new laws, but were instead working in a manner, "imbued with the spirit of the old law," to fuse *droit écrit* and the *coutumes* into a single text that could be the unified law of all of France. In that regard, civil law codification has always been, to a degree, an effort at both unification and amalgamation—an exercise in synthesizing multiple legal orders into a single, unifying document.[30] It is perhaps for this reason that continental civil law has always demonstrated a unique capacity to be exported and assimilated into other legal milieus. Since the advent of the modern civil code, civil law jurists (and comparativists) in various places throughout the world have acted as "synthesists," working to create a civil code based on the French model but retaining a sufficient degree of organic legal substance so as to be faithful to the legal traditions of the jurisdiction. These "synthesists" include the Haitian-born Louisiana jurist, Louis Casimir Elisabeth Moreau-Lislet, who, as early as 1806, along with another jurist named James Brown, was charged with creating a civil code for what was then called "the Territory of Orleans."[31] As Professor Alain Levasseur demonstrates in his illuminative book on the topic, Moreau-Lislet was given the task of creating a civil code based on the laws in force in Louisiana at that time, the substance of which was Spanish in origin. It is all the more remarkable as this Louisiana jurist was charged with this duty almost contemporaneously with the promulgation of the *Code Napoléon*.[32] To accomplish this task, Moreau-Lislet was perhaps the first civil law jurist to synthesize the French civil code with non-French law (the Spanish law that was at that time in force). In this effort, "[a]nterior laws were repealed, so far only as they were contrary to or irreconcilable with any of the provisions of the new."[33] As discussed more fully in the pages that follow, such a method is akin to the method used in crafting Tunisian civil law.

It is also important to note the degree to which Roman law served as a vital source and influence for the jurists drafting the *Code Napoléon*. Much of the organic French law synthesized during the codification process was suffused with Roman law (due to its continuing influence among learned jurists and its influence on customary law). In addition, the drafters of the primordial French code drew directly from Justinian's Digest. On that score, commentators have noted that Napoleon actually had some knowledge of Roman law and Justinian's Digest and frequently presided over the commission, which created the code. During those sessions, Napoleon was said to have engaged in discussions regarding Justinian's Digest, impressing the jurists enough that one was said to have asked, "Where did the First Consul get his knowledge of Roman Law?"[34] As a result, principles of Roman law were incorporated into the *Code Napoléon* such as the basic idea of a legal obligation, the elements of a valid contract, the rules governing the formation and dissolution of contracts, etc. The provisions in which these Roman law ideas were crystallized were, thereafter, passed on to subsequent civil codes based on the French model. Roman law, transmuted into the French code, was given global reach and lasting vitality.

CIVIL CODES

As noted above, one of the chief characteristics of a civil law jurisdiction is the existence of a civil code. Augustìn Parise has noted, "[c]odification, as understood today, finds its origins in Europe, where it experienced a significant development during the eighteenth and nineteenth centuries."[35] Founded on ideas and concepts from Roman law, but inspired by the philosophy of the Enlightenment, the codification movement "advocated for a new presentation and form of laws which would replace existing provisions, while grouping different areas in an organic, systematic, clear, accurate, and complete way."[36] This meant compiling existing civil law into a single text that unified the law and made it both accessible and comprehensible.

Civil law codification, however, is to be distinguished from the compilations of laws in other jurisdictions that are casually referred to as codes, such as tax codes, commercial codes, criminal codes, and the California Civil Code. These are not codes in the sense civil law jurists use the term. The use of the term code to civilian jurists conveys something specific: it is a tradition, a particular way of thinking about the law and codification.

What is meant by the term "code" ... is to designate an analytical and logical statement of general principles of the law to be applied by deduction to specific cases and extended by analogy to cases where the aphorism *au-delà du Code*

Civil, mais par le Code Civil (beyond the civil code but by the civil code) can be applied.[37]

Merryman, moreover, reminds us that civil codes and their styles may differ. Beneath the rubrics of "civil law system" and "civil code," there exists some level of diversity.[38] The French civil law tradition has been the most influential and most replicated civil law model—but it is not the only model. Indeed, commentators have distinguished various "families" or types of civil law systems, such as the French (or Romanistic), German,[39] Scandinavian,[40] and a "socialist-transition legal family, which is based on the legal tradition that emerged from the breakup of the Soviet Union."[41]

Each of these systems, of course, has its own unique history, influences, and characteristics. For example, with regard to the German system—one largely considered to be among the most influential—its seminal moment was the adoption of the German Civil Code in 1900. Much like its French counterpart, the German legal tradition is based on Roman civil law and was subsequently exported to other countries.[42] Unlike the French civil code, however, the German code also incorporated customary German law into its provisions. Moreover, the French code, consistent with its revolutionary ethos, was authored to be usable by the laity, while the German civil code "was thought of as a tool to be used primarily by professionals of the law."[43] Chibli Mallat has commented on the stylistic dissimilarities of the French and German codes, stating, "In contrast to the German [civil code], one finds in the French Civil Code lapidary formulas which tend to sacrifice legal precision to the profit of a literary, mnemonic style."[44] Such differences between French and German civil codes stem from the fact that "[t]he former is based on the principles of rationalism and ius-naturalism, whereas the latter is scientific, technical, and heavily influenced by the Pandectist system."[45]

By contrast, the Scandinavian legal tradition, which developed relatively independently in the seventeenth and eighteenth centuries, is less closely linked with Roman civil law and has not spread widely throughout the world. This tradition is largely isolated to the Nordic countries of Denmark, Norway, Finland, and Sweden and is notable for its separate evolution which was based on Germanic—rather than Roman—legal ideals.[46] Although robust codification was never undertaken in these countries, the Scandinavian legal tradition does find articulation in "Nordic legal cooperation" which has produced documents such as the "Law of contracts and other legal transactions in the law of property and obligations," which came into force across various countries in the region between 1915 and 1929.[47]

In addition, civil law scholars have recently begun focusing on hybrid civil law systems that incorporate elements of two or more legal traditions. On that score, Seán Patrick Donlan has described "mixed legal systems" as "diverse state laws [that] emerge from different legal traditions."[48]

> Neither the hybridity nor the diffusion of laws is new. Within Europe, law predated the state and the creation of genuinely national laws; a legal "system" centered on the modern nation-state, and the elimination of competing jurisdictions and marginalization of non-legal norms was a very long historical process. Especially before the nineteenth century, there were multiple contemporaneous legal orders co-existing in the same geographical space and at the same time. Modern national traditions are unique hybrids rooted in diverse customary or folklaws, summary and discretionary jurisdictions, local and particular iura propria, the Romano-canonical "learned laws" or ius commune, and other trans-territorial iura communia (including feudal law and the lex mercatoria).[49]

Yet another important family of civil code that has gained recent attention in the past decades is that which stems from the work of Abd al-Razzaq Al-Sanhūrī, a Middle Eastern comparativist. Considered to be "the Arab World's foremost comparative lawyer,"[50] Sanhūrī has been described as "the legendary arch-codifier who drafted many a law for many a newly independent Arab state."[51] Sanhūrī was part of an intellectual movement in the Middle East that simultaneously identified with European countries and traditions while maintaining a nationalistic ideology that valued Middle Eastern culture and identity.[52] His work is characterized by an eclectic blend of European and Islamic legal principles and a preoccupation with incorporating the Islamic legal tradition and existing Middle Eastern frameworks, some of which were Ottoman law, into modern civil codes. He is best known as the drafter of the Egyptian code, which was enacted in 1949 and the Iraqi Civil Code, which entered into force in 1953.[53] His codification also became a surrogate for the spread of the French legal tradition into other Arab countries, such as Libya and Syria.[54]

Civil law systems, therefore, span Europe, North America, Africa, Asia, and the Middle East. To invoke the concept of civil law is to reference a global, interconnected family of legal systems that exists under the aegis of a common tradition—one that transcends a variety of other cultural and linguistic barriers to provide juridical linkages and a shared understanding of law and its operation.

CONCLUSION

Civil law systems are highly systematized and structured legal systems that are based on legal concepts, categories, and rules derived from Roman law.

There are a variety of systems and codes, such as the French, German, and Scandinavian models. There are also hybrid civil law systems and other civil law models such as the Middle Eastern civil codes authored by Al-Sanhūrī. As this book will demonstrate, however, there is another distinct family of civil code that exists in Tunisia, Morocco, and Mauritania. The chapters that follow will describe the origin of these civil codes in the nineteenth century, their unique provisions that find no parallel in other civil law systems, and the societal needs the codes were designed to address. Importantly, these codes descend from the first modern civil code to blend continental civil law and Islamic legal concepts.

NOTES

1. *See* Roscoe Pound, *The Influence of the Civil Law in America*, 1 LA. L. REV. 4 (1938), http://digitalcommons.law.lsu.edu/lalrev/vol1/iss1/14. ("The history of the civil law begins in the Italian universities in the twelfth century.")
2. *See Proceedings of the Degree Ceremony: The Honorable John R. Brown, Doctor of Laws,* 54 TUL. L. REV. 263 (1980).
3. *See* MARY ANN GLENDON ET AL., COMPARATIVE LEGAL TRADITIONS: TEXT, MATERIALS, AND CASES ON WESTERN LAW 52 (3d ed. 2007).
4. *See* JOHN HENRY MERRYMAN ET AL., THE CIVIL LAW TRADITION: EUROPE, LATIN AMERICA, AND EAST ASIA (2d ed. 1994).
5. *See* William Tetley, *Mixed Jurisdictions: Common Law v. Civil Law (Codified and Uncodified),* 60 LA. L. REV. 677 (2000).
6. *Id.*
7. ALAIN LEVASSEUR, DECIPHERING A CIVIL CODE: SOURCES OF LAW AND METHODS OF INTERPRETATION 11 (2015).
8. *Id.*
9. *Id.* at 22.
10. *Id.* at 24.
11. *Id.*
12. *Id.*
13. *Id.* at 25.
14. Helmut Coing, *The Roman Law as ius commune on the Continent*, 89 L.Q.R. 505 (1973).
15. *See* UC Berkley School of Law, *Roman Legal Tradition and the Compilation of Justinian* 3, https://www.law.berkeley.edu/library/robbins/pdf/RomanLegalTradition.pdf
16. *See* Merryman et al., *supra* note 4, at 9.
17. *Id.*
18. *See* Levasseur, *supra* note 7, at 28.
19. *Id.* at 29.

20. *See* KONRAD ZWEIGERT & HEIN KÖTZ, AN INTRODUCTION TO COMPARATIVE LAW 77 (Tony Weir trans., 1998).

21. *See* Alain Levasseur, *Code Napoleon or Code Portalis?*, TUL. L. REV 763 (1969).

22. *See* Zweigert & Kötz, *supra* note 19, at 80 (citing *Oeuvres de Voltaire* VII [1838] Dialogues 5).

23. *See* Levasseur, *supra* note 20, at 762–63.

24. *Id.* at 764.

25. *See* Levasseur, *supra* note 7, at 45. *See also* Jean-Louis Halpérin, *The Civil Code* (trans. David Gruning); Olivier Moréteau, *Codes as Straight-Jackets, Safeguards, and Alibis: The Experience of the French Civil Code*, 20 N.C. J. INT'L COM. REG. 273 (1995).

26. *Id.*

27. *Id.* at 46.

28. *See* Zweigert & Kötz, *supra* note 20, at 74.

29. *See* MAURICE SHELDON AMOS & FREDERICK PARKER WALTON, INTRODUCTION TO FRENCH LAW 32 (1963).

30. *See* ALAIN A. LEVASSEUR, LOUIS CASIMIR ELISABETH MOREAU-LISLET, FOSTER FATHER OF LOUISIANA CIVIL LAW 80 (1996).

31. *Id.* at 64.

32. *Id.* at 65.

33. *See* WILLIAM L. BURDICK, THE PRINCIPLES OF ROMAN LAW AND THEIR RELATION TO MODERN LAW 12 (1938).

34. *See* AUGUSTÌN PARISE, PRIVATE LAW IN LOUISIANA: AN ACCOUNT OF CIVIL CODES, HERITAGE, AND LAW REFORM IN THE SCOPE AND STRUCTURE OF CIVIL CODES 441 (Julio Cesar Rivera, ed., 2013).

35. *Id.*

36. *See* JOHN H. TUCKER, JR., FOREWORD TO THE LOUISIANA CIVIL CODE (2004).

37. *See* Merryman et al., *supra* note 4, at 2.

38. *See* Zweigert and Kötz, *supra* note 20, at 133.

39. *See* Mathias M. Siems, *Legal Origins: Reconciling Law & Finance and Comparative Law*, 52 MCGILL L.J. 55, 59 (2007).

40. *Id.*

41. *Id.*

42. *See* Merryman et al., *supra* note 4, at 32.

43. CHIBLI MALLAT, INTRODUCTION TO MIDDLE EASTERN LAW 297 (2007).

44. Maria Luisa Murilla, *The Evolution of Codification in the Civil Law Legal Systems: Towards Decodification and Recodification*, 11 J TRANSNAT'L L. POL'Y 6 (2001).

45. *See* Zweigert and Kötz, *supra* note 20, at 284.

46. *Id.* at 281.

47. *See* Seán Patrick Donlan, *The Mediterranean Hybridity Project: Crossing the Boundaries of Law and Culture*, 4 J. CIV. L. STUD. 359–60 (2011).

48. *Id.* at 356.

49. See AMR SHALAKANY, Sanhuri and the Historical Origins of Comparative Law in the Arab World (Or How Sometimes Losing Your Asalah Can be Good for You), in RETHINKING THE MASTERS OF COMPARATIVE LAW 152 (Annelise Riles ed., 2001).

50. *Id.*

51. *See* Lama Abu-Odeh, *Modernizing Muslim Family Law: The Case of Egypt*, 37 VAND. J. TRANSNAT'L L. 1043, 1092–93 (2004).

52. *See* Dan E. Stigall, *Iraqi Civil Law: Its Sources, Substance, and Sundering*, 16 J. TRANSNAT'L L. POL'Y 13 (2006).

53. *See* Nabil Saleh, *Civil Codes of Arab Countries: The Sanhuri Codes*, 8 ARAB L.Q. 161, 162–63 (1993).

Chapter 2

Islamic Law

The civil codes to be discussed in this book are in force in geographic regions known, respectively, as the Maghreb and Sahel. These regions differ from many of the European countries referenced in the previous chapter (France, Italy, etc.) in many mays, including their cultural and religious contexts. Most significantly, the people who live in the countries of the Maghreb and Sahel are overwhelmingly Muslim. As explained in the chapter that follows, this fact implicates another system of law that has applicability and legal influence in the region—Islamic law.

Islamic law (or Shari'a) is considered, after common law and civil law systems, to be one of the major world legal systems.[1] Its nascence coincides with the rise of Islam in the early seventh century,[2] though it should be noted that long before that time there were legal practices and institutions in the region known today as the Middle East.[3] Chibli Mallat notes that the legal culture of the region dates back to Mesopotamia, when the Code of Hammurabi was enacted in the mid-eighteenth century BC.[4] Mallat also illuminates, to great effect, the influence of the fifth-century Syro-Roman law book, a compendium of Roman law and local custom,[5] which applied in the area of modern-day Syria[6] and influenced several areas of Islamic law. In addition, prior to the time of Muhammed, customary law and relatively sophisticated legal regimes (mainly associated with trade) were in force in commercial centers such as Mecca and Yemen.[7] "As early as the first century BC, the Yemen had already produced a sophisticated system of law. The Qatabanian kingdom was in possession of a trade code, including a Law Merchant, which, among other things, applied to foreign merchants in their dwelling places outside the city gates."[8] Although there was not an organized judicial system in the region during that early period, such legal practices were used to settle disputes in developed areas while, elsewhere, disputes were resolved using the ancient Arabian tribal system and private justice.[9]

A fertile legal landscape, therefore, existed in the seventh century, during the period of late antiquity, when Muhammad emerged to found the new religion of Islam and its accompanying political order.[10] Muhammad was born in Mecca in 570 into an esteemed tribe known as the Quraysh. The Quraysh held a special place in society and were the guardians of a sacred shrine in Mecca.[11] Around the age of thirty, Muhammad began preaching a religion of strict monotheism based around the idea that there was one god (Allah) and that he, acting as Allah's messenger, was conveying to humanity God's word (given to him by the archangel Gabriel).[12] His message earned him both followers and enemies, leading him to leave Mecca in 622 for Medina.[13] Muhammad's life is, thus, typically viewed in two phases: the Meccan period (610–622 CE) when he lived in the city of Mecca and the subsequent Medina period (622–632 CE).[14]

It is this history and the records produced during these times that form the bedrock of Islamic law. Islamic law is not, however, ossified in history. Despite its ancient origins—and contrary to the distorted image of Islamic law espoused by murderous extremists or viewed through the misty ignorance of social media feeds—Islamic law has always been surrounded by a vibrant intellectualism which continues to shape it and permit it to evolve. Since the days of its origins, the work of jurists has expanded on what was established in the early years of Islam to further define and elaborate on Islamic law and philosophy. In their work on Islamic intellectual activism, John L. Esposito and John O. Voll have highlighted the way in which Muslim activist intellectuals continue to shape contemporary Islam.[15]

> Their ideas provide the foundations for many of the programs of Islamic movements throughout the world. Even for those who disagree with them and dispute their claims, these activist thinkers have shaped the conceptual world and set the terms of most debates in the Muslim world. These people, their organizations, and their modes of thinking have been part of the heart of what has come to be called the Islamic resurgence of the end of the twentieth century.[16]

Such dynamism within the Islamic legal and philosophical tradition is made possible, in part, through the recognition of a diverse array of methodological tools that have permitted Islamic jurists for centuries to adapt ancient teachings to contemporary legal issues. This judicial approach and legal tradition has also served to shape modern legislative efforts in countries across the Middle East, Africa, and Asia. An understanding of it is, therefore, essential to any comparative legal analysis of such regions with significant Muslim populations.

ISLAMIC LEGAL CONCEPTS

The term Shari'a references Islamic law in a general sense.[17] The meaning of Shari'a (originally "the place from which one descends to water") developed over time to mean "the law of water" and, eventually grew to encompass all issues considered vital to human existence.[18] Shari'a is principally derived from two written sources: "the Qur'an, the divine Book revealed to the Prophet Muhammad in the late sixth century CE, and the sunna, which is the reported compilation of the conversations (hadith) and deeds of the Prophet collected after his death from his Companions."[19] Other primary sources of Islamic law based on an interpretive process are what is called ijma' (consensus) and analogy (qiyas). Together, the Qur'an, sunna, ijma', and qiyas are considered the "roots" of Islamic law.[20] Aside from those principal sources of law, Islamic law is also formed from numerous other subsidiary sources of law, such as public interest (maslaha) and custom ('urf).[21]

THE QUR'AN

David Santillana, in his famous *Istituzioni di Diritto Musulmano*, notes that "[t]he supreme source of Islamic law is the Qur'an." The Islamic faith holds that the Qur'an was incrementally revealed to Muhammad over a period of twenty-two years, ending with his death in 632 CE. It consists of 114 chapters (suras) which are further divided into various verses (aayat). Some chapters were revealed while Muhammad was in Mecca and others while he was in Medina. The style of content of the chapters revealed in those two different times and locations differ in style, substance, and focus. "Prior to his arrival in Medina, Muhammad did not, in all probability, have in mind the establishment of a new polity, much less a new law or legal system."[22] It is only around AD 626 that Muhammad began to consider the idea that the Islamic community might possess its own distinct law.[23]

> The Muslims in Mecca were a small, scattered, and persecuted minority, and there was no Muslim community that needed legal norms to regulate its affairs. Thus, the verses revealed in Mecca contained principles of the faith and rules of morality, with little or no specific socio-legal provisions. These were revealed mostly during the Medina period, when Medina became a Muslim city-state with the Prophet acting both as religious leader and as a head of state.[24]

Thus, the oldest chapters of the Qur'an—the Meccan chapters—are shorter and almost exclusively religious in content while the later chapters—the Medinese chapters—contain most of the political and legal precepts. With regard to that latter group of chapters, commentators note that the Qur'an contains somewhere between 80 and 500 verses that deal with legal matters—depending on how law and legality are defined.[25] David Santillana posited a more expansive number: "[O]f 6219 verses contained in the 114 chapters (or suras) about 600 ... [maximum] deal with legislation in the strict sense."[26] M. Cherif Bassiouni and Gaman M. Badr note that seventy verses focus on family and inheritance law; seventy verses focus on obligations and contracts; thirty verses on deal with criminal law; and twenty verses address procedure.[27] As a result, though it remains the primary legal document in Islamic law, it is hardly comprehensive in its legal scope. This is, in part, because, during his lifetime, "Muhammad made no attempt to elaborate anything like a code of law," opting instead for *ad hoc* solutions.[28] This necessarily results in challenges for jurists seeking to distill rules of law from its pages. As Werner Minski notes, "Since the Qur'an is not a Napoleonic code, finding guidance on 'the law' inevitably involved human agents."[29] Accordingly, methodologic tools and other sources were developed to formulate solutions for legal issues faced by Muslim communities.

SUNNA

The concept of sunna refers to the actions, sayings, and opinions of Muhammad and his oldest disciples. The sunna (literally "beaten path") are considered the second source of law in the Islamic legal hierarchy and it is the duty of Muslims to abide by the precepts and guidance found therein.[30] The concept of sunna, however, is an ancient one that predates the Muslim faith. Ignaz Goldziher notes that the ancient pagans of the period before Islam understood sunna to be "those rules which were in conformity with the traditions of the Arab world and the ancestral manners and customs."[31] With the rise of Islam, this ancient usage was transformed to mean anything that could be proven to have been the practice of the Prophet.[32] The importance of sunna as a source of law was solidified during the early days of the Islamic faith such that sunna are considered on par with the Qur'an in the Islamic hierarchy of legal authority.[33] Serving as the Prophetic example, they stand alongside the revelations in the Qur'an and have similar normative force.

HADITH

The related concept of hadith, in turn, refers to "a report attributed to the Prophet Muhammad, describing his words and actions and representing the chief source for knowing his authoritative precedent (Sunna)."[34] Each hadith

consists of two parts: (a) the chain of informants through which the communication was transmitted (the sanad or isnad) and (b) the text with the substance
of the hadith (the matn).[35]

> The concrete details of the Sunna—that is, what the Prophet had done or said,
> or even tacitly approved—took the form of specific narratives that became
> known as [hadith] (at once a collective and singular noun, referring to the body
> of hadith in general and to a single hadith, according to context). For example,
> the Sunna of the Prophet generally promotes the right to private property, but
> the precise nature of this right was not made clear until the pertinent hadiths
> became known.[36]

The difference between hadith and sunna can sometimes be difficult
to discern. Ignaz Goldziher posited that the distinction is that hadith are
oral communications traced back to Muhammad while sunna is a usage
or practice on a point of law or religion (without the necessity of an oral
communication).[37] Other scholars, however, opine that the distinction
lies in the method of validation. The best way to envision the distinction,
however, is that a hadith is an individual report, and sunna is the corpus
of traditions referring to the Prophet, chiefly in his sayings, but also in his
reported actions and, more rarely, in his silence. "The Sunna was recorded
in thousands of disparate reports of the Prophet's words and actions, called
hadith[.]"[38] The hadith, therefore, differ from sunna in concept but are used
as mechanism for elucidation and clarification of the sunna. In practice and
as a technical matter, however, the difference between sunna and hadith
is slight.

QIYAS

The term qiyas refers to deductive reasoning—a methodological tool used by
jurists encountering legal issues not explicitly covered by other legal sources.
Such reasoning has been employed in Islamic law since its earliest days to
solve emerging legal issues, though it was only permitted as a legal recourse
if no solution could be found in the Qur'an, the sunna, or ijma'.[39] Qiyas can
be used to reason *a pari ratione* between two cases and find that a rule for
one case should be applied to another similar case.[40]

> In its most rudimentary form, qiyas is a form of analogical reasoning through
> which prescribed norms in the Qur'an, Sunna or Ijma' can be extended to
> unregulated legal problems if they share the same 'illa, or ratio legis. The most
> typical example here is the Qur'anic prohibition on drinking wine. While the
> holy text does not touch on other forms of alcohol, jurists argued that the 'illa of

prohibiting wine-drinking lay in the substance's intoxicating effect, and relying on qiyas extended the wine prohibition to all other intoxicating substances.[41]

Qiyas, of course, has limitations. As a subsidiary source of law, qiyas may not conflict with a provision in the Qur'an.[42] Even so, commentators have noted that, within the main sources of Islamic law, qiyas holds the greatest potential as a mechanism to permit legal change and evolution.[43]

IJTIHAD

The related concept of ijtihad is a term that, in its technical legal sense, denotes "personal reasoning."[44] David Santillana explained that this sort of reasoning is not the mere "arbitrary subjective and personal opinion of the jurist," but is, rather, a jurist's opinion based on the meaning and spirit of the law.[45] It is, otherwise stated, a juristic effort to derive a rule from the source. As with other methods of reasoning, ijtihad can only be used where primary sources of Islamic law are silent. Moreover, to engage in ijtihad, a jurist must have a thorough knowledge of Islamic theology and the revealed texts, the ability to engage in sophisticated legal reasoning, and a thorough knowledge of Arabic.[46] Some commentators have posited that ijtihad has, however, been less in use since the tenth century AD when the respective schools of Islamic law cohered and "the door of ijtihad" was "closed."[47] According to these commentators, the effect of this was to greatly limit the degree to which a single jurist's personal reasoning would have any normative force. For instance, Ibn Khaldun remarked, "The person who would claim independent judgment nowadays would be frustrated and have no adherents."[48] Chibli Mallat, however, has noted that the idea that "the door of ijtihad" was somehow "closed" was somewhat exaggerated and that, while canonization of Islamic law had an impact on its interpretation, "a 'legal closure' in any society or civilization, since silence itself is interpretation, cannot be sustained."[49] Ijtihad, therefore, retains a place in Islamic law as a methodological tool.

ISTIHSAN AND ISTISLAH

Two other jurisprudential tools used, albeit more sparingly, in Islamic law are that of istihsan and istislah. These methods of reasoning, permitted only by the Hanafi and Maliki schools of Islamic law (discussed below), are "to be used only when the hadith offers no explicit solution, qiyas does not lend a satisfactory answer, and there is some necessity or reason for applying the alternative rule."[50] Istihsan is defined as a "reasoned distinction of authority" or "either (1) the preference for a recognized source of law over reasoning by analogy (qiyas), or (2) the preference for one reasoning by analogy over another that is considered weaker."[51] Istislah, in turn, is defined as "the process of selecting one acceptable alternative solution over another because the former appears more suitable for the situation at hand, even though the selected solution may be technically weaker than the rejected one."[52] This requires a jurist to determine what is best for the welfare of human beings "and select the judgment that will promote it."[53] Otherwise stated, such methods permit a limited deviation from established precedent if adherence to that precedent would result in an injustice or, in the opinion of the jurist, undermine the spirit of the law. Istislah is akin to istihsan in terms of its purpose, scope, and practice.[54]

IJMA'

Ijma' refers to the "infallible consensus of the community."[55] Where the Qur'an and sunna do not provide specific guidance on an issue, the Muslim community may deduce the law through reasoning.[56] This can be done through collective reasoning or through individual reasoning,[57] though it is usually through qiyas, or analogical reasoning, deployed by jurists from the four orthodox schools. When it is done through the former of these avenues (collective reasoning), the result is called ijma'—and it is considered the third foundation of Islamic law. Ijma' is defined as "the agreed opinion and teachings of the acknowledged Islamic jurist-theologians of a given period."[58] It, therefore, must be the consensus of the learned—not merely popular opinion. Some commentators maintain that ijma' may be obtained when the recognized jurists of an era express an opinion on a point of law, when there is demonstrated unanimity in practice, or, alternatively, when only a few recognized jurists express an opinion and others remain silent and do not controvert that opinion. That said, the idea of ijma' and its applicability remains contested space among Islamic scholars.[59] As one commentator has remarked, "there is no ijma' about ijma'."[60]

Ijma' has been diminished in its practical impact on Islamic law due to political and geographic divisions in the Muslim world that make obtaining a consensus view somewhat difficult.[61] On that score, while Irshad Abdal-Haqq notes that the practice of reaching a legal decision by consensus after mutual consultation (shura) was established by the companions of Muhammad (the Sahaba), the modern world possesses no real mechanism to obtain a global Islamic opinion on a point of law.[62] Accordingly, ijma' today—to the extent it remains relevant at all—is generally determined through retrospection.[63]

FIQH

To distill detailed legal rules from the sources explained above requires rigorous analysis and interpretation of those Islamic legal sources. The result of this arduous effort by Muslim legal scholars is known as fiqh.[64] Fiqh literally means "understanding,"[65] but is defined in its technical legal sense as "the knowledge of the subsidiary rulings of religion (shar), or the ascertainment of practical duties through detailed proofs (al-adala al-tafsilia/dalayil-i tafsili)"; and as "knowledge of the subsidiary rulings of religion based on a proof-text (dalil)."[66] Fiqh is generally found in comprehensive compendia that are characterized by complex and elaborate language.[67] As to its place in the hierarchy of the sources of law, Chibli Mallat notes that "the shari'a encompasses fiqh, whereas fiqh as a hybrid of jurists' jurisprudence and substantive 'textbook' law is only one of the several forms taken by Islamic law as a whole, the shari'a."[68] Asifa Quraishi has expounded on the topic in an illuminative manner:

> The core principle of Islamic jurisprudence is that sharia, God's Law, cannot be known with certainty. Literally meaning "street," or "way," the term "sharia" in the Quran denotes the perfect Way of God—the way God advises people to live a virtuous life. This Way of God is described in the Quran and the Prophet Muhammad's life example. But of course not everything is clearly answered in those two sources, so Muslim scholars perform "ijtihad" (rigorous legal reasoning) to extrapolate from those sources more detailed guidance for life according to sharia. This guidance comes in the form of detailed legal rules called "fiqh" (literally "understanding"). Muslims never established any clerical establishment or central institution to establish Islam's official religious doctrine, so the religious rules of Islam are the result of the work of a diverse community of fiqh scholars operating according to their own collective standards of integrity and professionalism.[69]

The concept of fiqh is, therefore, analogous to jurisprudence or, perhaps more precisely, doctrine.[70] Quraishi emphasizes that fiqh represents "the doctrinal rules of Islamic law," and are a subsidiary source of law because "they are the result of ijtihad, a fallible human effort, representing the best 'understanding' of God's Law by Muslim legal scholars."[71]

QANUN

The concept of qanun equates to "law as statutes and as positive legal provisions in actual operation in a contemporary Middle Eastern society or state."[72] The qanun is, otherwise stated, positive law created through political institutions (legislatures, councils, courts, etc.).[73] Primary sources of the qanun include constitutions, statutes, cases, regulations, and—importantly for purposes of this book—civil codes.[74] Commentators note that the legitimacy bestowed on the qanun can vary from one Muslim state to another.[75] In secular states, for instance, "the qanun may prohibit what the Shariah allows and may allow what the Shariah prohibits. In such states, secular law asserts precedence over both fiqh and the Shariah."[76] And, of course, the opposite may hold true in less secular states. This has led many scholars to treat qanun as "separate but complimentary" to Islamic law.[77] Others, however, argue that, in practice, there are "synthetic connections" between Islamic law and qanun—conceptual overlaps between qanun and Islamic jurisprudential interpretation—which make the boundary between the two at most illusory and, at minimum, somewhat porous.[78] The analysis of Santillana's work in the pages that follow, in fact, reinforces this view. In any event, qanun represents the law of the state—and, by consequence, the law that the institutions of the state will apply and enforce.

CUSTOM ('URF)

Finally, custom ('urf), the common practice or usage within a community, is considered the oldest source of law in Islamic law. While custom in Islamic law is not a primary source of law, it is nonetheless important to Islamic legal scholars, having roughly the normative force of ijma'.[79] Santillana has emphasized the importance of custom in Islamic law, noting:

> It is a kind of unwritten rule which has the power of making law and even modifying it. "What the Muslims approve, is approved of God." When it is uniform, enduring, and is not *contra bonos mores*, or against the general rules of law, usage has the same force as law itself; and becomes part and parcel of it.[80]

Custom must, however, generally meet certain qualifications to have legal force: (a) it must be "of ancient and general prevalence"; (b) it must exist within the territory of the country in which the question of its validity arises; (c) it must not be immoral or against public policy; (d) it must be continuous and invariable (absence of long breaks in adherence to the custom); and (e) it must not be against Islamic law.[81]

Custom has been a particularly strong force in the legal reasoning of the Hanafite and Malikite traditions (discussed below).[82] In his introduction to the *Avant-Projet*, Santillana highlights the important role of custom in Islamic law and cites to Zarqani's statement: "Usage ('urf) is, according to us (Malikites), a branch of the law (Shari'a) that brings specificity to what, in the law, is general and tempers what is absolute."[83]

SIYAR (INTERNATIONAL LAW)

The concept of Siyar, in the technical legal sense, refers to the classical traditions of the Muslim law of nations or, otherwise stated, international law.[84] Commentators note that, in a strict sense, Islamic law does not recognize a distinct category of international law apart from the central body of Islamic law. Siyar, rather, describes "the sum total of the principles, rules and practices governing Islam's relationships with the other nations[.]"[85] It entails "elaborate rules of war, peace, treaty and neutrality governing the relationship of Muslim and non-Muslim states[.]"[86] Interestingly, this body of law developed far earlier than its Western corollary.

> The Siyar was compiled by the Islamic cleric Shaybani (750–805 C.E.) who, like Hugo Grotius, was the first to consolidate an ordered and coherent theory of international law within the realm of Islam. Like his Western counterpart, Shaybani became the father of Islamic international law, but "preceded Grotius (d. 1645) by some eight centuries and composed his works on a system of law whose appeal to students of the history of law is greater than to students of the modern law of nations." Before Shaybani, there existed no Islamic law of nations although components of it, most notably the jihad, were popularly examined by several Islamic clerics and scholars[.][87]

It has been posited that early European international law commentators, such as Vitoria and Grotius, were acquainted with Siyar and that their scholarly work may have even been influenced by it.[88] It is perhaps too soon to say whether such assertions can be proven definitively. Even so, the fact remains that Shaybani's work exists as a forerunner in many respects to the corpus of international law that would develop in later centuries.

SCHOOLS OF ISLAMIC LAW

During the Abbasid period, there was a struggle between Islamic scholars and caliphs over the issue of religious authority.[89] It was the scholars who prevailed in this struggle, and attained primacy in legal authority as a collective over time. As a result, Islamic law is considered "jurists law"—law that is made by jurists (not the state) and which, therefore, stands independent from the state. It was also during the Abbasid period that the various approaches to Islamic jurisprudence cohered into various schools of law.[90] These schools (madhabs) were initially determined geographically but would later become associated with the name of the jurist around which the school formed.[91] From this phenomenon arose the four major orthodox schools of Islamic law in the Sunni tradition: the Hanafi, Maliki, Shafi'i, and Hanbali schools.[92] These schools are generally in accord with fundamental issues associated with Islamic law but do diverge in various ways and in their approach to certain legal issues.[93]

HANAFI

The Hanafi madhab emerged in Baghdad among jurists who associated themselves with the writing and teaching of Abu Hanifa al-Nu'man ibn Thabit al-Taymi (80–150 AH/699–767 CE).[94] Considered "the oldest and most liberal of the schools of thought,"[95] the Hanafi madhab considers ijma' and qiyas to be valid methods of legal reasoning,[96] and likewise make use of istihsan and istislah as jurisprudential tools.[97] It was favored by the early Abbasid caliphs and became the preferred school of the Turks during the era of the Ottoman Empire. On that score, due to Ottoman influence, Hanafite doctrine has continuing relevance in many countries as a legacy of Ottoman rule.[98] This is so even in countries where the majority of the population follows another school.[99] The Hanafi madhab is followed widely today in Pakistan, India, Central Asia, Iraq, Syria, Jordan, and Turkey.[100]

MALIKI

The Maliki madhab emerged in Medina among jurists who associated themselves with the writing and teaching of Abu Abd Allah Malik ibn Anas (97–179 AH/713–795 CE).[101] The second most prevalent Islamic school of thought, it is considered somewhat more conservative than the Hanafi School in ways,[102] but is still considered quite moderate and is known to permit methods of interpretation beyond those recognized by the other three orthodox schools.[103]

The Malikis were the second distinct legal school to become institutionalized, having emerged out of the jurisprudence of the People of Tradition. Malik b. Anas al Asbahi was born in the year 718 A.D. in Medina and became recognized as Medina's most accomplished man of learning, particularly in the field of jurisprudence. He authored various books on jurisprudence, such as his famous al-Muwatta, in which he arranged various hadith texts according to topics of law.[104]

While Maliki jurists do not reject qiyas as a source of legal reasoning, it is afforded less weight than in, for instance, the Hanafi madhab.[105] Maliki jurists, however, make recourse to "customary practice, analogical reasoning, public interest, and traditional opinions in their legal analysis," and tend to emphasize the customary practices of Medina.[106] Notably, they also permit both istihsan and istislah.[107] The Maliki madhab prevails in most of Muslim Africa, including the countries of the Maghreb and Sahel.[108] Ergo, and importantly for purposes of this book, it is the school of jurisprudence that prevails in Tunisia, Morocco, and Mauritania.

SHAFI'I

The Shafi'i madhab emerged in Baghdad among jurists who associated themselves with the writing and teaching of Muhammad ibn Idris al-Shafi'i (150–204 AH/767–819 CE), who later moved to Cairo.[109] Considered the third most prevalent school of Islamic thought, the Shafi'i madhab is known as a highly formalistic school in its approach to legal interpretation which was more limiting in, for instance, the use of ijma' as a source of law.[110] Similarly, the Shafi'i madhab does not consider methods such as istihsan to be valid methods of legal interpretation because the philosophy of the school "considers it to be a method that makes laws—something, according to Shafi'i, a jurist is not supposed to do."[111] While the Shafi'i madhab does not exclude the use of qiyas as a method of legal reasoning, it "has a specific set of rules under which it may be used."[112] The Shafi'i madhab is followed widely today in Jordan, Syria, Yemen, Northern Iraq, East Africa (Somalia, Kenya, and Tanzania), Indonesia, Malaysia, Singapore, Sri Lanka, Maldives, and Palestine.

HANBALI

The Hanbali madhab also emerged in Baghdad among jurists who associated themselves with the writing and teaching of Ahmad ibn Hanbal al-Shaybani (164–241 AH/780–855 CE).[113] The Hanbali madhab is the smallest school of Islamic law and is considered the most conservative of the four major orthodox schools.[114] Today it is frequently associated with a "'literalist' approach, meaning that it focuses on the literal meaning of the original sources of law, the Qur'an and the Sunna."[115] Hanbali scholars only recognize ijma' of the Sahaba—and only use analogical deduction as a last resort.[116] Mallat is careful to note, however, that "the equation of classic Hanbalism with arid conservatism does not hold true," and that a review of Hanbali legal texts reveals that "it does not differ in its treatment of various subjects in any 'qualitative' manner from other classical texts."[117] Moreover, Mallat asserts that Hanbalism is unusual as a legal school, representing "more of an intellectual current than a proper legal school."[118] The Hanbali madhab is associated with Saudi Arabia, the United Arab Emirates, and Qatar.[119]

SHI'I SCHOOLS

In addition to the four orthodox Sunni schools of Islamic law, noted above, there are also Shi'i schools such as the Ja'fari madhab.[120] The Ja'fari madhab is the most prevalent Shi'i legal school. Named for the fifth and sixth Shi'i imams—Abu Ja'far Muhammad Al-Baqir and Ja'far al-Sadiq—it is regarded as the "fifth school" of Islamic legal jurisprudence.[121] The Ja'fari madhab recognizes the key sources of Islamic law as well as reports from of the imams, who are considered infallible.[122]

The Ja'fari madhab is followed by Shi'i Muslims in Iran, Iraq, and Lebanon—as well as by the Shi'i minorities in Saudi Arabia and Syria. There are also other surviving Shi'i schools of law, notably the Zaydi and Isma'ili madhabs.[123] The Zaydi madhab is followed by Shi'as in Yemen while the Isma'ili school is followed by Shi'as in the Middle East (such as Syria) Central and South Asia, and East Africa.[124]

IBADISM

Another distinct sect of Islam—one that is neither Sunni nor Shi'i—is that of Ibadism. Ibadism developed out of a seventh-century Islamic sect (known as the Khawarij) and claims to be the oldest sect in Islam.[125] It survives today in Oman (the only country in which it is dominant), as well as East Africa, Algeria, Libya, and on the island of Djerba in Tunisia.[126] The aim of Ibadism as a religious philosophy is to create a righteous Muslim society, and it is notably moderate as a branch of Islam.[127] With regard to its approach to law and legal reasoning, Valerie J. Hoffman notes, "The principles of jurisprudence are the same in Ibadism as in Sunni and Shi'i Islam," though Ibadis do not accept the obligation to follow opinions of earlier scholars and are permissive with regard to ijtihad and analogical reasoning.[128]

SUFISM

The term "Sufism" encompasses a range of practices which are associated
with mysticism and which emphasizes "the inward life and call to spiritual
purification and closeness to God."[129] Sufism originated in the thirteenth century "in reaction to the orthodox emphasis on law and its denial of the mystical or emotional needs of the human spirit."[130] Sufism contains some mystical
elements which tend to blend Islamic beliefs and pre-Islamic religious concepts, such as the recognition of "intercessors" between the worshipper and
God, "which led to the formation of brotherhoods (tariqas, or "ways") and
recognition of holy men (marabouts)."[131] Sufism also recognizes the veneration of saints or walaya—a term which "denotes closeness and intimacy
with God, as well as protection by God."[132] Sufis are frequently organized
into "orders" within which there are a number of apprentices (murid) under
the direction a spiritual master (sheykh or pir).[133] Sufism, however, does not
denote a distinct madhab or theological sect—merely a difference in philosophical emphasis and religious practice.[134]

ISLAMIC LAW AND PLURALISM

As the discussion of the various schools above has demonstrated, Islamic
law has always tolerated a degree of dissonance and diversity among the
various Muslim schools. Moreover, Islamic law has long contended with the
questions of non-Muslims living in Muslim territory and how to reconcile
the need to enforce its directives vis-à-vis Muslims with the fact that those
directives do not apply to every person of every faith. An important Islamic
legal concept, elucidated by Professor Haider Hamoudi, is that of the aman,
a historic juristic idea that granted non-Muslims the right of temporary free
passage in the Muslim state to trade, etc. so long as the covenant lasted.[135]

> The concept of the aman can readily be developed in a fashion that permits
> considerable interaction and coexistence as between Muslims and non-Muslims.
> Hence, for example, what began as a plainly recognized, but temporary, right
> to travel to the House of War to trade and engage in other similar activities
> developed into a more robust juristic recognition of permanent residence in
> non-Muslim states. Similarly, but in reverse, as early as the sixteenth century
> the Ottoman empire widely granted revocable "ahdnames" pursuant to which
> European merchants enjoyed covenants of security. The seeds of a new, more
> interdependent world were already sown by that time.[136]

Hamoudi notes that early classical jurists generally limited the duration of
the aman to one year, highlighting the fact that "the residence of a Muslim in

non-Muslim lands was generally viewed as temporary."[137] This notion developed in Islamic thought and contributed to the rules relating to the permanent presence of non-Muslims in Muslim territories and vice versa.[138]

In addition, during the period of Islamic conquest, the Islamic state reconciled the fact of religious plurality through the "dhimmi" system.[139] Dhimma literally means "a compact which the believer agrees to respect, the violation of which makes him liable to dhamm (blame)."[140] Through this system, certain religious minorities in Muslim territory who were not Muslim but were still considered "people of the book"—such as Jews, Christians, and Zoroastrians—were granted a degree of protection and autonomy in exchange for their agreement to accept an inferior status and to assume certain obligations, such as the required payment of a dhimmi tax (jizyah).[141] Mark L. Movsesian notes, "[T]he contours of the dhimma, and the status of the dhimmis, were systematized as part of fiqh in the eighth and ninth centuries."[142]

Pagans and polytheists were not permitted to have dhimmi status.[143] Those who were given status dhimmis, however, could practice their religions and—quite importantly—follow their own community's laws, though "in cases where non-Muslim law conflicted with the Shari'a, Islamic law controlled."[144] As Timur Kiran notes, "From the rise of Islam to the secularist reforms of the nineteenth century, [dhimmis] were entitled to choice of law, except on criminal matters, which fell exclusively within the jurisdiction of Islamic courts. Although the doctrinal basis for this choice varied over time, its fundamental principles remained fixed."[145]

> Islamic law thus dealt with the dhimmis as members of a non-Muslim religious community. The law of the dhimmis regulated their relationships to each other, and each of the dhimmi communities was led by its religious functionaries. Out of this concept developed the so-called *millet* system of the Ottoman Empire under which the various *dhimmi* communities lived according to their own laws within and as subjects of the Ottoman Empire. Remnants of this system are found today in most Arab states and in parts of the Muslim world where matters of family relationships and frequently also inheritance are regulated by the law of the individual community and not by legal rules applicable to all citizens of the state. This constitutes a survival of the concept of the personality of laws in an age when legal relationships are generally regulated on the basis of the territoriality of the law.[146]

This system persisted in the Ottoman Empire until the Tanzimat reforms of the nineteenth century and the effort to create secular courts and modernized legal codes.[147] These reforms also sought to grant dhimmis legal equality.[148] This rather revolutionary change in the way Islamic governance addressed non-Muslims was announced in the Hatt-i Sherif of Gülhane of 1839 and in the Hatt-i Humayun of 1856.[149] By the middle of the nineteenth century, therefore, the dhimmi system—and its accompanying legal pluralism—was fated for oblivion.

INTERNATIONAL LAW, EXTRATERRITORIAL PROTECTION, AND PLURALITY

It is also worth noting that international law in the eighteenth and nineteenth century permitted a degree of legal autonomy for religious minorities. Prior to the more developed notion of territorial statehood—in which sovereignty implies absolute legal control of a territory—it was common practice for states to grant certain categories of foreigners special rights and immunities.[150] Powers of this sort were commonly conferred by treaties that were widespread in both geographic and temporal terms. As early as the fifth century AD, commentators note that the Visigoths in Spain conceded to foreign merchants a special jurisdictional right to be tried by "judges selected from among their own countrymen."[151] This practice was, likewise, recognized during the Byzantine Empire, prevailed among the Italian City States, and was even a general practice during the Crusades.[152] A global review of such treaties finds them, at various times, present in Egypt and throughout North Africa, Turkey, Persia, China, Siam, and the Malay States.[153] This jurisdictional scheme, based in the ancient notion of "personality of law,"[154] is, however, most popularly identified with the "capitulations"—the voluntary grants of various rights by Ottoman sultans to European sovereigns in the sixteenth century, including the right of Europeans in Ottoman territory to remain subject to the jurisdiction of their country and immunity from Ottoman jurisdiction.[155] The rights were initially granted from a more powerful sovereign to a lesser one and did not, as the term "capitulation" may seem to imply to the modern reader, indicate a concession of power and control from a weaker government to some stronger power. Indeed, the name for these treaties derives from the word *capitulatio* which merely means "chapters" and was a term commonly used to denote an agreement. Moreover, scholars have noted that the Ottoman Capitulations of the sixteenth century merely recognized the prevailing international practice. In fact, when one of the original treaties of this type was negotiated between Francis I and Suleiman the Magnificent in 1535, "the granting state was much the stronger of the two."[156] Norman Bentwich, a professor of International Relations in the Hebrew University of Jerusalem during the 1930s, noted that Turkish authorities had no desire to exercise jurisdiction over "the Christian resident alien" and that Ottoman law "was to him what the *Ius Civile* was to the Roman under the Republic—the privilege of the citizen."[157]

In the sixteenth century, pursuant to the capitulatory regime, European states began to register Ottoman-born, non-Muslim subjects as *protégés*—protected subjects of European powers.[158] For European powers, such *protégés* "were viewed as valuable vehicles for the expression—and, at times, the expansion—of European interests."[159] For the persons who were *protégés*, it was considered "a canny investment and a hedge against an unstable world."[160] The arrangement, thus, benefitted European countries who wanted to benefit from the networks of *protégés* and the consular taxes they paid, while the *protégés* gained protection which emanated from a foreign power and, from that same source, what can be described as extra-territorial rights.[161]

Timur Kuran, a professor Duke University also posit that this state of affairs was possible due to the uniquely Islamic system of governance that facilitated a degree of legal plurality.

> Under the Islamic system of governance, non-Muslim subjects were allowed to conduct business outside the jurisdiction of the Islamic court system and, absent Muslim involvement, to seek adjudication in autonomous courts. This choice of law gave Christians and Jews a huge advantage as the West developed the legal infrastructure of the modern economy. Minorities advanced economically simply by adopting Western business methods, forming economic alliances with westerners, and using Western courts to settle disputes. Traditionally denied the same choice of law, Muslims could not take advantage of modern institutions as individuals; they had to wait for collectively generated legal reforms, and the delay left them economically handicapped. The observed bifurcation in communal economic standings was thus an unintended and unforeseeable consequence of a pluralistic legal system designed, paradoxically, to help Muslims by giving Islamic courts jurisdiction over all their legal affairs.[162]

The international legal context of the time was, therefore, one in which groups could exist as legal islands with a degree of autonomy and even outside protection in a world of colliding and overlapping authorities. Such a legal framework necessitates a certain degree of legal cosmopolitanism for those who must live within a territory with one set of laws; seek to administer itself by its own set of laws; seek the protection of a country with yet another set of laws; and navigate each of these legal systems to the greatest benefit.

Islamic law in its classical form, therefore, recognizes the idea of the personality of laws—allowing certain religious minorities to be governed by their own law and legal institutions. Early international law, likewise, fostered a degree of legal pluralism through the capitulatory system and through tolerance for the exercise of foreign authority (judicial and otherwise) vis-à-vis foreign citizens and *protégés* (often religious minorities) in Ottoman territory.

ISLAMIC LAW AND CONTRACTS

The fundamental tenet of Islamic law relating to contracts is the Qur'anic verse which commands, "O ye who believe! Fulfill (all) obligations."[163] While Islamic law never fully developed a general theory of obligations or contracts in the same way as continental civil law, rules to govern transactions have developed—most of which were modeled on the contract of sale.[164] These rules began to develop in the seventh century and, as noted, in the context of a region already surging with trade, commerce, and organic rules used to regulate transactions.[165] Schacht notes that the city of Mecca had a more developed commercial life and, therefore, a more developed commercial law than other places.[166] "An important source of information on commercial law and practice in Mecca in the time of Muhammad is provided by the Koran, in its extensive use of commercial technical terms, many of which are legally relevant."[167] On that score, part of Muhammad's focus was on reforming what he saw to be abusive trade practices in Mecca and elsewhere. The original focus of Islam's founder, therefore, was not on creating a general theory of contracts and obligations, but on reforming what was then in place.

In the course of time, however, Islamic jurists were required to address questions related to contractual disputes. This accretion of decisions and practical experience resulted in some development in the field of Islamic contract law. Some general principles of Islamic contract law, therefore, emerged as the discipline developed. For instance, Islamic contract law generally promotes the idea of contractual liberty—giving parties the freedom to determine the terms and conditions of a contract.[168] Likewise, for a contract to be formed, Islamic law requires the existence of an agreement; existence of the subject matter (mahall) or consideration; that the parties have contractual capacity (ahliyah); that the contract must conform to Islamic law; the existence of genuine assent of the contracting parties; and that the contract be concluded in the prescribed form.[169]

> In other words, a contract requires that there should be two or more parties to it, that one party make a proposal and the other accept it, that there be a meeting of the minds as to the object and purpose of the contract, and that the object of the contract be considered legal.[170]

It should be noted that some commentators disagree on the question of whether Islamic law also generally requires that there be consideration (in the Anglo-American understanding of the concept) in order for a contract to be binding.[171] Even so, the basic form and requirements of a contract under Islamic law should be familiar to many Western jurists from both common law and civil law backgrounds.

Islamic contract law also, however, has limitations and protections. For instance, the consent of the parties to the contract must be free of error, fraud, or coercion—the presence of which will invalidate any contract under Islamic law.[172] Most notable among these limitations and protections are the two "cardinal doctrines" of Islamic contract law: riba and gharar.[173] The concept of gharar refers to something whose future is not yet known or, in other contexts, something for which the future is concealed. In the context of Islamic contract law, it is most frequently associated with uncertain consideration of object of a contract.[174] Riba, in turn, relates to the Islamic prohibition on contracts that entail "a monetary advantage without a countervalue"[175] or, otherwise stated, interest. And, as noted, the contract cannot be for a reason that is violative of Islamic law in other ways, such as a contract to sell alcohol among Muslims, a contract relating to illegal sexual intercourse, etc.[176]

CONCLUSION

Islamic law entails a specific set of religiously inspired imperatives; a rich, autonomous legal method; and a comprehensive system of legal and moral rules that seek to govern the behavior of each individual Muslim vis-à-vis the rest of the world (Muslim and non-Muslim). It is notable for its normative force in the Muslim countries around the globe and even among Muslim citizens living outside such countries. Today, it is estimated that there are 1.57 billion Muslims globally.[177] Data indicate that roughly 60% of Muslims are in Asia and about 20% are found in the Middle East and North Africa.[178] Moreover, numerous countries consider Islam to be a core feature of their national identity.

> Four states worldwide are officially called "Islamic," the Islamic Republics of Afghanistan, Iran, Mauritania and Pakistan. On 11 December 2015, the small African state The Gambia also declared itself to be an Islamic republic; however, its secular constitution remains unaltered. In a further 22 states, Islam is the official or state religion (Algeria, Bahrain, Bangladesh, Brunei, Comoros, Djibouti, Egypt, Iraq, Jordan, Libya, Kuwait, Maldives, Malaysia, Morocco, Oman, Palestine, Qatar, Saudi Arabia, Somalia, Tunisia, United Arab Emirates and Yemen).[179]

This unique set of rules and juridical method, therefore, is of relevance in discussing the legal context of countries throughout the world, including those of the Maghreb and Sahel.

An in-depth exploration of Islamic law reveals that it is frequently (perhaps strangely) familiar to Western jurists, especially those trained in the continental civil law tradition. Though the terminology and methods obviously differ, international lawyers and many Western practitioners should sense some familiarity with the contours of a legal system in which a textual document is the primary source of law; in which custom and past practices can become a source of law; and in which jurists employ a variety of methods of reasoning to fashion solutions to legal problems. After all, Article 38 of the Statute of the International Court of Justice sets forth a similar legal hierarchy for the international legal system, and international jurists employ a variety of methods of reasoning in crafting decisions.[180] The same is true on many levels of both common law and civil law systems that prevail in the West. As our focus shifts from a general description to a detailed analysis of substantive law, the vague outlines of familiar concepts will resolve into clear commonalities. That discussion will demonstrate how many of the rules that are considered emblematic of continental civil law align with Islamic law in both substance and judicial approach. Thus, while Islamic law differs from Western legal systems in many respects, to insist that it is somehow completely alien, or that it does not share values common to Western legal systems, is to persist in a grandiloquent illusion. This is because, as Santillana has noted, the same Roman law that serves as the root of that legal tradition influenced the formation of Islamic law in various respects.[181] This sameness and shared lineage will be illuminated further in the chapters that follow.

NOTES

1. *See* Hossein Esmaeili, *The Nature and Development of Law in Islam and the Rule of Law Challenge in the Middle East and the Muslim World*, 26 CONN. J. INT'L L. 329, 330 (2011).

2. WAEL B. HALLAQ, THE ORIGINS AND EVOLUTION OF ISLAMIC LAW 1 (2005).

3. *Id.*

4. *See* Chibli Mallat, *From Islamic to Middle Eastern Law A Restatement of the Field (Part i)*, 51 AM. J. COMP. L. 699, 701 (2003).

5. *See* MICHAEL MAAS, READINGS IN LATE ANTIQUITY: A SOURCEBOOK 294 (2012).

6. *See* EDWARD GIBBON, THE HISTORY OF THE DECLINE AND FALL OF THE ROMAN EMPIRE 546 (Cambridge University Press, 2013).

7. *See* JOSEPH SCHACHT, AN INTRODUCTION TO ISLAMIC LAW 6 (1982).

8. *See* Hallaq, *supra* note 2, at 18.

9. *See* Schacht, *supra* note 7, at 7.

10. *See* Hallaq, *supra* note 2, at 8.

11. *See* HUGH KENNEDY, THE GREAT ARAB CONQUESTS: HOW THE SPREAD OF ISLAM CHANGED THE WORLD WE LIVE IN 45–46 (2007).

12. *Id.*

13. *Id.*

14. *See* M. Cherif Bassiouni & Gamal M. Badr, *The Shari'ah: Sources, Interpretation, and Rule-Making,* 1 UCLA J. ISLAMIC & NEAR E. L. 135, 148 (2002).

15. JOHN L. ESPOSITO & JOHN O. VOLL, MAKERS OF CONTEMPORARY ISLAM 3 (2001).

16. *Id.*

17. *See* Mallat, *supra* note 4, at 718–19.

18. *Id.* at 719.

19. CHIBLI MALLAT, INTRODUCTION TO MIDDLE EASTERN LAW 33 (2007).

20. *See* J.N.D. ANDERSON, LAW AS A SOCIAL FORCE IN ISLAMIC CULTURE AND HISTORY 15 (1957).

21. *See* MUHAMMAD MUNIR, ISLAMIC INTERNATIONAL LAW (SIYAR): AN INTRODUCTION, HAMDARD ISLAMICUS 18 (2012), http://works.bepress.com/muhammad_munir/21/

22. *See* Hallaq, *supra* note 2, at 19–20.

23. *Id.* at 20.

24. *See* Bassiouni & Badr, *supra* note 14, at 148.

25. *See* Mallat, *supra* note 4, at 719.

26. David Santillana, 1 *Istituzioni di Diritto Musulmano Malichita,* 32–33 (trans. and quoted in HERBERT J. LIEBESNY, THE LAW OF THE NEAR & MIDDLE EAST 13 [1975]).

27. *See* Bassiouni & Badr, *supra* note 14, at 149.

28. WERNER MINSKI, COMPARATIVE LAW IN A GLOBAL CONTEXT: THE LEGAL SYSTEMS OF ASIA AND AFRICA 295 (2006).

29. *Id.* at 294.

30. *See* xiii YUSUF AL-QARADAWI, APPROACHING THE SUNNAH: COMPREHENSION & CONTROVERSY (2007).

31. Ignaz Goldziher, 2 *Muhammedanische Studien,* 13 (trans. and quoted in Liebesny, *supra* note 26, at 13).

32. *Id.*

33. *Id.*

34. *See* JONATHAN A. C. BROWN, HADITH: OXFORD BIBLIOGRAPHIES ONLINE RESEARCH GUIDE 3 (2010).

35. *See* Goldziher, *supra* note 31, at 14.

36. *See* WAEL B. HALLAQ, AN INTRODUCTION TO ISLAMIC LAW 16 (2009).

37. *See* Ignaz Goldziher, 2 *Muhammedanische Studien,* 11 (trans. and quoted in Liebesny, *supra* note 26, at 14).

38. *See* Intisar A. Rabb, *"Reasonable Doubt" in Islamic Law,* 40 YALE J. INT'L L. 41, 94 (2015). The author must also specifically thank Professor Haider Hamoudi for his elucidation of this distinction.

39. *See* M. Cherif Bassiouni et al., Reporter, *Islamic Law A Survey of Islamic International Law Contracts and Litigation in Islamic Law the Sources of Islamic Law,* 76 AM. SOC'Y INT'L L. PROC. 55, 67 (1982).

40. *See* Yasir Billoo, *Change and Authority in Islamic Law: The Islamic Law of Inheritance in Modern Muslim States,* 84 U. DET. MERCY L. REV. 637, 642 (2007).

41. *See* Amr. A. Shalakany, *Islamic Legal Histories,* 1 BERKELEY J. MIDDLE E. ISLAMIC L. 1 (2008), http://scholarship.law.berkeley.edu/jmeil/vol1/iss1/1

42. *See* Billoo, *supra* note 40.

43. *Id.*

44. *See* David Santillana, 1 *Istituzioni di Diritto Musulmano Malichita,* 46 (trans. and quoted in Liebesny, *supra* note 26 at 18).

45. *Id.*

46. *See Oxford Islamic Studies Online,* http://www.oxfordislamicstudies.com/article/opr/t125/e990

47. *See* J.N.D. Anderson, *Law as a Social Force in Islamic Culture and History* 16 (1957).

48. Ibn Khaldun, 3 *The Muqaddimah* 8–9 (trans. and quoted in Liebesny, *supra* note 26 at 27).

49. *See* Mallat, *supra* note 19, at 110.

50. *See* Haider Ala Hamoudi, *Muhammad's Social Justice or Muslim Cant?: Langdellianism and the Failures of Islamic Finance,* 40 CORNELL INT'L L.J. 89, 108–109 (2007).

51. *See* John Makdisi, *A Reality Check on Istihsan as a Method of Islamic Legal Reasoning,* 2 UCLA J. ISLAMIC & NEAR E.L. 99 (2003).

52. *See* Irshad Abdal-Haqq, *Islamic Law: An Overview of Its Origin and Elements,* 7 J. ISLAMIC L. & CULT 27, 57 (2002).

53. *See* Andra Nahal Behrouz, *Transforming Islamic Family Law: State Responsibility and the Role of Internal Initiative,* 103 COLUM. L. REV. 1136, 1148 (2003).

54. *See* Hamoudi, *supra* note 50.

55. *See* C. Snouk Hurgoneje, *Le Droit Musulman,* 225–27 (trans. and quoted in Liebesny, *supra* note 26, at 17).

56. *See* Abdal-Haqq, *supra* note 52, at 17.

57. *Id.*

58. *See* Ignaz Goldziher, *Vorlesungen uhrer den Islam,* 52–53 (trans. and quoted in Liebesny, *supra* note 26, at 17).

59. *See* Vandenhoeck & Ruprecht, World Peace Through Christian-Muslim Understanding: The Genesis And Fruits Of The Open Letter "A Common Word Between Us And You" 136 (2016).

60. *Id.*

61. *See* Abdal-Haqq, *supra* note 52.

62. *See* Gustav Von Grunebaum, *Medival Islam* 149–51 (trans. and quoted in Liebesny, *supra* note 26, at 17).

63. *Id.*

64. *See* Asifa Quraishi, *On Fallibility and Finality: Why Thinking Like A Qadi Helps Me Understand American Constitutional Law,* 2009 MICH. ST. L. REV. 339, 341 (2009).

65. *Id.*

66. *See* Sayyid Mohsen Sa'idzadeh, *Fiqh and Fiqahat,* 1 UCLA J. ISLAMIC & NEAR E.L. 239, 241–41 (2002). *See also* 3 *Ibn Khaldun, The Muqaddimah* 30–32 (trans. and quoted in Liebesny, *supra* note 26, at 21). ("Jurisprudence is the knowledge of the classification of the laws of God, which concern the actions of all responsible Muslims, as obligator, forbidden, recommendable, disliked, or permissible. These [laws] are derived from the Qur'an and the *Sunna* [traditions], and from the evidence of the Lawgiver [Muhammad] has established for the knowledge of [the laws]. The laws evolved from the [whole] of this evidence are called 'jurisprudence' [*fiqh*].")

67. *See* Mallat, *supra* note 19, at 41.

68. *Id.*

69. *See* Asifa Quraishi-Landes, *Islamic Constitutionalism: Not Secular. Not Theocratic. Not Impossible*, 16 Rutgers J. L. & Religion 553, 554 (2015).

70. *See* Mallat, *supra* note 4, at 718–19.

71. *See* Quraishi, *supra* note 69, at 341.

72. *See* Mallat, *supra* note 4, at 718–19.

73. *See* Liaquat Ali Khan, *Jurodynamics of Islamic Law*, 61 RUTGERS L. REV. 231, 272 (2009)

74. *Id.*

75. *Id.* at 272.

76. *Id.* at 281.

77. *See* BOGAC A. ERGENE, *Qanun and Sharia*, in THE ASHGATE RESEARCH COMPANION TO ISLAMIC LAW 117–18 (Peri Bearman, ed., 2016).

78. *Id.*

79. *See* RAKESH KUMAR SINGH, TEXTBOOK ON MUSLIM LAW 44 (2011).

80. *See* DAVID SANTILLANA, *Law and Society*, *in* THE LEGACY OF ISLAM 36 (Thomas Walker Arnold, Sir, & Alfred Guillaume, eds., 1931).

81. *See* Singh, *supra* note 79.

82. *See* LISBET CHRISTOFFERSEN & JØRGEN S. NIELSEN, SHARI'A AS DISCOURSE: LEGAL TRADITIONS AND THE ENCOUNTER WITH EUROPE 7 (2016).

83. *See* M.D. SANTILLANA, AVANT-PROJET DU CODE CIVIL ET COMMERCIAL TUNISIEN III, n.3. (1899) [hereinafter AVANT-PROJET].

84. *See* Christopher A. Ford, *Siyar-Ization and Its Discontents: International Law and Islam's Constitutional Crisis*, 30 TEX. INT'L L.J. 499, 500 (1995).

85. *Id.* citing Majid Khadduri, trans., *introduction* to MUḤAMMAD IBN-AL-ḤASAN AS̄- S̄AIBAN̄I, THE ISLAMIC LAW OF NATIONS: SHAYBANI'S SIYAR 8 (1966).

86. *Id.; see also* Shameem Akhtar, *An Inquiry into the Nature, Origin and Source of Islamic Law of Nations*, 6 KARACHI L.J. 63, 71 (1970).

87. *See* Khaled Ali Beydoun, *Dar al-Islam Meets "Islam As Civilization": An Alignment of Politico-Theoretical Fundamentalisms and the Geopolitical Realism of This Worldview*, 4 UCLA J. ISLAMIC & NEAR E. L. 143, 152 (2005).

88. *See* Munir, *supra* note 21, at 25. *See also* MUHAMMAD-BASHEER A. ISMAIL, ISLAMIC LAW AND TRANSNATIONAL DIPLOMATIC LAW: A QUEST FOR COMPLEMENTARITY IN DIVERGENT LEGAL THEORIES 45–46 (2016).

89. *See* Babak Rod Khadem, *The Doctrine of Separation in Classical Islamic Jurisprudence*, 4 UCLA J. ISLAMIC NEAR E.L. 95, 128 (2005).

90. *Id.*

91. Liebesny, *supra* note 26, at 20.

92. *See* Khadem, *supra* note 89.

93. Liebesny, *supra* note 26, at 20–21.

94. *See* Bassiouni & Badr, *supra* note 39 at 161.

95. *See* DANA ZARTNER, COURTS, CODES, AND CUSTOM: LEGAL TRADITION AND STATE POLICY TOWARD INTERNATIONAL HUMAN RIGHTS AND ENVIRONMENTAL LAW 132 (2014).

96. *Id.*

97. *See* Hamoudi, *supra* note 50, at 108–109.

98. Majid Khadduri & Herbert J. Liebesny, *Origin and Development of Islamic Law* (1955), 68–69.

99. *Id.*

100. *See* Zartner, *supra* note 95.

101. *See* Bassiouni & Badr, *supra* note 14, at 161.

102. *See* Zartner, *supra* note 95.

103. Stephen S. Zimowski, *Consequences of the Arab Spring: How Shari'ah Law and the Egyptian Revolution Will Impact Ip Protection and Enforcement*, 2 PENN ST. J.L. & INT'L AFF. 150, 158 (2013).

104. *See* Khadem, *supra* note 89, at 130.

105. *See* Zartner, *supra* note 95, at 132.

106. *See* Amna Arshad, *Ijtihad as a Tool for Islamic Legal Reform: Advancing Women's Rights in Morocco*, KAN. J.L. & PUB. POL'Y 129, 133–34 (Winter 2006–2007).

107. *See* Zimowski, *supra* note 103, at 158.

108. *See* Khadduri & Liebesny, *supra* note 98, at 69.

109. *See* Bassiouni & Badr, *supra* note 14, at 161.

110. *See* Zartner, *supra* note 95, at 132.

111. *See* Ali Khan, *The Reopening of the Islamic Code: The Second Era of Ijtihad*, 1 U. St. THOMAS L.J. 341, 363–64 (2003).

112. *See* Zartner, *supra* note 95, at 132.

113. *See* Bassiouni & Badr, *supra* note 14, at 161.

114. *See* Zartner, *supra* note 95, at 132.

115. *Id.*

116. *Id.*

117. *See* Mallat, *supra* note 19, at 113.

118. *Id.*

119. Sayyid Rami Al Rifai, Who is the Main Body of the Ummah?: Muslim Demographics 6 (2015)

120. *Id.*

121. *See* HISHAM M. RAMADAN, UNDERSTANDING ISLAMIC LAW: FROM CLASSICAL TO CONTEMPORARY 29 (2006).

122. *See* Mohammad Fadel, *Islamic Politics and Secular Politics: Can They Co-Exist?*, 25 J.L. REL. 187, 201 (2010).

123. Khaled Abou El Fadl, *Muslims and Accessible Jurisprudence in Liberal Democracies: A Response to Edward B. Foley's Jurisprudence and Theology*, 66 FORDHAM L. REV. 1227, 1231 (1998).

124. *See generally*, A MODERN HISTORY OF THE ISMAILIS: CONTINUITY AND CHANGE IN A MUSLIM COMMUNITY (Farhad Daftary, ed., 2010) ABU UMAR FARUQ AHMAD, THEORY AND PRACTICE OF MODERN ISLAMIC FINANCE: THE CASE ANALYSIS FROM AUSTRALIA 84 (2010).

125. *See* VALERIE J. HOFFMAN, THE ESSENTIALS OF IBADI ISLAM 20 (2012).

126. *Id.* at 14.

127. *Id.* at 8–11.

128. *Id.* at 41–42.

129. SADEK HAMID, SUFIS, SALAFIS AND ISLAMISTS: THE CONTESTED GROUND OF BRITISH ISLAMIC ACTIVISM 12 (2016).

130. ROBERT EARL HANDLOFF, MAURITANIA, A COUNTRY STUDY 92 (1990).

131. *Id.*

132. CARL W. ERNST, SUFISM: AN INTRODUCTION TO THE MYSTICAL TRADITION OF ISLAM 30–31 (1950).

133. LLOYD RIDGEON, SUFIS AND SALAFIS IN THE CONTEMPORARY AGE 43 (2015).

134. DIANE MORGAN, ESSENTIAL ISLAM: A COMPREHENSIVE GUIDE TO BELIEF AND PRACTICE 236 (2010).

135. *See* Haider Ala Hamoudi, *"Lone Wolf" Terrorism and the Classical Jihad: On the Contingencies of Violent Islamic Extremism,* 11 FIU L. REV. 19, 29 (2015).

136. *Id.*

137. *Id.*

138. *Id.*

139. *See* Melanie D. Reed, *Western Democracy and Islamic Tradition: The Application of Shari'a in A Modern World,* 19 AM. U. INT'L L. REV. 485, 508 (2004).

140. *See* Majid Khadduri, *War and Peace in the Law of Islam,* 175–77 (trans. and quoted in Liebesny, *supra* note 26, at 9).

141. ABDULLAHI AHMED AN-NA'IM, TOWARD AN ISLAMIC REFORMATION: CIVIL LIBERTIES, HUMAN RIGHTS, AND INTERNATIONAL LAW 89 (1996).

142. *See* Mark L. Movsesian, *Elusive Equality: The Armenian Genocide and the Failure of Ottoman Legal Reform,* 4 U. ST. THOMAS J.L. PUB. POL'Y 1, 6 (2010).

143. *See* Khadduri, *supra* note 140.

144. *See* Reed, *supra* note 139, at 508.

145. Timur Kuran, *The Economic Ascent of the Middle East's Religious Minorities: The Role of Islamic Legal Pluralism,* 33 J. LEGAL STUD. 475, 484 (2004).

146. Liebesny, *supra* note 26, at 10.

147. *See* Movsesian, *supra* note 142, at 6.

148. *Id.*

149. *Id.*

150. *See* Norman Bentwich, *The End of the Capitulatory System,* 14 BRIT. Y.B. INT'L L. 89, 89–91 (1933).

151. *See* Nasim M. Soosa, *The Historical Interpretation of the Origin of the Capitulations in the Ottoman Empire,* 4 TEMP. L. Q. 360 (1929–1930) (footnote omitted).

152. *Id.* at 360–64.

153. *See* Bentwich, *supra* note 150, at 90.

154. *Id.* at 89 (internal quotation marks omitted).

155. *Id.*

156. R.G. Surridge & Rebecca Matthews, *Extraterritoriality—A Vanishing Institution,* 3 Cum. Dig. Int'l L. & Rel. 81, 81 (1934).

157. *See* Bentwich, *supra* note 150, at 89.

158. *See* Sarah Abrevaya Stein, *Extraterritorial Dreams: European Citizenship, Sephardi Jews, And The Ottoman Twentieth Century* 1 (2016).

159. *Id.* at 1–2.

160. *Id.* at 2.

161. Daniel J. Schroeter, The Sultan's Jew: Morocco And The Sephardi World 40 (2002), 40.

162. *See* Timur Kuran, The Long Divergence: How Islamic Law Held Back The Middle East 170 (2012).

163. Qur'an, Sura 5.

164. Liebesny, *supra* note 26, at 210.

165. *See* Ramadan, *supra* note 121, at 96–97.

166. *See* Schacht, *supra* note 7, at 6.

167. *Id.*

168. *See* Abdur Rahim, The Principles Of Muhammadan Jurisprudence According To The Hanafi, Maliki, Shafii And Hanbali Schools 282 (1911). *See also* Hiroyuki Yanagihashi, *Socio-Economic Justice,* in The Ashgate Research Companion To Islamic Law 153 (Rudolph Peters, ed., 2014).

169. *See* Imran Ahsan Khan Nyazee, Outlines Of Islamic Jurisprudence 246 (1998).

170. *See* Rahim, *supra* note 168, at 282.

171. *See, e.g., id.* at 166 and 105 (indicating that Islamic law requires consideration); and at 2 (stating that Islamic law does not require "mutuality of advantage"); Khadduri & Liebesny, *supra* note 98, at 195 (noting that "Muslim jurists have disagreed over the question of consideration, including the meaning of the term and the extent of its effect on the contract.").

172. *See* Khadduri & Liebesny, *supra* note 98, at 193.

173. *See* Ramadan, *supra* note 118, at 96–97.

174. *See* Nyazee, *supra* note 169, at 256.

175. *See* Schacht, *supra* note 7, at 145.

176. *See* Nyazee, *supra* note 169, at 255.

177. European Parliament, *Briefing: Understanding the Branches of Islam: Sunni Islam* (Feb. 2016), http://www.europarl.europa.eu/RegData/etudes/brie/2016/577963/eprs_bri(2016)577963_en.pdf.

178. *Id.*

179. *Id.*

180. United Nations, *Statute of the International Court of Justice* (Apr. 18, 1946), article 38, http://www.refworld.org/docid/3deb4b9c0.html (accessed May 14, 2017).

181. *See* Avant-Projet, *supra* note 83, at IV.

Chapter 3

The Genesis of the Santillana Codes

An analysis of the Santillana Codes is a necessarily complex undertaking. It is an endeavor that entwines the histories of multiple countries, cultures, and legal systems. An understanding of the geographic and historic context of the places where the Santillana Codes are in force helps to explain how and why the codes were created and adopted. Similarly, as the elaboration of his work in the chapters that follow demonstrate, the contribution of Islamic legal scholars in Tunisia influenced the seminal Tunisian approach to codification and helped produce the magnificent, syncretistic style that characterizes Santillana's work.

The three countries relevant to this comparative excursus (Tunisia, Morocco, and Mauritania) are African countries that are considered part of what is called the Maghreb—the region in Africa which is closest to Europe and thus "a ready bridge for the exchange of influences in both directions."[1] Tunisia and Morocco are the most similar and "share a core of historic characteristics" that make them quite different countries from Mauritania, which is considered both part of the Maghreb and the Sahel.[2] Each of the three countries, of course, is different in important ways, with its own history, culture, and political challenges. Those historical differences, in turn, influence the way their laws are received and implemented. As one nineteenth-century commentator has noted, "Law stands foremost among the practical sciences as an aid to history, and history in turn becomes the interpreter of law."[3] It is, therefore, helpful before delving too deeply into the civil law of Tunisia, Morocco, and Mauritania, to note some key aspects of each country's legal history and observe some political and social developments that have served to shape and continuously influence their respective legal physiognomies.

TUNISIA

Tunisia is a North African country that borders the Mediterranean Sea, between Algeria and Libya.[4] The geographic territory that we associate today with the modern country of Tunisia[5] is one with a rich history of diverse people and successive empires, all of which have influenced modern Tunisia's fascinating legal culture. Tunisia has historically been predominantly Muslim but has always had a degree of religious diversity.[6] For instance, parts of the first Jewish community in Tunisia could potentially date back to the destruction of the First Temple in Jerusalem in 566 BCE.[7] Christians likewise have historically had a presence in Tunisia as ancient Carthage was a center of Christianity in the region,[8] though that population shrank dramatically in the thirteenth century.[9] It is because of the traditional presence of such religious minorities and ethnic groups throughout its history that Tunisia has been a place "characterized by ethno-religious diversity"[10]—a complex cultural tapestry rather than a mundane monolith.

The Punic Wars brought Tunisia under the Roman Empire in 149 BC.[11] Tunisia's subsequent "integration into the Roman and Byzantine Empires led to the Christianization of the region in the first several centuries CE."[12] Arab Muslim armies, however, "conquered Tunisia in the late seventh century and initiated the spread of Islamic influences throughout the country."[13] Coextensive with that series of rulers, Roman law prevailed, until the Arab conquest in the seventh century effectively replaced Roman law with Islamic law.[14] During the Aghlabite period, among the predominantly Muslim population, the Maliki school of Islamic law became most prominent, though a notable minority of adherents to the Hanafite School also existed in the region.[15] Islamic law, however, applied only to Muslims. The Jewish population was still governed by Mosaic law and Christians, in turn, were governed by ecclesiastic law (which retained elements of Roman law).[16] Professor Faouzi Belknani, a legal scholar who has served on faculties in both Tunisia and Qatar, notes that, in the twelfth century, Muslim jurists compiled collections fatwas and juridical opinions on diverse questions of law,[17] such as the Hanafite compilations of Alhindiyya and Alamkîrya or the Malikite collection called Al-Mi'yâr by the jurist al-Wanshârisi.[18]

Modern Tunisia has, it turns out, always had an intellectual climate that inspired innovative codifications. The modern administration of Tunisia began in the nineteenth century,[19] which saw the creation of multiple distinct jurisdictions and courts, the applicability of which depended on the religion of the party. For instance, Muslims had access to Malikite or Hanafite courts, while Jews had access to rabbinical courts, etc.[20] As a general matter, civil law in Tunisia was largely regulated by Islamic law.[21] In the nineteenth century, however, interesting efforts to codify Tunisian law began. For instance,

Figure 3.1   Map of Tunisia: CIA World Factbook, Tunisia.

the Civil and Penal Code promulgated in 1861 by Sadek Bey contained provisions inspired by both Maliki and Hanafi schools of Islamic law,[22] but was short lived and was repealed by 1864.[23] Despite its brief life, it stands out as a demonstration of Tunisian legal innovation and a signal of what could be realized with regard to codification.

Many other reforms during this period were attempted by Khayr al-Din al-Tunisi (Khayr al-Din) an Ottoman Tunisian political reformer and modernist. Khayr al-Din became Prime Minister of Tunisia in 1873 and pressed economic and administrative reforms to address Tunisia's growing

financial crisis. Although exiled in 1877, his tenure in Tunisia is notable
for his efforts at judicial reform and modernization. Other intellectual currents, however, were also at work and continued the Tunisian march toward
legal modernity. A notable moment occurred in 1885, with the promulgation of the Tunisian *Code Foncier*—a legislative achievement that marked
the beginning of a process of progressive diminution of Islamic law's
applicability in Tunisia.[24] Building off the experience of years of legal
experimentation and an innovative intellectual tradition, the momentum
toward codification in Tunisia had begun and would only garner force.

As the global movement toward codification began, perhaps the most significant early attempt at codification of Islamic law came in 1876 with the
promulgation of the Ottoman code known as the Mejelle.[25] It is interesting to
note that the Mejelle, though frequently characterized as the first codification
of Islamic civil law, is predated in Tunisia by Sadek Bey's Civil and Penal
Code of 1861. The Mejelle, however, would have no immediate influence on
the development of Tunisian law and was never fully in force in the region
today associated with modern Tunisia—a region which, as noted, was deeply
immersed in its own legislative initiatives by the time the Mejelle was promulgated.[26] In that regard, commentators note that the Ottoman legal reforms of
the late nineteenth century occurred parallel to Tunisian legal developments,
but did not have significant impacts in Tunisia, which "retained substantial
autonomy under the rule of the Husaynid Bey."[27] Nonetheless, as discussed
further below, the Mejelle would come to influence modern Tunisian civil law
in later years.

In 1881, with the Treaty of Bardo, Tunisia's period as a French protectorate began. During this time, the Ottoman Bey maintained power in theory,
but was effectively under the power of a foreign (French) sovereign.[28] French
legal influence became more pronounced in 1883 after signing of the Treaty
of Marsa formally established the French protectorate and permitted France
to directly undertake legislative reforms.[29] This opened the door to far more
expansive and ambitious legal projects, among the first of which was an effort
to codify Tunisia's civil and commercial law based on the French model of
codification. These political developments would set the stage for the codification that Santillana and his team of jurists would undertake.

MOROCCO

Morocco is also a North African country that borders the North Atlantic
Ocean and the Mediterranean Sea, between Algeria and Western Sahara.[30]
"Its citizens are Arab, Berber, and often a blend of both, and remnants of the
old Jewish community still remain."[31] Jews arrived in Morocco before the

arrival of the Romans,[32] while Christianity arrived during the Roman era.[33] Like Tunisia, Morocco has been described as a country of "profound cultural diversity and separate human landscapes in which the legacy of distinctive cultural development remains strong."[34]

Morocco's history, so closely linked with that of Tunisia, is equally rich and diverse. During antiquity, the Phoenicians and Carthaginians established staging areas and trading posts in the area before the Romans founded, in what is now northern Morocco, the province of Mauritania Tingitana.[35] Roman domination of the area ended in the early part of the fifth century with the arrival of the Vandals.[36] However, no prior group would impact the cultural and social physiognomy of North Africa in the same way as the Arabs who came to the area in the seventh century. As early as the eighth century, a series of dynasties began to attempt to bring Morocco under the control of a central government, including a succession of Berber dynasties that had intermittent success.[37] Unlike Tunisia and other areas of the Maghreb, however, the area of modern-day Morocco never fell under Ottoman control.[38] This distinction meant that this part of the Maghreb would develop without extensive Ottoman influence (to include the Ottoman legal innovations such as the Mejelle).[39]

The sixteenth century saw the ascendance of the Saadians—a group which emphasized its Sharifian descent from the Prophet Muhammad "and its commitment to the enforcement of a purer form of Islam."[40] The Saadian dynasty eventually brought most of the area known today as Morocco under their control,[41] though they would call the area under their control the Sharifian Empire.[42] The Saadians were succeeded by the Alawite dynasty around

Figure 3.2   Map of Morocco: CIA World Factbook, Morocco.

1659[43] and by the eighteenth century, the area of modern-day Morocco was experiencing protracted civil war and a prolonged period of political instability.[44] It was during this period that Morocco's technical and military capabilities fell behind those of the French and Spanish, a fact that permitted greater European encroachment into Moroccan sovereignty in the nineteenth century, when French colonial ambitions increased.[45] As Dwight Ling notes, "With the termination of the Franco-Prussian War, France turned its attention even more seriously to North Africa viewing the Maghreb as the gateway to Africa."[46]

It is also during this time that both Tunisia and Morocco became heavily indebted to European countries.[47] At such an economic and technical disadvantage, "Morocco entered the 20th century unable to resist becoming a pawn in the intensified European diplomatic maneuvers."[48] Such ambitions were expressed in the *Entente Cordiale* of 1904 between Britain and France that gave France the right to "preserve order … and provide assistance in Morocco."[49] In 1906, at an international conference in the Spanish town of Algeciras, much of the sultan's authority was effectively ceded to France. In 1911, French troops were deployed to Morocco at the request of the sultan who was facing revolt, ushering in a new period of intensified French involvement.[50] Finally, in 1912, Sultan 'Abd al-Hafiz signed the Treaty of Fez, the first article of which stated that the French government and the sultan would agree to institute new administrative, judicial, educational, financial, and military regimes in Morocco that were deemed needed by French authorities.[51]

Throughout its history, Islamic law (mainly Malikism) held sway in Morocco.[52] Susan Gilson Miller, in her excellent book on Morocco, notes that the period from 1900 to 1912—though frequently considered a period of decline—actually represented an intellectually dynamic time for "nonstate actors [in Morocco] who rose up in the interstices of society and seized the opportunity created by the vacuum of power to advance a different version of how Morocco's past and future might be jointed."[53] Morocco was becoming receptive to European and Western culture during this era and young Moroccans who studied abroad were returning with ideas of reform that could be applied to domestic institutions.[54] This period of intellectual and cultural awakening included the work of legal scholars who advanced reformist ideas.[55] Morocco in 1913 was, therefore, vulnerable to French legal influence, but simultaneously experiencing a period of robust intellectual and cultural fecundity that prepared the Moroccan polity to receive a legal code that blended Islamic law with continental civil law.

MAURITANIA

The Islamic Republic of Mauritania is a large, arid, and sparsely populated country in West Africa.[56] It borders the North Atlantic Ocean, between

Senegal and Western Sahara.[57] As noted, Mauritania is technically considered part of the Maghreb, but is also considered a Sahelian country. While it is geographically, historically, and culturally dissimilar from both Tunisia and Morocco, there are some similarities and shared characteristics. Unlike its northern neighbors, however, there is very little religious diversity in Mauritania, with some reports noting that it is 100% Islamic.[58] On that score, Robert Dowd notes that Mauritania numbers among several Muslim countries with "essentially no effective sub-religious groups."[59]

Long before it was called "Mauritania," it was an area in West Africa of lesser interest to European explorers, which they called the *Pays Maures* (Moor Country).[60] Within this territory, Islamic law—notably the Maliki madhab—has long had a strong influence.[61] As one commentator noted in 1969, "While Islamic law has not governed crimes in Mauritania since 1946, it would appear to be the general law of the land in civil matters, with the written modern law being applied only by way of exception."[62]

In the fifteenth and sixteenth centuries, European traders sought to obtain gum arabic (a substance obtained from acacia trees that was used for a variety

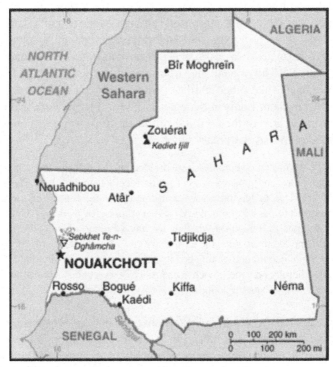

Figure 3.3   Map of Mauritania: CIA World Factbook, Mauritania.

of purposes) from areas in the southern part of this area.[63] Coastal trade, however, was the primary focus of European engagement in the region and there was little effort expended to facilitate inland exploration or to establish permanent settlements.[64] The primary European country to influence the region was France, which established a settlement at Saint Louis at the mouth of the Senegal River in 1678.[65] French sovereignty over the area encompassing the Senegal River and the Mauritanian coast was recognized by the Congress of Vienna in 1815,[66] though, at that time, the area that would eventually become Mauritania was wrongly considered by French authorities to be something of a wasteland that did not merit the expense or effort to occupy and develop.[67]

On June 16, 1895, France established a central government to administer its eight territories in Western Africa (including Mauritania) in a federation that would be simply called French West Africa (*Afrique Occidentale Francaise*).[68] In 1830, French authorities made the French Civil Code applicable throughout that entire region.[69] French law, therefore, including the French Civil Code, began to have applicability in Mauritania in the nineteenth century.

In 1901, France implemented a plan of "peaceful penetration" of the areas north of the Senegal River under the suzerainty of the Maures, a primarily Arab-Berber ethnic group.[70] This plan, authored by Xavier Coppolani, purposefully exploited conflicts among key Maure leaders and established military posts in the central region of southern Mauritania.[71] Thereafter, in October 1904, France "recognized Mauritania as an entity separate from Senegal and organized it as a French protectorate under a delegate general in Saint Louis."[72] This meant that Mauritania was judicially and administratively organized like other similarly situated French territories in Africa, though run from Saint Louis in Senegal.[73] The legal framework that emerged during this era to govern the civil life of this territory was a fascinating mixture of French law and customary law.[74]

> The inhabitants of French colonies were divided into two groups: persons subject to customary law and persons subject to the received French law. The former were characterized as having a customary status (*statut coutumier*), while the latter were said to possess French civil status (*statut civil français*). Until 1946, a person's status depended on whether he was a French citizen. The received French law applied to citizens; the customary law governed non-citizens. Generally speaking, when France established its African colonies, the colonial population did not thereby become French citizens. They were considered subjects and customary law consequently continued to govern their affairs.[75]

After the Second World War, Mauritania became an overseas territory in French West Africa with membership in the French Union.[76] Thereafter, in November 1958, Mauritania became a republic and an autonomous member of the French Community.[77] Finally, Mauritania became an independent republic on October 19, 1960,[78] and immediately the leaders of this new country were faced with the question on which law should govern within their young borders.[79] For instance, a Code of Civil, Commercial, and Administrative Procedure was enacted in Mauritania in 1962.[80] The code, however, had gaping lacunae in terms of its applicability and noted that Islamic law would generally govern in civil matters, with the exception of eight categories.[81]

Mauritania's first president, Moktar Ould Daddah, ruled until 1978 when he was ousted (and later exiled) by a military coup.[82] After a tumultuous period of succeeding military regimes, on December 12, 1984, Chief of Staff and former Minister of Defense Maaouiya Ould Sid 'Ahmed Taya rose to power through another palace coup.[83] President Taya would rule Mauritania from 1984 until he too was ousted by a military coup in 2005.[84] Though much of what occurred during his time in office was objectionable,[85] commentators note that there was a progressive aspect to his regime and that "in Mauritania in the mid-1980s traditional outlooks based on custom, family ties, and Islam were gradually giving way to a more modern set of political views based on codified laws and procedures, achievement, and a national consciousness." Mauritania in the 1980s, therefore, was ready for a degree of institutional reform and—despite obvious challenges—was slowly starting to tilt in spirit toward legal modernity.

THE 'ULAMA OF THE MAGHREB AND SAHEL

An important group in the Maghreb and Sahel which was critical to legal life in those regions was that of the 'ulama or "scholars of religion, especially the law [Shari'a] whose training (and piety) lent them the ability to interpret the law authoritatively."[86] Throughout the Muslim world, the 'ulama derived authority from their role as custodians and interpreters of Shari'a and the physical institutions which facilitated its practice and study—mosques, Shari'a courts, and schools.[87] While, as one might expect, the role of the 'ulama varied across the Maghreb and Sahel, there are some areas of commonality. For instance, the populations of each country are overwhelmingly Muslim and, from a historical perspective, Islam has played a critical role in the history and formation of each country. In addition, the main school of Islamic law across the Maghreb and Sahel is the Maliki madhab—though other madhabs have also had considerable influence. Religious practices in each country also were tinged with Islamic mysticism and indigenous practices which clashed with orthodoxy and efforts by the Salafiyya movement to "reform" Maghrebi and Sahelian Islamic practices.[88]

The 'ulama in Tunisia "formed the core of the Tunisian religious establishment and served as the guardians of the Islamic high cultural tradition."[89]

As an institutional body, however, the Tunisian 'ulama was more akin to an academic group than a formal institution.[90] To be counted as an alim (scholar) and be considered part of the 'ulama was an honorific title—one bestowed on learned men by virtue of their learning and erudition.[91] It was, even so, a title that came with recognition and a role as legal authority.[92]

> The ulama prized strict observance of traditionally established behavior patterns. An alim was expected to live an exemplary life in conformity with the precepts of Islam, free of scandal. He should affect a certain gravity, avoid the popular cafes, and not let himself be seen in public laughing, speaking in a loud voice, or eating.[93]

At the center of this elite group of scholars in the Tunisia was the Zeituna Mosque, the oldest and largest mosque in Tunisia.[94] The Zeituna Mosque (pictured on the cover of this book) had an esteemed university that provided religious education and was the primary educational pathway for one seeking to be considered part of the 'ulama in Tunis.[95] It was an intellectual pillar of the Islamic world and a renowned center of learning.

Although the prevailing school of Islamic law in Tunisia was the Malikite madhab, Ottoman authority meant that the Hanafite madhab would also find a role in Tunisian religious society. In that regard, the Ottoman deys afforded recognition to Tunisia's religious institutions but stressed the formal supremacy of the Hanafite over the Malikite madhab. This meant that both madhabs coexisted within Tunisian religio-social space.[96] Jamil M. Abun-Nasr notes that the Hanafites in Ottoman Tunisia were, in religious and legal matters, dependent on the help of Malikite scholars. For instance, most Hanafite religious scholars of Tunisia in the seventeenth and eighteenth century had Malikite teachers, and the Hanafite muftis often sought help from their Malikite colleagues in dealing with complex legal matters.[97]

Another important aspect of Islam in nineteenth-century Tunisia was the Sufi influence on Tunisian religious practices. In fact, those educated at Zeituna were often the children of Sufi shaykhs, meaning that—as they ascended into the 'ulama—they brought with them their "maraboutic origins."[98] Moreover, many orthodox religious leaders in Tunisia were identified as members of Sufi orders.[99] Leon describes the situation by noting that Hussainid Tunisia in the early nineteenth century was "still living in the period of accommodation between orthodoxy and mysticism."[100]

As previously discussed, the nineteenth century brought many attempts by the Ottoman Empire to reform the law and administration of Ottoman territories—and some of the Tunisian 'ulama resisted such reforms.[101] Later, however, many 'ulama "emerged to support the modernizing initiatives of Khayr al-Din, reformist Prime Minister of Tunisia during the mid-1870s."[102]

This vacillation between support and opposition would continue throughout the century. The French occupation in 1881 would temporarily suspend indigenous reform efforts, and parts of the Tunisian 'ulama would again be an initial source of resistance to the extension of French control during the period of the protectorate.[103] Some sought to obstruct early French reform efforts but later "began to give themselves over to reformist pursuits in cooperation with the French liberals, advocates of *'la politique d'association.'*"[104] Commentators note, however, that the cooperation between the 'ulama and reformers (especially the French) was always somewhat fragile and uneasy.[105] Such uneasiness is entirely understandable given the fact that most reforms served to undermine the 'ulama's influence. Arnold H. Green notes, "[W]hen Western-inspired law codes and courts were introduced, the 'ulama's judicial powers were suppressed or severely reduced; and when secular schools were established, the 'ulama's monopoly over education was broken[.]"[106]

Notable members of the Tunisian 'ulama were those given the title shaykh al-Islam, which literally means "master of Islam."[107] This honorific title was bestowed on the "chief jurisconsult of a city or realm," and the legal opinions of person bearing such a title carried considerable force.[108] Many of these individuals were exceptionally well-traveled and cosmopolitan thinkers. One family that had many of its line bear this title was the Bayram family—a scholarly Hanafite family which Green describes as the most prestigious and important 'ulama dynasties in Tunisia.[109] Its founder arrived in Tunis with the Ottomans in 1574 and the family soon thereafter "devoted itself to religious pursuits."[110] In fact, Muhammad Bayram IV (d. 1861) "was the first Tunisian religious dignitary to bear the title of Shaykh al-Islam."[111]

Perhaps the most famous of the Bayram family was Mohammed Bayram al-Khamis V. Like most of his influential family of 'ulama, he was educated at Zeituna Mosque[112] and engaged in a variety of academic, journalistic, and literary pursuits. For instance, he was appointed as the editor of the official gazette in Tunisia, directed the state printing office, and organized the library at Zeituna University. He was also a prolific writer on a variety of topics, including Islamic law and political geography, and was widely viewed as a reformist who wished to harmonize Islam and modern society.[113] In addition, he is known to have traveled to Europe on various occasions—visiting both Paris and London—and held a deep appreciation for European art and culture.[114] Green notes, "In 1879 he emigrated to Egypt where he devoted the remainder of his life to Islamic justice and journalism."[115] Nineteenth-century British statesman Evelyn Baring, in fact, met Mohammed Bayram al-Khamis in Egypt and wrote effusively of his fondness and admiration for Bayram's intellect and demeanor:[116]

He was, moreover, one of the most remarkable types with which I have met in the course of my Eastern existence. He looked like a thorough gentleman.

I have rarely seen a more striking figure than that of this grave Oriental, with
his high intellectual forehead, refined features, melancholy eyes, dignified
mien, exquisite manners, and graceful costume, who would sit with me by the
hour and sing a dirge over the decadence of Islam. Moreover, Sheikh Mohammed Beyram not only looked a gentleman; he was one. In no country have I
come across a man of more elevated and refined feelings, or one whose opinions and actions were less tainted with worldly self-interest than this Tunisian
aristocrat.[117]

Another notable Tunisian to bear the title of shaykh al-Islam was Ahmad
Ibn al Khūja. Born in Tunis in 1834 as the son of another shaykh al-Islam,[118]
Ibn al Khūja was described by French resident-general Paul Cambon as a
"prominent individual" with considerable influence in Tunisia and it is noted
that he once attended New Year's Eve festivities at Cambon's residence in
Tunis.[119]

Ahmad b. Khuja was a alim of the solid traditional formation, well versed in
usul al-fiqh and in tafsir (exegesis). He acquired a great reputation in Tunis as
a teacher, and continued to teach the work on tafsir by al-Baydawi even after
he became Shaikh al-Islam. The renowned Malikite alim Muhammad al-Fadil
b. Ashur extolled in a biography of Ahmad b. Khuja the meticulous care with
which he documented the fatwas he wrote and which made him famous outside
Tunisia. He was also a reformist thinker who, upon a suggestion from Khayr
ad-Din, wrote two essays, showing the compatibility of Islam with modern
civilization, and defending reform in general and Khayr ad-Din's program in
particular. According to Ibn Ashur, Ibn Khuja played a determinant role in the
changes introduced under the Resident-General Paul Cambon in the early period
of the French protectorate in the Tunisian system of law[.][120]

Moreover, Green notes that Ahmad Ibn al Khūja was a member of the
court of appeals in Tunis along with other members of the 'ulama such as
Muhammad al-Shāhid, Ahmad Ibn al Khūja, Muhammad al-Sattārī, Mahammad al-Nayfar, and Hasan Abbās. Perhaps most interestingly, it is noted that
Ahmad Ibn al Khūja assisted Cambon in creating a mixed Franco-Tunisian
property court.[121] The Tunisian 'ulama of the mid-nineteenth century was,
therefore, already engaging with government authorities on comparative
legal efforts.
    A succeeding shaykh al-Islam in Tunis was another (though less known)
member of the Bayram family named Mahammad Bayram.[122] The cousin of
Mohammed Bayram al-Khamis V and the son of a qadi, he too studied at Zeituna Mosque and served as an imam, a teacher, Hanafi qadi, and eventually
served as the mufti of the Zeituna Mosque. Green notes that "[Mahammad
Bayram] became Shaykh al-Islam in 1897, and he died in 1900."[123] Before

his death, however, he would interact with David Santillana and, through the guidance and insight that he provided to Tunisian codification effort, he would have a lasting impact on Tunisian law.

The Zeituna Mosque in Tunisia was one of the two most famous madrassas in the Maghreb. The other was the Qarawiyin Mosque in Fez, Morocco.[124] The Tunisian and Moroccan 'ulama and their roles were, however, somewhat different. This was, in part, because of the many cultural and political differences between the two countries. At the outset, Morocco was not a part of the Ottoman Empire and, thus, had its own cultural and national identity.[125] It was never pressed to shape its approach to political or religious life to accommodate Ottoman views. Moroccan Muslims in the nineteenth century also approached Islam a bit differently from their Tunisian contemporaries. For instance, commentators have noted that Moroccan Islam has maintained certain "anthropolatrous" practices that were prevelant among rural Moroccan tribes.[126] This imbued Moroccan Islam with more pronounced elements of mysticism and various Sufi-inspired practices such as the veneration of saints who serve as supernatural intermediaries between Allah and the worshiper.[127] Moroccan Islamic practice also recognized the shurafa—direct descendants of the Prophet who formed a sort of religious aristocracy who maintained special legal and social status.[128] Since the Idrisid dynasty, this group formed a separate power center wielding its own political authority—the power of which increased during the Merinid dynasty.[129]

> The more anthropolatrous popular Islam ... stressed hierarchy and mediation between the believer and God. The mediators were sufi shaykhs, saints, and shurafa'. This form of Islam was characterized by ritual indulgence, in contrast to the puritanism of urban orthodoxy.[130]

In addition, the sultan of Morocco was a descendant of the Prophet and, accordingly, considered himself to be the legitimate head of the religious community (umma) in Morocco.[131] The Moroccan 'ulama was technically under the supervision of the sultan though it did enjoy considerable autonomy. For instance, the Chief Qadi of Fez had the responsibility of appointing all the professors and teachers of the university at Qarawiyin Mosque and controlled the waqf properties of the city of Fez.[132] The sultan could not interfere in the content or form of education or otherwise interfere in matters under the Chief Qadi's control.[133] That said, in the later nineteenth century, sultans Hassan I and 'Abd al-'Aziz implemented measures to restrict the Chief Qadi's ability to appoint judges and forced the Chief Qadi to share his jurisdiction over parts of Fez.[134]

The structure of Moroccan society and Moroccan Islam, therefore, meant that religious authority was dispersed and contested in a competitive power structure in which "knowledge ('ilm) was not the sole provenance of the lawyers but also included others who derived authority and privilege from their status as people of knowledge[.]"[135] Within this context, the Moroccan 'ulama consisted of "the usual panoply of judicial and educational officials which one would expect to find in a Muslim country, and they were arranged in a roughly hierarchical organization."[136] But Edmond Burke III notes that the 'ulama in nineteenth-century Morocco was a more nebulous construct.[137]

[I]t is even possible to say that the ulama as an identifiable corporate group did not exist in Morocco. Only if the term is restricted in its employ to refer to the seventeen to twenty major professors at the Qarawiyin university (a limitation that considerably distorts the way the term is actually used) is it possible to distinguish a clearly defined group of ulama.[138]

During the era of French colonization, the Moroccan 'ulama was rather passive and offered little resistance.[139] In fact, during the initial part of the colonial period, the Moroccan 'ulama were generally supportive of the French administration.[140] Developments in the early nineteenth century—such as perceived French imperialism and the reform efforts of 'Abd al 'Aziz which threatened many of the 'ulama's traditional interests—briefly served to galvanize the Moroccan 'ulama as a group.[141] The years 1903–1912 witnessed several instances of the Moroccan 'ulama opposing government reform efforts and even directing intervention into political affairs, such as their intervention on behalf of 'Abd al-Hafiz whom they proclaimed sultan of Morocco.[142] This surge in the Moroccan 'ulama's coherence and political will was, however, short lived. After the ascendance of 'Abd al-Hafiz as sultan, "the Moroccan ulama once again receded into the background."[143] In 1912, when Morocco became a French protectorate and Moulay Youssef was made sultan, the Moroccan 'ulama was no longer a formidable political force.

Mauritania, of course, also possessed a group of learned religious clerics. This is no surprise due to the rich history of intellectual exchange in the Sahara since Islam first spread to the region in the ninth century with the movement of Muslim traders and artisans. This important intellectual tradition facilitated the trans-Sahara book trade and the "desert libraries" which served as remote fortresses of knowledge and repositories of ancient manuscripts. This also gave rise in the Sahara to the specialized professionals who facilitated intellectual life.

The demand for specific services and skills generated by the trans–Saharan book trade gave rise to professional figures such as copyists, scribes, calligraphers, illuminators, bookbinders, and booksellers. Some of them were highly regarded and well remunerated, while others had a more entrepreneurial profile that required a combination of business acumen, managerial skills, and cultural awareness. Booksellers would often combine the functions of "publisher," dealer, and collector, maintaining a workshop of calligraphers, illuminators, and binders, while also sending agents to various parts of West Africa to buy or copy works.[144]

With respect to Mauritania, the approach to Islam in that country was forged by the historic influence of the Almvorids who spread the Maliki madhab throughout the Sahara and, later in time, the ascendance of two dominant Sufi brotherhoods: the Qadiriyya and the Tijaniyya.[145] These Sufi orders facilitated "the popular establishment of Islam and the development of a religious framework in the society."[146] In fact, commentators note that "brotherhoods and the marabouts were perhaps the most important elements in the growth and development of Islam in West Africa."[147]

With particular regard to the Qadiriyya, that order was founded in Mesopotamia in the twelfth century by Abd al Kader al Jilani and spread to Africa in the fifteenth century.[148] "Like all brotherhoods, the Qadiriya includes some emotional mystical elements, but it also stresses learning and Islamic education as the way to find God. All members of the Qadiriya are directed to follow the precepts of humility, generosity, and respect for their neighbors regardless of religious beliefs or social standing."[149] The Qadiriyya order ascended in importance in Mauritania and influenced and, by the nineteenth century, it was associated with the Mauritanian 'ulama in important centers of learning.[150]

On that score, from its earliest history, there have been—and remain—many important religious centers and places of learning in Mauritania. Perhaps the most important (culturally and historically) is the Chinguetti Mosque. Chinguetti, known as the seventh holy city of Islam, was already known for its libraries by the thirteenth century and was a stopover for pilgrims making the hajj to Mecca[151] as well as caravans carrying gold, salt, dates, and ivory across the Sahara.[152] It was also, quite interestingly, the site of a major meteorite impact.[153] By the eighteenth century, Chinguetti had developed into an intellectual center for the Sahelian region.[154] Visitors voyaging through the sands of Chinguetti were frequent, and brought with them the vibrancy that generally follows on the wheels of travelers.[155] By the eighteenth century, Chinguetti reportedly had twelve mosques, twenty-five madrassas, five libraries, "and a distinguished population of scholars and poets."[156] Its main library housed over 1,300 calligraphic manuscripts and illuminations.[157] On the Rue des Savants of the city, hundreds of scholars regularly gathered to discuss law, religion, and esoterica.[158] The most famous of Chinguetti's mosques remains the Friday Mosque of Chinguetti, "an ancient structure of dry stone featuring a square minaret capped with five ostrich egg finials."[159]

Other important center of learning also were scattered throughout Mauritania in places such as Boutilimit in southern Mauritania.[160] Boutilimit was historically considered a major center of Islamic learning due to its "substantial zaqiya (marabout) presence, and the fact that it hosts one of the largest and most comprehensive libraries of Islamic manuscripts and books in the entire region."[161] In 1955, the Institute of Islamic Studies, the only Islamic institution of higher learning in West Africa, was founded in Boutilimit—though it was moved to the capital city of Nouakchott after independence.[162]

Boutilimit was also the home of Sidiyya al-Kabir ("Sidiyya the Great"), nineteenth-century Mauritanian jurist and a key figure in the Qadiriyya order. Born in 1789, Sidiyya al-Kabir studied in Timbuktu with renowned Kunta marabouts during his youth and became a renowned Islamic legal scholar, mystic, and Saharan bibliophile. Among his many achievements during his lifetime were his travels to Morocco where he purchased approximately two hundred books in Marrakech on subjects ranging from Islamic jurisprudence to language, mysticism, Sufi literature, and medicine.[163] These accumulated manuscripts and books "formed the basis for the vast Sidiyya library of the late nineteenth and twentieth centuries."[164] This library (which still exists in southern Mauritania) is considered among the most important libraries in the Sahel, holding in excess of 1,195 works, including 683 printed books (which were relatively uncommon in such libraries.).[165]

During the period of French colonization, the Mauritanian 'ulama was divided between those who supported colonial authorities "and detractors who were suspicious of the colonial administration."[166] Zekeria Ould Ahmed Salem notes that Mauritanian religious authorities recognized the French political powers—but at a careful distance. "The orthodox ulema tended to participate in the religious functioning and establishment of an independent republic, which was proclaimed to be 'Islamic' from the outset. Religious figures were at best notables."[167] Records indicate, however, that the Qadiriyya Sufi order under the leadership of Shaykh Sidiyya Baba, grandson of Shaykh Sidiyya al-Kabir, was inclined to cooperate with French authorities.[168]

In modern times, religion has continued to play a role in Mauritanian politics and in its legal development. Religion has become an especially salient topic since the 1980s when, after almost two decades of drought and a military defeat in the 1970s Western Sahara war, Mauritanian political regimes "sought to increase their legitimacy by associating the state with Islam, in particular by making the legal system more compliant with sharia law." [169]

DIVERGENCES AND COMMONALITIES

There are, accordingly, important similarities in the legal histories of Tunisia, Morocco, and Mauritania. Each country has a history and culture that has traditionally given a special place to Islamic law—specifically the Maliki school of Islamic law. None of the countries were heavily impacted by the nineteenth-century Ottoman legal reforms. In fact, of the three, only Tunisia was ever technically under Ottoman control. Each country, however, did experience French colonialism and, through that experience, was subjected to French legal influence. In addition, each country, at varying stages and in varying periods, reached a point at which the idea of a modern civil code could be received and implemented within the structure of the country's domestic law. Nevertheless, important cultural and historical differences mark each country, including the degree to which each country has been required to address culturally and religiously diverse components of its society. These are the legal, cultural, and historical landscapes in which the Santillana Codes were developed, enacted, and where they still remain in force.

SEPHARDIC JEWS

An understanding of the legal histories of the relevant countries is important—but one must also briefly understand the ethnic group to which Santillana belonged in order to fully understand the legal and philosophical context in which he worked. That history is, at times, somewhat apart from the places where the history plays out. On that score, to review the history of Sephardic Jews (Sephardim) is to engage in a fascinating, transnational exploration of a group of people who were repeatedly and forcefully displaced over the course of hundreds of years. Though the word "Sephardic" comes from the Hebrew word for Spain,[170] the history of Sephardic Jews transcends borders. The Jewish community arrived in the Iberian Peninsula during antiquity and lived there under both Roman and, later, Visigothic rule.[171] Jews were able to prosper in *Hispania*, the Roman name for the Iberian Peninsula, and by the third millennium, Spain was a place in which Christians, Muslims, and Jews lived together in a state of harmony which commentators now call *la covivencia* ("the Coexistence").[172] During this period, the Jewish community in Spain created a rich and unique culture. "The lingua franca of Spanish Jewry was a melodious blend of Hebrew and Spanish known as Ladino, and their music carried the notes and rhythms of both Iberia and the Maghreb."[173] Still, as Dolores Sloan poignantly notes, coexistence did not mean that Jewish existence in Spain was not, in many ways, precarious. "They were to be outsiders always, thriving or surviving at the pleasure or displeasure of the host people, who changed with the waves of conquest and reconquest through the centuries."[174]

Indeed, after centuries of such coexistence in Spain, the shadow of the Inquisition would fall across the continent, changing the political dynamic and imperiling the vibrant Jewish community. Ultimately, the grand inquisitor of the Spanish Inquisition, Tomas de Torquemada, convinced the joint Catholic Monarchs of Spain, Isabella I of Castile and Ferdinand II of Aragon, to issue a decree that would offer the Jewish community a cruel ultimatum: convert to Christianity or be expelled from Spain.[175] This decree was known as the Alhambra Decree (also known as the Edict of Expulsion).[176] The Catholic rulers of Spain, thus, "by a stroke of the pen, put an end to the largest and most distinguished Jewish settlement in Europe."[177]

While some Jews converted and remained in Spain, many fled to Portugal, which was then under the rule of King John II—a ruler who was only somewhat tolerant of Jewish subjects and even less so of the Iberian immigrants who sought refuge in his territory. Even so, many Jewish families fled to Portugal although the conditions there and requirements for entry were less than hospitable. Historians note that all Jews who wished to come from Spain to Portugal ("children at the breast excepted") were obligated to pay eight crusados or were forced to become slaves to the king.[178] "Armourers, smiths, and braziers, who would remain in the kingdom, were only to pay four crusados each."[179] Under these conditions, Jewish exiles from Spain were permitted to remain in Portugal for eight months or else become slaves.[180]

Circumstances for Jewish exiles in Portugal were harsh. Even so, during that time of temporary succor, the Jewish intellectual community thrived. Writing in the nineteenth century, E.H. Lindo specifically noted jurisprudence as one of the areas in which the displaced Jewish community maintained strong intellectual interest.[181]

> The Jews had seized with avidity an art that afforded the means of disseminating knowledge. The printing presses of the Jews were not confined to theological and religious books. Works of every description on *jurisprudence*, history, and medicine were printed from the manuscripts that circulated among the Hebrew people in the bright age of their literature.[182]

Of course, the time for the Iberian exiles to leave Portugal eventually came. Yale Strom notes that, of the 150,000 Jews that fled from Spain to Portugal, only those able to pay large bribes to King John II were permitted to remain.[183] The rest were "forced to board unworthy seaworthy ships for destinations unknown. Most perished at sea. A few landed in Morocco. Today, there are a number of Moroccan Jews who trace their ancestry back to those fortunate few."[184]

Many Jews fleeing Spain eventually made their way to Livorno, Italy, an area which where the grand duke of Tuscany, Ferdinand I, encouraged foreigners (including Jews) to settle by granting special rights and privileges.[185] This progressive policy was designed to expand the trade of the new port. In 1593, Jews were expressly given such privileges in a charter called the

Livornina—a document referred to by some commentators as the Magna Carta of the Jews of Livorno.[186] The Jewish community in Livorno was self-governing and its members could either become naturalized (as subjects of the Grand Duke of Tuscany) or otherwise remain and still enjoy his protection.[187] Scholars have noted the legal complexity that resulted from the web of interactions such legal pluralism occasioned, creating a legal world in which "Jews and Muslims had their own comprehensive bodies of law, yet they interacted with one another and with Christians."[188]

From Livorno, some members of the Sephardic diaspora went to live in other cities "throughout the Mediterranean basin, sometimes establishing 'colonies' that kept their distinctive identities, though they were known by a variety of names[.]"[189] Schroeter notes that important Jewish commercial establishments from Livorno were found throughout the region, "and most importantly in Tunis."[190] The expulsion of Jews from the Iberian Peninsula, therefore, resulted in a diaspora that crossed Portugal and expanded through the Mediterranean and North Africa, enriching the places to which its members fled.

SEPHARDIC JEWS IN NORTH AFRICA

As discussed above, the capitulations permitted European countries to extend protections extraterritorially to individuals or groups in Ottoman territories. Stein notes that, "[a]mong the first Jews to pursue foreign protection were Tuscan merchants of Livornese and Iberian origin who came to Ottoman lands in the eighteenth century as French protégés, thereby earning themselves the Ladino moniker *Franko* [a term meaning, loosely speaking, 'European'] and the appellation *Grana* in North Africa."[191] Indeed, in Tunisia, the Jewish community was divided into the *Granas* (European Jews) and the *Twansa* (the indigenous Jews.)[192] *Granas* is the plural Arabic noun for a group of Europeans while *Twansa* is the plural Arabic for a group of Tunisians.[193] The two were distinguished by their style of dress as well as their language. While both had the status of being dhimmis,[194] permitting a degree of autonomy and protection from local authorities,[195] Granas, by virtue of a treaty signed in 1846, were also granted protection under the Consul of Tuscany. The 1846 treaty, which consisted of only one article, written in both Italian and Arabic, was "signed by the Tuscan Consul Enrico Nyssen and by the Bey Ahmed Bascià, sealed with a wax seal of the Consulate General of Tuscany," and "was ratified by the Grand Duke of Tuscany Leopold the II on the 29 of January 1847."[196] This treaty modified a previous 1822 treaty between the two countries, which had given to the Jews from Livorno the same status of Tunisian Jews and placed them under the jurisdiction of the Ottoman Bey. According to the new treaty, Granas who registered in the

Tuscan Consulate were placed under Tuscan jurisdiction and protection.[197]
Jewish life in Tunisia was, therefore, a dense entanglement of cultures, countries, and overlapping jurisdictions.

Domestic events would provoke even more extensive extraterritorial
entanglement. In 1857, a rather mundane street altercation between a Jew and
an Arab Tunisian led to more legal developments that granted additional protections to Tunisian Jews. Around that time, historians note that, in a rather
banal confrontation on the street, and in a moment of impatience, a Tunisian
Jew named Batou Sfez said to an Arab citizen some words to the effect of
"Que Dieu maudisse la religion de ton père!"[198] This was an insult used even
by some Muslims in the community at that time and was considered to be
roughly the French equivalent of *"Le diable l'emporte!"*[199] Whether or not the
language used was offensive, the punishment meted out was extraordinarily
harsh and strikingly unusual in the context of that time and place.

> It was the first time in the nineteenth century that the law punishing blasphemy
> had been invoked and applied. The sentence was severe because Mohammed
> Bey (r. 1855–59) was probably looking for a pretext to target the Jewish com-
> munity. A Muslim had been executed sometime before for the murder of a
> Jew—a course of action that had sparked resentment in the city through faction
> conflicts[.][200]

In short, riots erupted against the Jewish community as a result of the
execution of a Muslim for killing a Jew and the Bey took drastic action "at
the expense of the first jew against whom a pretext could be found."[201] The
incident triggered an angry response from European powers who wished to
intervene and protect the Jewish community. In August 1857, under the threat
of French military action, Muhammed Bey agreed to guarantee the basic
liberties of his subjects in what was known as the Fundamental Pact.[202] This
pact, among other things, granted equality of taxation, religious freedom, and
equality of all subjects (Muslim, Christian, or Jew) before the law. It also
gave foreign subjects property rights, allowing European powers to intensify
their grip over Tunisian affairs.[203] This equality among citizens was later
enshrined in the Tunisian Constitution of 1861.[204]

DAVID SANTILLANA AND HIS CODIFICATION

It is within this convulsive political, social, and legal context that David
Santillana's family arrived and prospered in Tunisia.[205] As noted, Santillana
is among the least studied civil law and comparative law innovators—and his
background is frequently the victim of oversimplification or misrepresentation. For instance, he is sometimes described as an Italian jurist who worked

Figure 3.4 Portrait of Sir Richard Wood.[206]

in Tunisia. In fact, while he later did acquire Italian citizenship, Santillana was born in Tunis, Tunisia in 1855.[207] As his name indicates, however, his family was neither of Tunisian nor Italian origin. Rather, Santillana was from a Jewish family of Spanish ancestry[208]—he was a Sephardic Jew. He was born and raised Tunisian; had historic links to Spain; was educated internationally; acquired Italian citizenship; and later taught in Rome and elsewhere across the globe. Santillana was therefore a profoundly cosmopolitan jurist—and his work is very much a reflection of the man.

Historical records note that his great grandfather (M. Santillana) came to Tunisia from Livorno, Italy.[209] His grandfather, David Diaz Santillana, was born in Tunis in 1780 and served as a translator for the British Consulate General.[210] Santillana's grandmother was from a Jewish family that fled Portugal and had been living in Great Britain since the seventeenth century.[211] Santillana's grandparents, therefore, lived in Tunisia but had significant connections to Great Britain.

The family of M. Santillana and David Diaz Santillana briefly moved to France for some time, where M. Santillana died, but then returned to Tunisia in 1800.[212] Thereafter, records show that in 1849, "in consideration of his long services as interpreter," David Diaz Santillana was placed on the list of British-protected subjects.[213] Thus, Santillana's grandfather, a Jew from Livorno who lived in Tunisia, became a British protégé—obtaining the protection of a foreign power while he lived on Tunisian soil.

Santillana's father, Moses Santillana, succeeded his grandfather as consular interpreter[214] in the Court of Bardo,[215] and, in 1857, applied to be a
naturalized citizen of Britain. He was refused, but was able to acquire letters
of denization—a mechanism by which foreign persons could obtain certain
rights akin to those otherwise enjoyed by British subjects, including the right
to own land.[216] With this status of a British protégé, Moses entered into the
service of the consulate of Great Britain in Tunis,[217] and, thereafter, even
resided for some time in Great Britain and eventually became a close companion of Sir Richard Wood, the British Consul in Tunisia.[218]

It was into this cosmopolitan family with considerable political influence
that David Santillana was born in 1855. Santillana's family maintained its
strong connections with Great Britain, and Sir Richard Wood was extremely
fond of the young David Santillana.[219] Sir Richard ensured that Santillana was
initially educated at an Italian school in Tunis,[220] and helped Santillana travel
to England to complete his secondary studies.[221] David Santillana returned
to Tunisia after completing his education in England and, in 1873, at the age
of 18, he assumed the lofty role of Secretary of the *Commission financière
internationale*,[222] a commission created in 1869 to address Tunisia's fiscal
problems and ensure the payment of Tunisia's debts.[223] It is likely no coin-
cidence that his father, Moses Santillana, was elected as a member of this
commission in 1872.[224]

During this same period, David Santillana was also pursuing his government career, serving as an interpreter to the Bey in the *département des
Affaires étrangères*.[225] In that capacity, Santillana became acquainted with
Odoardo Maggiorani, an Italian jurist and member of the bar of Florence who
would eventually become legal counselor to the Bey in 1875.[226] Together,
Maggiorani and David Santillana would find themselves at the heart of most
of the major political affairs of the era—though largely in diplomatic capaci-
ties.[227] Maggiorani would also become one of Santillana's best friends and
Santillana even eventually married Maggiorani's daughter, Emilia.[228]

David Santillana was able to attend the University of Rome after he was
awarded a chance to obtain legal training in Rome by virtue of a *formation
diplomatique universitaire*.[229] He resigned from his post as the Bey's second
translator and enrolled at the University of Rome in 1880.[230] After graduat-
ing in 1883,[231] he began work as an attorney both in Rome and Florence.[232]
While in Rome he obtained Italian nationality and became enamored with
Roman law.[233] Santillana became noted for his ability as a lawyer in Italy
and, throughout his career, he continued to play a role in controversial legal
matters across North Africa, such as the legal defense of Ahmed Orabi, an
Egyptian military officer who staged a revolt against the British and French
presence in Egypt.[234] He also briefly taught at the University of Cairo but, for
reasons relating to declining health, returned to Italy where he taught Islamic

law at the University of Rome from 1913 to 1923.[235] He lived the life of an academic adventurer and died in 1931.

THE TUNISIAN CODIFICATION

When the Commission for the Codification of Tunisian Laws was established in 1896, Santillana was a natural choice to preside over the commission along with four French legal scholars. Those scholars, all of which had roles in the Tunisian government and/or judiciary, were S. Berge, MM. Roy, Padoux, and Anterrieu.[236] This commission would produce a draft civil code (presented in an *Avant-Projet*) which would form the basis for the code to come.[237] To create this remarkable piece of legislation, Santillana and his team would draw on a plurality of sources, namely the French civil code,[238] the German civil code,[239] the Italian civil code, several schools of Islamic jurisprudence (especially the Malikite and Hanafite schools),[240] and the Ottoman Mejelle.[241] Their work was further influenced by Tunisian custom, French jurisprudence, and the jurisprudence of French courts that were active in Tunisia during its time as a French protectorate.[242] The character of the Tunisian code, therefore, is as diverse and cosmopolitan as its principal author.

In 1899, David Santillana and S. Berge submitted the draft code to a mixed commission composed of Tunisian jurists—professors from the University of Zeituna and Tunisian magistrates[243]—which modified the proposed code's provisions before it was finalized. This commission, which represented the Tunisian 'ulama, was led by the Hanafite shaykh al-Islam, Mahammad Bayram,[244] and was also staffed by Ahmed Chérif (a Malikite mufti) and Mahmoud Bel-khouja (a Hanafite mufti).[245] The professors from Zeituna Mosque who were part of the commission were Mustapha Radhouan and Salem Bou Hâheb.[246] Raja Sakrani notes that this second commission included Tunisia's religious elite—with representatives from both the Malikite and Hanafite schools—so that its conformity with Islamic law could be evaluated and confirmed.[247] The process, therefore, benefitted from input and expertise from a broad cross-section of the French and Tunisian legal community.

From the earliest phases of this novel project, Santillana and his team fully understood that this undertaking presented both legal challenges and challenges related to the bias of some who did not believe a synthesis of European and Islamic law was possible. In the introduction to the *Avant-Projet* of the Tunisian code, Santillana noted, "That portion of the objective of this work that related to Islamic law presented special difficulties. According to a widely held view, it would be chimerical to attempt at conciliation between our law and the doctrines of Islam."[248] In response to such bias, Santillana noted that there is a perceived rigidity to Islam that makes such synthesis impossible, but that all religions have fixed dogmas that cannot be changed—and that nothing in Islamic law or the Muslim faith served as an obstacle to his task.[249]

It is worth noting that Tunisia's unique legal history and development resulted in a somewhat different approach to codification than what is seen elsewhere in civil law jurisdictions. Rather than a single, cohesive code governing all civil law—or even the "codal dualism"[250] that characterizes countries in the Middle East and North Africa with codes drafted by Abd al-Razzaq Al-Sanhūrī—Tunisian legal development has been characterized by what has been called "thematic codification."[251] For instance, Tunisian property law is now largely governed by the law of 12/2/1965 which enacted the Code of Real Rights,[252] the Personal Status Code governs "personal status law" such as marriage, divorce, and successions.[253] As a result, a notable aspect of the Tunisian Code of Obligations and Contracts is its intensely subject-specific focus.

The creation of such a code—successfully addressing the needs of so diverse a polity—was a complex endeavor. An analysis of his work demonstrates that Santillana and his team synthesized diverse sources of continental civil law with Islamic law and Tunisian custom through four primary methods. The first of these was by direct incorporation of Islamic law and legal devices into the codal text. The second method was through exploiting the natural correlates that exist between Islamic law and continental civil law. In that regard, scholars have noted that "Islamic Law is rooted in Arabic and Middle Eastern legal traditions, but through its evolution, it has assimilated elements of Roman law."[254] The third method present in the Santillana Codes, one which was influenced by Santillana's review of the code with the Tunisian 'ulama, consisted of excepting Muslims from aspects of the civil law which might violate the tenets of Islamic law and, thereby, permitting certain transactions between Muslims to occur in a way that comports with Islamic law. The fourth method used in the Santillana Codes involved imparting a religious dimension to otherwise secular legal devices, a technique which, in the context of the Maghreb and Sahel, naturally tilts in favor of Islamic law. The result is a codification of civil law that, adheres to the modern civil law model inspired by the French civil code, yet, at the same time, is also uniquely Tunisian.

Centered, as its name implies, on the formation of obligations and contracts, the Tunisian Code lacks provisions of broader applicability to persons and things that characterize most modern civil codes. In that regard, the Tunisian Code consists of only 1531 total articles which are divided into two books: Book I (Obligations in General)[255] and Book II (Different Contracts and Quasi-Contracts Relating Thereto).[256] Commentators have noted that this division, in essence, divides the Tunisian code into a "general part" and a "special part," each of which reflects a diversity of sources as explicated more fully below.[257]

The Tunisian codification was a success that has lasted to this day. Since its promulgation in 1906, it has been described as "the first durable codification of Tunisian civil law."[258] Its replication in Morocco and Mauritania are a testament to the ability and foresight of its principal drafter. That said, though Santillana was the main intellectual force behind the Tunisian code, it is clear that he was not the only force, nor were all of his proposals finally accepted. Though the Tunisian code is still generally considered to be principally the work of Santillana,[259] other jurists such as S. Berge, shaykh al-Islam Mahammad Bayram, and the representatives of the Tunisian 'ulama certainly left their mark on the substance of the code and ensured its compatibility with Islamic law.

MOROCCAN CIVIL LAW AND CODIFICATION

Morocco was the first country to base its laws on Tunisia's Code of Obligations and Contracts. Before the establishment of the French Protectorate in Morocco, the law in force was officially Islamic law, with glimpses (largely in personal status matters) of Hebraic law, local custom, and foreign law.[260] This was due to a certain level of respect afforded to the *Gens du Livre*—the People of the Book—who were adherents to the great monotheistic religions.[261] With the establishment of the Protectorate, however, Morocco underwent a juridical revolution during which Franco-Moroccan authorities adopted a number of legislative measures and codes inspired principally from French law but also other European legal systems such as those of Germany and Switzerland.[262]

> After establishing the protectorate, the French moved quickly to endow it with a basic body of legislation patterned after that of Europe. At the suggestion of Resident-General Lyautey, legislative commissions composed of imminent French jurists were established in Paris to draft a series of codes on the basis of proposals prepared by the French services in Rabat.[263]

Interestingly, S. Berge (who worked with Santillana on the Tunisian code) was appointed by the French Ministry of Foreign Affairs to sit on the organizing committee of a legislative program that would be submitted to the approval of the government before proposing its adoption to the Sultan.[264] To craft the needed legislation, a "commission of jurisconsults" was presided over by Louis Renault, a professor of international law at the Faculté de droit de Paris, and numerous other French jurists.[265] From this process emerged the *Dahir des obligations et des contrats*, which still exists as the primary legislation governing obligations and contracts in

Prof. Meloni - Prof. Santillana - Prof. Nallino

Figure 3.5   Photograph of David Santillana: Emmanuele Paldi, Il Principe Fuad e l'Universita egiziana (1911). Emmanuele Paldi, Il principe Fuad e l'universita egiziana (1911).

Morocco. Promulgated in 1913 by the sultan Moulay Youssef,[266] the *Dahir* (hereinafter referenced as the Moroccan code) is "a shortened version of the Tunisian code," which "d[oes] not include procedural rules, commercial law regulations, and a number of other matters that had been contained in the Tunisian code."[267]

Maati Bouabid notes that the Moroccan code omitted certain provisions that were viewed as derived from specifically Tunisian norms and which were viewed as not fully adaptable to Moroccan society.[268] Other parts of the Tunisian code were kept but modified by the sub-commission that assembled the Moroccan code so that it could exist in harmony with other laws already in place.[269] The version of the Moroccan code still in force consists of 1250 articles which are divided into two books—the first of which ("Obligations in General") is subdivided into seven titles and the second of which ("Different Specific Contracts and Quasi-Contracts") is subdivided into twelve.

MAURITANIAN CIVIL LAW AND CODIFICATION

The most recent country to adopt laws based on Santillana's model is Mauritania. With respect to codified law, the law applicable to civil matters after Mauritanian independence was, for decades, a blend of customary law, Islamic law, and the French civil code.[270] This changed on September 14, 1989 with the enactment of the Mauritanian Code of Obligations and Contracts.[271] Ould Mohamed Salah, in describing the Mauritanian code, notes that it contains significant influence from Islamic law but was enacted in an effort to modernize Mauritanian law and reconcile Mauritanian civil law with Western legal norms, most notably the French system.[272] It was enacted as part of "the vast movement of recodification which began in the early 80's with a view toward a return to the principles of Islamic Sharia."[273] Salah further notes that the Mauritanian code was based on the Moroccan code which, in turn, was based on the Tunisian code.[274] The code consists of 1182 articles which are divided into two books—the first of which (General Dispositions) contains only the first 21 articles and the second of which is subdivided into 13 titles.

CONCLUSION

David Santillana was a nineteenth-century jurist and lawyer who was part of the Sephardic Jewish community in Tunisia. His education was markedly international in scope and comparativist in nature, traversing Tunisia, England, and finally Rome. Moreover, his experience during the era in which he was raised and educated was notably transnational in nature due to his linkage to a community forced to move across frontiers yet able to establish enclaves of legal autonomy—a world of overlapping legal authority and normative diversity. Santillana experienced this personally as the child of British *protégés* living in Tunisia. On that score, as a skilled jurist who had worked as the Bey's second translator, Santillana would have been aware of the legal and political frameworks in which Tunisian subjects (including the Jewish community) existed. He would have necessarily been acutely aware of the "world of multiple normative communities"[275] in which the Ottoman subjects in Tunisia lived, the advantages of such a situation, and its disadvantages.

Moreover, the jurists who later contributed to Santillana's codification project were learned Islamic legal scholars who trained at Zeituna, including shaykh al-Islam Mahammad Bayram. These scholars also had a deep sense of how Islamic law regulated civil life, its doctrines permitting pluralism, and the Islamic legal tradition of allowing religious minorities to be governed by their own law and legal institutions. These combined legal experiences would indelibly color the Tunisian codification, imbuing it with elements that had never yet been experienced in the context of a modern civil code. This code would then, in turn, serve as the template for the civil codes of Morocco and Mauritania.

NOTES

1. *See* MICHAEL WILLIS, POLITICS AND POWER IN THE MAGHREB: ALGERIA, TUNISIA AND MOROCCO FROM INDEPENDENCE TO THE ARAB SPRING 9 (2014).

2. *Id.* at 5.

3. *See* H.H. Wilson, *The Relation of History to the Study and Practice of Law* (1887). Transactions and Reports, Nebraska State Historical Society. Paper 15, 17, http://digitalcommons.unl.edu/nebhisttrans/15

4. *CIA World Factbook, Tunisia,* https://www.cia.gov/library/publications/the-world-factbook/geos/ts.html

5. Although this book, for the sake of clarity, consistently refers to "Tunisia," it is important to keep in mind Professor Lisa Anderson's admonition that it is an anachronism to refer to Tunisia when discussing the nineteenth century. Until it was occupied by the Europeans, it was simply known by the names its capital city, Tunis. LISA ANDERSON, THE STATE AND SOCIAL TRANSFORMATION IN TUNISIA AND LIBYA, 1830–1980 13 (1986).

6. *See* Fanack, *Chronicle of the Middle East & North Africa, Tunisia,* https://chronicle.fanack.com/tunisia/population/

7. *See* 1 MARK AVRUM EHRLICH, ENCYCLOPEDIA OF THE JEWISH DIASPORA: ORIGINS, EXPERIENCES, AND CULTURE 509 (2009).

8. *See* BETTY JANE BAILEY & J. MARTIN BAILEY, WHO ARE THE CHRISTIANS IN THE MIDDLE EAST? 176 (2003).

9. *See* Fanack, *supra* note 6.

10. *See* JULIA CLANCY-SMITH, NORTH AFRICA, ISLAM AND THE MEDITERRANEAN WORLD: FROM THE ALMORAVIDS TO THE ALGERIAN WAR 190 (2013).

11. *See* The Berkley Center for Religion, Peace, and World Affairs, *Tunisia: From the Roman Empire to Ottoman Rule,* http://berkleycenter.georgetown.edu/essays/tunisia-from-the-roman-empire-to-ottoman-rule

12. *Id.*

13. *Id.*

14. *See* AFIF GAIGI, *Tunisia,* in YEARBOOK OF ISLAMIC AND MIDDLE EASTERN LAW 417 (1994).

15. *Id.* at 417–18. *See also* Mounira M. Charrad, *Tunisia at the Forefront of the Arab World: Two Waves of Gender Legislation*, 64 WASH. LEE L. REV. 1513, 1520 (2007). ("Prior to 1956, the Maliki school of Islamic law applied to the overwhelming majority of the Muslim population in Tunisia.")

16. *Id.* at 418.

17. *See* FAOUZI BELKNANI, *Code Des Obligations et des Contrats et la Codification*, in LIVRE DU CENTENAIRE DU CODE DES OBLIGATIONS ET DES CONTRATS 1906–2006 12 (2006).

18. *Id.*

19. *See id.*, note 44, at 14.

20. *See* Gaigi, *supra* note 14, at 418.

21. *See* Belknani, *supra* note 17, at 14.

22. *See* Gaigi, *supra* note 14, at 418.

23. *Id.* at 419.

24. *See* Belknani, *supra* note 17, at 14.

25. *Id.*

26. *See* Maaike Voorhoeve, *Judges in a Web of normative Orders: Judicial Practices at the Court of First Instance Tunis in the Field of Divorce Law 52* (2011) (Ph.D. dissertation, University of Amsterdam).

27. *Id.*

28. *See* Afif Gaigi, *supra* note 14, at 419.

29. *Id.*

30. *CIA World Factbook, Morocco*, https://www.cia.gov/library/publications/the-world-factbook/geos/mo.html

31. Ann Elizabeth Mayer, *Conundrums in Constitutionalism: Islamic Monarchies in an Era of Transition*, 1 UCLA J. ISLAMIC NEAR E. L. 183, 188 (2002).

32. *See* HAÏM ZAFRANI, TWO THOUSAND YEARS OF JEWISH LIFE IN MOROCCO 3 (2005).

33. *See* RAPHAEL CHIJIOKE NJOKU, CULTURE AND CUSTOMS OF MOROCCO 34 (2006).

34. *See* James Miller, *Imlil: A Moroccan*, POLITICAL QUARTERLY, March 1, 1984, at 27, 28.

35. *See* JESWALD SALACUSE, AN INTRODUCTION TO LAW IN FRENCH-SPEAKING AFRICA, VOLUME II, NORTH AFRICA 211 (1975).

36. *Id.*

37. *Id.* at 212.

38. *See* Willis, *supra* note 1, at 14.

39. *Id.* at 14–16.

40. *Id.* at 16.

41. *See* Salacuse, *supra* note 35, at 212.

42. *Id.*

43. *See* Willis, *supra* note 1, at 16.

44. SUSAN GILSON MILLER, A HISTORY OF MODERN MOROCCO 8–9 (2013).

45. DWIGHT L. LING, MOROCCO AND TUNISIA: A COMPARATIVE HISTORY 41 (1979).

46. *Id.*

47. *Id.* at 42.

48. *Id.* at 43.

49. *See* Miller, *supra* note 34, at 72.

50. *Id.* at 78.

51. *See Traité pour L'organisation du Protectorat Français dans L'empire Chérifien* (Fès, Mars 30, 1912) ("Article premier. Le Gouvernement de la République française et Sa Majesté le sultan sont d'accord pour instituer au Maroc un nouveau régime comportant les réformes administratives, judiciaires, scolaires, économiques, financières et militaires que le Gouvernement français jugera utile d'introduire sur le territoire marocain."), http://mjp.univ-perp.fr/constit/ma1912.htm

52. Abdulaziz H. Al-Fahad, *From Exclusivism to Accommodation: Doctrinal and Legal Evolution of Wahhabism*, 79 N.Y.U. L. REV. 485 FN 10 (2004).

53. *See* Miller, *supra* note 34, at 87.

54. *Id.* at 81.

55. *Id.* at 87.

56. *See* Salacuse, *supra* note 35, at 170.

57. *CIA World Factbook, Mauritania*, https://www.cia.gov/library/publications/the-world-factbook/geos/mr.html

58. *Index Mundi, Mauritania*, http://www.indexmundi.com/mauritania/demographics_profile.html

59. ROBERT A. DOWD, CHRISTIANITY, ISLAM, AND LIBERAL DEMOCRACY: LESSONS FROM SUB-SAHARAN AFRICA 60 (2015).

60. *See* Office of the Geographer, Bureau of Intelligence and Research, *International Boundary Study*, No. 78–July 15, 1967, Mauritania–Senegal Boundary (Country Codes: MR-SN) at 3 (hereinafter *International Boundary Study*).

61. *See* Salacuse, *supra* note 35, at 178.

62. *Id.*

63. See ROBERT EARL HANDLOFF, MAURITANIA, A COUNTRY STUDY XX (1990).

64. *Id.* at 12.

65. *Id.* at 11.

66. *Id.* at 3.

67. *Id.* at 16.

68. *International Boundary Study*, 2.

69. *See* SIDY MOHAMED SECK, LES CULTIVATEURS "TRANSFRONTALIERS" DE DÉCRUE A LA QUESTIONS FONCIÈRE IN LA VALLÉE DU FLEUVE SÉNÉGAL: EVALUATIONS ET PERSPECTIVES D'UNE DÉCENNIE D'AMÉNAGEMENTS, 1980–1990 297(1991). *See also* JEFFREY WHITE, RURAL TRANSITION: AGRICULTURAL DEVELOPMENT AND TENURE RIGHTS: A CASE STUDY IN THE SENEGAL RIVER VALLEY (2000). ("In 1830, the French West African governor in Saint-Louis at the mouth of the Senegal river, declared the Civil Code over all territorial possessions.")

70. *See* Handloff, *supra* note 63, at 14.

71. *Id.* at 15.

72. *Id* at 16.

73. *See* Kalidou Gadio, *Codification and Modernization of Law: A Case Study of Mauritania* 9 (April 30, 1987) (unpublished J.D. thesis, Harvard Law School).

74. *See* Salacuse, *supra* note 35, at 49.

75. *Id.*

76. *See International Boundary Study, supra* note 68, at 5.

77. *Id.*

78. *Id.*

79. *See* Gadio, *supra* note 73, at 6. ("In 1960, the year in which almost all French African colonies became independent, the question that African lawmakers were facing was whether the legal systems they had inherited from the French administration should be left untouched or, if no, to what extent codification should intervene.")

80. *See* Salacuse, *supra* note 35, at 178.

81. *Id.* at 178, citing the Mauritanian Code of Civil, Commercial, and Administrative Procedure, Law No. 62—052 of February 2, 1962, JORIM, September 19, 1962, at 394, noting that the eight categories were: (1) matters relating to expropriation of property by public authorities; (2) matters relating to certain immoveable property that was subject to the registration system; (3) cases related to aircraft, ships, boats, and motor vehicles; and cases relating to a contract in which the parties voluntarily agree to have disputes regulated by "the rules of modern law;" (4) commercial matters in which one party was a commercial entity or "a merchant registered at the commercial registry;" (5) administrative matters not within the jurisdiction of the Supreme Court; (6) matters involving nationality law; (7) matters relating to personal status when the parties are foreigners and Islamic law was not applicable; and (8) matters under the purview of article 3 of the Code of Criminal Procedure as well as matters relating to the payment of damages caused by any type of vehicle.

82. *See* Handloff, *supra* note 63, at 121.

83. *Id.* at 122.

84. *Mauritanian President Overthrown in Bloodless Military Coup*, The Telegraph (Aug. 3, 2005), http://www.telegraph.co.uk/news/1495419/Mauritanian-president-overthrown-in-bloodless-military-coup.html

85. *Id.*

86. Abdulaziz H. Al Fahad, *The Prince, the Shaykh—and the Lawyer*, 32 CASE W. RES. J. INT'L L. 307, 308 (2000).

87. *See* ARNOLD H. GREEN, THE TUNISIAN ULAMA 1873–1915 6–7 (1978).

88. FRANZ KOGELMAN, *Maghreb*, in ISLAM IN THE WORLD TODAY: A HANDBOOK OF POLITICS, RELIGION, CULTURE, AND SOCIETY 406 (2010).

89. LEON CARL BROWN, *The Religious Establishment in Hussainid Tunisia,* in SCHOLARS, SAINTS, AND SUFIS: MUSLIM RELIGIOUS INSTITUTIONS IN THE MIDDLE EAST SINCE 1500 100 (Nikki R. Keddie ed., 1972).

90. *See* Green, *supra* note 87, at 26.

91. *Id.* at 26–27.

92. LEON CARL BROWN, THE TUNISIA OF AHMAD BEY, 1837–1855 163 (2015).

93. *Id.* at 161.

94. JUAN EDUARDO CAMPO, ENCYCLOPEDIA OF ISLAM 721 (2009).

95. *See* Green, *supra* note 87, at 29.

96. Jamil M. Abun-Nasr, A History Of The Maghrib In The Islamic Period 171 (1987).

97. *Id.*

98. *See* Green, *supra* note 87, at 53.

99. *Id.*

100. *See* Brown, *supra* note 89, at 80.

101. *Id.* at 104–105.

102. *Id.* at 231.

103. *Id.* at 132–33.

104. *See* Abu-Nasr, *supra* note 96, at 232.

105. Götz Nordbruch, Transnational Islam In Interwar Europe: Muslim Activists And Thinkers 70 (2014).

106. *See* Green, *supra* note 87 at, 14.

107. Gerhard Böwering, Patricia Crone, Mahan Mirza, The Princeton Encyclopedia Of Islamic Political Thought 509 (2013).

108. *Id.*

109. *See* Green, *supra* note 87, at 70.

110. *Id.*

111. *Id.*

112. Abdul Azim Islahi, Economic Thinking Of Arab Muslim Writers During The Nineteenth Century 99–101 (2016).

113. Theodore Morison, *Can Islam be Reformed?* in The Nineteenth Century And After, Volume 64 (1908).

114. *See* Islahi, *supra* note 112, at 99–101.

115. *See* Green, *supra* note 87, at 244.

116. *See* Evelyn Baring, Modern Egypt 600 (1911).

117. *Id.*

118. *See* Green, *supra* note 87, at 256.

119. David Motadel, Islam And The European Empires 99 (2014).

120. Ernest Gellner, Islamic Dilemmas: Reformers, Nationalists, Industrialization: The Southern Shore Of The Mediterranean 80–81 (1985).

121. Jamil M. Abun-Nasr, *A History of the Maghrib in the Islamic Period* 293 (1985).

122. *See* Green, *supra* note 87, at 242–43.

123. *Id.* at 243.

124. Camron Michael Amin, Benjamin C. Fortna, Elizabeth B. Frierson, The Modern Middle East: A Sourcebook For History 480 (2006).

125. Edmund Burke, III, Prelude To Protectorate In Morocco: Pre-Colonial Protest And Resistance, 1860–1912 216 (2009).

126. Oxford Encyclopedia Of The Islamic World (John Esposito ed., 2008), Oxford Islamic Studies Online, http://www.oxfordislamicstudies.com.

127. *See generally* Dale F. Eickelman, Moroccan Islam: Tradition And Society In A Pilgrimage Center (2014).

128. A. Laroui, *Moroco from the beginning of the nineteenth century,* in Africa In The Nineteenth Century Until The 1880s 483 (J. F. Ade Ajayi, ed., 1989).

129. Stephen Cory, Breaking The Khaldunian Cycle? The Rise Of Sharifian-ism As The Basis For Political Legitimacy In Early Modern Morocco 83 (History Faculty Publications, 2008), http://engagedscholarship.csuohio.edu/clhist_facpub/83

130. *See Oxford Encyclopedia of the Islamic World, supra* note 126.

131. *See* Burke, *supra* note 125, at 216.

132. Edmund Burke III, *The Moroccan Ulama, 1860—1912: An Introduction,* in Scholars, Saints, And Sufis: Muslim Religious Institutions In The Middle East Since 1500 100 (Nikki R. Keddie ed., 1972).

133. A. Laroui, *Moroco from the Beginning of the Nineteenth Century,* in Africa In The Nineteenth Century Until The 1880s 483 (J. F. Ade Ajayi, ed., 1989).

134. Felicitas Opwis, *Changes in Modern Islamic Legal Theory: Reform or Reformation?,* in An Islamic Reformation? 31 (Michaelle Browers & Charles Kurzman ed., 2004).

135. Sahar Bazzaz, Forgotten Saints: History, Power, And Politics In The Making Of Modern Morocco 59 (2010).

136. *See* Burke *supra* note 132, at 100.

137. *Id.* at 101.

138. *Id.*

139. Brian Morris, Religion And Anthropology: A Critical Introduction 109 (2006).

140. *Id.*

141. *See* Burke *supra* note 132, at 117.

142. *Id.* at 125.

143. *Id.*

144. Graziano Krätli, *The Book and the Sand: Restoring and Preserving the Ancient Desert Libraries of Mauritania—Part 1,* World Libraries 14 (Spring 2004).

145. Ousmane Kane, Non-Europhone Intellectuals 21–22 (2012).

146. Zekeria Ould Ahmed Salem, *Les mutations paradoxales de l'islamisme en Mauritanie,* Cahiers d'études africaines, No. 206–207, 635–64 (2012).

147. *See* Handloff, *supra* note 63.

148. Rahal Boubrik, *Traditional 'Men of Religion' and Political Power in Mauritania,* ISIM NEWSLETTER, Feb. 2, 1999.

149. *Id.*

150. 7 C.C. Stewart, *Islam,* in The Cambridge History Of Africa, 209 (J.D. Fage & A.D. Roberts eds., 1986).

151. Ettagale Blauer & Jason Lauré, Mauritania 103 (2009).

152. *See* World Monuments Fund, *Chinguetti Mosque,* https://www.wmf.org/project/chinguetti-mosque

153. L. Lapaz & J. Lapaz, *The Adrar (=Chinguetti), Mauritania, French West Africa, Meteorite (CN=0127,202),* 1 METEORITICS 187 (1954).

154. *See* Blauer & Lauré, *supra* note 151, at 10.

155. Smith Hempstone, The New Africa 374 (1961).

156. U.B. Marvin, *Theodore Andrew Monod and the lost Feu de Dieu meteorite of Chinguetti, Mauritania,* in Four Centuries Of Geological Travel: The Search For Knowledge On Foot, Bicycle, Sledge And Camel (Patrick Wyse Jackson ed., 2007).

157. *See* Archnet, *Chinguetti*, https://archnet.org/authorities/5053

158. Thierry Defert, *Chinguitti ou l'appel des espaces radieux*, 71 BALAFON, July 1985 at 10–18; *see also* New World Encyclopedia, *Ksour*, http://www.newworldencyclopedia.org/entry/Ksour

159. *See* New World Encyclopedia, *Ksour*, http://www.newworldencyclopedia.org/entry/Ksour

160. 7 C.C. STEWART, *Islam*, in THE CAMBRIDGE HISTORY OF AFRICA, 209 (J.D. Fage & A.D. Roberts eds., 1986).

161. ANTHONY G. PAZZANITA, HISTORICAL DICTIONARY OF MAURITANIA 102 (2008).

162. *See* Handloff, *supra* note 63, at 70.

163. GHISLAINE LYDON, *Inkwells of the Sahara: Reflections on the Production of Islamic Knowledge in Bilad Shinqit*, in THE TRANSMISSION OF LEARNING IN ISLAMIC AFRICA 53 (Scott Steven Reese ed., 2004).

164. David Robinson, *Collaboration, Modernity and Colonial Rule: Sidiyya Baba and Mauritania*, http://aodl.org/islamicmodernity/sidiyyababa/essays/64—248-B/

165. *See* Lydon, *supra* note 163, at 60.

166. *See* Salem, *supra* note 146, at 635–64.

167. *Id.*

168. *See* Krätli, *supra* note 144, at 14.

169. Anouar Boukhars, *Mauritania's Precarious Stability and Islamist Undercurrent*, Carnegie Endowment for International Peace (Feb. 2016), http://carnegieendowment.org/files/CEIP_CP266_Boukhars_Final.pdf

170. *See* JONATHAN KIRSCH, *Foreword* to DOLORES SLOAN, THE SEPHARDIC JEWS OF SPAIN AND PORTUGAL: SURVIVAL OF AN IMPERILED CULTURE IN THE FIFTEENTH AND SIXTEENTH CENTURIES 2 (2009).

171. JANE S. GERBER, JEWS OF SPAIN: A HISTORY OF THE SEPHARDIC EXPERIENCE 8 (1994).

172. *Id.* at 1.

173. *Id.*

174. *Id.* at 1–2.

175. *Id.*

176. SAMUEL R. THOMAS, SEEKING THE SAINT, FINDING COMMUNITY: CELEBRATING THE HILLULA OF BABA SALI IN RELIGIOUS DIVERSITY TODAY: EXPERIENCING RELIGION IN THE CONTEMPORARY WORLD: EXPERIENCING RELIGION IN THE CONTEMPORARY WORLD (2015).

177. *See also Jewish History Sourcebook: The Expulsion from Spain, 1492 CE*, http://www.fordham.edu/halsall/jewish/1492-jews-spain1.asp

178. E.H. LINDO, THE JEWS OF SPAIN AND PORTUGAL 321 (1848).

179. *Id.*

180. *Id.*

181. *Id.* at 319–20.

182. *Id.* (emphasis added).

183. *See* YALE STROM, THE EXPULSION OF THE JEWS: FIVE HUNDRED YEARS OF EXODUS 143 (1992).

184. *Id.*

185. DANIEL J. SCHROETER, THE SULTAN'S JEW: MOROCCO AND THE SEPHARDI WORLD 39 (2002).

186. *Id.*

187. *Id.* at 40.

188. Brian Z. Tamanaha, *Understanding Legal Pluralism: Past to Present, Local to Global,* http://www.austlii.edu.au/au/journals/SydLawRw/2008/20.html

189. *See* Schroeter, *supra* note 185, at 40.

190. *Id.*

191. Sarah Abrevaya Stein, Extraterritorial Dreams: European Citizenship, Sephardi Jews, And The Ottoman Twentieth Century 13 (2016).

192. *See* Florence Renucci, *David Santillana, Acteur et Penseur des Droits Musulman et Européen*, 7 MONDE(S), Mai 2015, at 25–26.

193. Keith Walters, Education For Jewish Girls In Late Nineteenth And Early Twentieth Century Tunis And The Spread Of French In Tunisia, In Jewish Culture And Society In North Africa 261 (Emily Benichou Gottreich & Daniel J. Schroeter eds., 2011).

194. *See* Renucci, *supra* note 192, at 25.

195. *See* J. Liebesny, The Law Of The Near & Middle East 9 (1975). ("In the Muslim realm certain religious communities were tolerated and allowed to live according to their own religion and law, they were the so-called *dhimmis*.")

196. *See* Loredana Maccabruni, A Treaty Between The Regency Of Tunis And The Grand Duchy Of Tuscany, Concerning The Jurisdition Over Tuscan Jews Migrated To Tunisia In "Sharing History," Museum With No Frontiers, 2016, http://www.sharinghistory.org/

197. *See* Walters, *supra* note 193.

198. *See* Institut de Carthage (Tunisia), 14 REV. TUNISIENNE 139–40 (1907).

199. *Id.*

200. Nora Lafi, Challenging The Ottoman Pax Urbana: Intercommunal Clashes In 1857 Tunis, In Violence And The City In The Modern Middle East 100 (Nelida Fuccaro ed., 2016).

201. *Id.* at 101.

202. *See* Jacob Abadim, Tunisia Since The Arab Conquest: The Saga Of A Westernized Muslim State 282 (2012).

203. *Id.*

204. *See* Renucci, *supra* note 192, at 26.

205. *See* Nadhir Ben Ammou, L'avant Propos De L'avant-Projet De Code Civil Et Commercial Tunisien In Livre Du Centenaire Du Code Des Obligations Et Des Contrats 1906–2006, 60 (Mohamed Kamel Charfeggine ed., 2006). *See also* Jewish History Sourcebook: The Expulsion From Spain, 1492 CE, http://www.fordham.edu/halsall/jewish/1492-jews-spain1.asp

206. United Kingdom Government Art Collection, http://www.gac.culture.gov.uk/work.aspx?obj=13975.

207. *See* Ammou, *supra* note 205, at 65.

208. *Id.*

209. *See* Great Britain, Parliament, House of Commons, *Reports from Commissioners, Naturalization Commission, Appendix to the Report*, at 9 (1869).

210. *Id.*

211. *See* Renucci, *supra* note 192, at 27.

212. *See* Reports from Commissioners, Naturalization Commission, *supra* note 366.

213. *Id.*

214. *Id.*

215. *See* Renucci, *supra* note 192, at 26.

216. *See* 1 WILLIAM BLACKSTONE, COMMENTARIES, 354, 357–58, 361–62 (1809) ("A denizen is an alien born, but who has obtained *ex donatione regis* letters patent to make him an English subject: a high and incommunicable branch of the royal prerogative. A denizen is in a kind of middle state between an alien, and natural-born subject, and partakes of both of them. He may take lands by purchase or devise, which an alien may not; but cannot take by inheritance: for his parent, through whom he must claim, being an alien had no inheritable blood, and therefore could convey none to the son. And, upon a like defect of hereditary blood, the issue of a denizen, born before denization, cannot inherit to him; but his issue born after, may. A denizen is not excused from paying the alien's duty, and some other mercantile burthens. And no denizen can be of the privy council, or either house of parliament, or have any office of trust, civil or military, or be capable of any grant from the crown.").

217. *See* Renucci, *supra* note 192, at 26.

218. *Id.* at 27.

219. *See* Renucci, *supra* note 192, at 27.

220. *See* Ammou, *supra* note 205.

221. *Id.*

222. *See* Renucci, *supra* note 192, at 27.

223. *Id.*

224. *Id.*

225. *Id.*

226. *See* ERIC GOBE, LES AVOCATS EN TUNISIE DE LA COLONISATION A LA REVOLUTION (1883—2011): SOCIOHISTOIRE D'UNE PROFESSION POLITIQUE 35 (2013).

227. *See* Renucci, *supra* note 192, at 28.

228. *Id.* at 34–35. In 1902, Santillana and his wife would have one child, Giorgio Diaz De Santillana, who would travel to the United States and become a professor at the Massachusetts Institute of Technology (MIT) and the author of an esoteric book entitled: Hamlet's Mill, An Essay On Myth And The Frame Of Time.

229. *See* Ammou, *supra* note 205, at 66.

230. *Id.*

231. *Id.*

232. *Id.*

233. *See* RAJA SAKRANI, AU CROISEMENT DES CULTURES DE DROIT OCCIDENTALE ET MUSULMANE: LE PLURALISME JURIDIQUE DANS LE CODE TUNISIEN DES OBLIGATIONS ET DES CONTRATS 237 (2009).

234. ALEXANDER MEYRICK BROADLEY, HOW WE DEFENDED ARÁBI AND HIS FRIENDS: A STORY OF EGYPT AND THE EGYPTIANS 75 (1884) (referring to Santillana as "one of the most accomplished living Arabic scholars").

235. *See* Sakrani, *supra* note 233, at 237.

236. *See* M.D. SANTILLANA, AVANT-PROJET DU CODE CIVIL ET COMMERCIAL TUNISIEN 54 (cover page) (1899) [hereinafter AVANT-PROJET].

237. *See* GEORGE N. SFEIR, MODERNIZATION OF THE LAW IN ARAB STATES 39 (1998).

238. *See* Belknani, *supra* note 17, at 18.

239. *Id.*

240. *Id.*

241. *See* Belknani, *supra* note 17, at 12. It is important to note that, while it occupies a significant place in legal history as a major codification of Islamic law, the Mejelle was not an attempt to synthesize Islamic and continental civil law.

242. *See* Voorhoeve, *supra* note 26 at 54.

243. *See* MATTI BOUABID, *Preface to* FRANÇOIS PAUL BLANC, CODE ANNOTÉ DES OBLIGATIONS ET DES CONTRATS: LES OBLIGATIONS 10 (1981).

244. *See* Green, *supra* note 87, at 242–43; *see also* Sakrani, *supra* note 233, at 237.

245. *See* Sakrani, *supra* note 233, at 22–23.

246. *Id.*

247. *Id.* at 22–25.

248. *See* Avant-Projet, *supra* note 236, at III.

249. *Id.*

250. For a discussion of "codal dualism," *see* Dan E. Stigall, *Iraqi Civil Law: Its Sources, Substance, and Sundering,* 16 J. TRANSNAT'L L. POL'Y 71 (2006).

251. *See* Belknani, *supra* note 17, at 40.

252. *See* Afif Gaigi, *supra* note NOTEREF _Ref400287056 \h * MERGEFORMAT 14, at 426.

253. *See* Belknani, *supra* note 17, at 40. Given the diversification of codes in Tunisia, it must be emphasized that the Tunisian Code of Obligations and Contracts represents but one facet of the corpus of laws that comprise the entirety of Tunisian civil law. It is, nonetheless, a critical pillar in the architecture of the Tunisian legal system.

254. *See* Ayman Daher, *The Shari'a: Roman Law Wearing an Islamic Veil?,* 3 HIRUNDO: MCGILL J CL. STUD. 91, 92 (2005).

255. Republique Tunisienne, *Ministère de la Justice et des Droit de l'Homme, Code des Obligations et des Contrats* (Conformément à la loi n° 2005—87 du 15 août 2005) [hereinafter "Tunisian Code of Obligations and Contracts"], Livre Premier (Articles 1–563).

256. *Tunisian Code of Obligations and Contracts, Livre II* (Articles 564–1531).

257. *See* Belknani, *supra* note 17, at 14.

258. *Id.*

259. Santillana was the reporter and author of the AVANT-PROJET for the Tunisian code, and successive scholars—including his contemporaries—have acknowledged Santillana as the principle intellectual force behind the Tunisian code. *See, e.g.,* 11 F. Gény, *La Technique Législative dans la Codification Civile Moderne,* in Le Code Civil. 1804–1904. Livre Du Centenaire 1004 (1904).

260. *See* L. Messaoudi, *Grandeurs et limites du droit musulman au Maroc,* 47 Rev. Int'l. DE DROIT COMPARE (Janvier–Mars 1995), at 149.

261. *Id.*

262. *Id.*

263. *See* Salacuse, *supra* note 35, at 257.

264. *See* Bouabid, *supra* note 243, at 8.

265. *Id.* Bouabid lists numerous other French jurists as being part of this commission, including: Herbaux, Berge, Boulloche, Romieu, Grunebaum-Ballin, Jean Labbe, Chardenet, Colavet, Albert de Geouffre, Georges Teissier, Cruchon Dupeyrat, and Kammerer.

266. *See* Nicole Souletie, Le Mot De Madame Nicole Souletie In Le Centenaire Du Dahir Formant Code Des Obligations Et Contrats (Doc) 1913–2013 15 (2013).

267. Liebesny, *supra* note 195, at 114.

268. *See* Bouabid, *supra* note 243, at 10.

269. *Id.*

270. *See* Gadio, *supra* note 73, at 39. *See also* Salacuse, *supra* note 35, at 62 ("Despite the fact that a person having customary status had not, prior to 1946, become a French citizen, or after 1946, had not completely renounced customary law, he could during the entire colonial period nevertheless opt for the application of French law to individual transactions and matters.").

271. *See* Ould Mohamed Salah, Droits Des Contrats En Mauritanie 2 (1996).

272. *Id.*

273. *Id.* at 10.

274. *Id.* at 12.

275. Paul Schiff Berman, *Global Legal Pluralism*, 80 S. CAL. L. REV. 1155, 1157 (2007).

Chapter 4

The Sources of Law

A preliminary matter in the analysis of a legal system is a review of its sources of law. The phrase "sources of law" is susceptible to more than one meaning. For instance, Roman law, cannon law, and customary law influenced the development of continental civil law, and, therefore, are considered historical sources of law in the sense that they are bodies of law that were the sources contributing to the formation of that legal system. Another meaning of this phrase, however, relates to which legal sources the jurists operating in such legal systems may call upon and utilize for the resolution of legal questions. In that regard, perhaps the most distinguishing feature of civil law, to the common law jurist, is the civil law system's hierarchy of legal sources.[1] This hierarchy was forged through years of history and by the revolutionary context in which civil law developed. Merryman notes that the continental civil law legal model was born amid the chaos of revolution—a time when "the social and economic injustices of the old order were brought into direct conflict with the desire of egalitarianism."[2] It was during this time that the idea that the law was divine in origin began to lose its vitality. Eclipsing that pre-revolution ideology was the ascending, positivist idea that law emanates from the modern, sovereign nation-state.[3]

> Roman Catholic natural law had lost its power to control the prince. Secular natural law, while providing many of the ideas that were the intellectual fuel of the revolution, was ineffectual as a control on the activity of the state. It was backed by no organization and had no sanctioning power. The perennial controversy between natural lawyers and legal positivists (familiar to all students of legal philosophy) thus was decisively resolved, for operational purposes at least, in favor of the positivists.[4]

75

A result of this revolutionary ethos was an emphasis on the strict separation of powers. Civilian doctrine crystallized around the idea that legislation
was the primary source of law in contrast to "secondary sources of law, such
as jurisprudence, doctrine, conventional usages, and equity that may guide
the court in reaching a decision in the absence of legislation and custom."[5]
As the Louisiana Civil Code expresses the idea, "Legislation is a solemn
expression of legislative will,"[6]—and only the legislature can make the law.[7]
The primary source of law for civil law jurists, therefore, is legislation or,
otherwise stated, "statutes enacted by the legislature."[8] Jurisprudence in civil
law systems is relegated to the lot of secondary sources along with doctrine
and equity. The effect of this is that the concept of *stare decisis* is foreign to
the civil law.[9]

Another source of law in the majority of modern civil law systems today
is custom. Custom as a source of law, however, was a contested concept in
the past—and, even today, it can be somewhat difficult to understand and/or
identify as a matter of practice. Civil law jurists note that custom develops
over time from repeated practice with "the conviction that the practice has
the force of law."[10] Determining when custom obtains the force of law, however, can be a difficult endeavor "because society must sufficiently acquiesce
in the conduct, a requirement with few quantifiable features."[11] Despite this
difficulty, contemporary civil law courts have routinely turned to custom as
an authoritative source of law when crafting decisions.[12] The way in which
civil law jurisdictions have approached the sources of law, however, has not
remained static through time. In fact, civil law methodology since the nineteenth century has experienced exciting and dramatic evolutions.

SOURCES OF LAW, INTERPRETATION, AND EVOLUTION

The judicial use of legal sources beyond the text of legislation has been an
area of significant change for civil law jurisdictions over the years. Interestingly, the archetypal French *Code Civil* does not define custom, nor does it
give it a special place in the juridical order as some civil codes do. The French
code, in fact, contains no provisions articulating the sources of law. This is
because French legal scholars have generally considered the sources of law
to be "a matter of legal science not requiring definition by the Legislature."[13]
Beyond that rather technical point, however, even though the *Projet de Code
Civil* initially included custom as a source of law and even defined it,[14] the
revolutionary ethos that permeated the intellectual atmosphere at the time
the French code was adopted was such that the French code's implementers
sought to rid themselves of the ancient customs they disdained.[15] So although
French customary law was incorporated into the substance of the French civil

code—and while that code retained references to custom in the context of property law—custom is not defined in the French code, nor is it otherwise prominently featured in the codal text. It was only later that the role of custom as a source of law would grow in French law.[16]

Similarly, while the French code was not absolutely bereft of provisions relating to the interpretation of the law, it is correct that it contains relatively few provisions of that kind—especially in comparison with civil codes that succeeded it. Although the *Projet de Code Civil* initially included some didactic provisions that guided judges in the interpretation of the law, those provisions were not adopted in the final draft of the French code.[17] This left a role for juridical doctrines to guide judges in how to interpret the code's provisions. In that regard, early French doctrine favored an "exegetical" method of judicial interpretation in which it was required that "every solution be based on the enacted legislative texts."[18] While this method—one that prevailed throughout the nineteenth century—still permitted judicial interpretation, it did so under a framework that securely fastened judicial thought to the enacted legislative text. Through his method the judge could seek to "discover and apply legislative will," but in a way that emphasized the primacy of legislative authority. [19]

The German Civil Code, consistent with its French cousin, does not include provisions on the sources of law, nor guidance to judges on where to look to resolve legal matters. As famed comparativist Roscoe Pound noted, "[t]he German Civil Code of 1900 contains no provisions as to interpretation, thus leaving the matter in the hands of the courts."[20] Writing in 1956, Léon Julliot de la Morandière noted that neither the French or German civil codes "contain general provisions dealing directly with the existence of sources of law other than legislation, or with the role of the judge in applying rules of law," though other civil codes "deal in a more or less detailed way with sources of law in addition to legislation, and with the role of the judge." [21]

Certain codes based on the French model, however, diverged from that paradigm and incorporated more extensive procedural provisions. Looking again across the ocean to Louisiana, the Digest of 1808 provided that custom could be a source of law and articulated detailed guidance for judges in the interpretation of law, including an article that stated:

> In civil matters, where there is no express law, the judge is bound to proceed according to equity. To decide equitably an appeal is to be made to natural law and reason, or received usages, where positive law is silent.[22]

Another early example is the Italian *Codice Civile*, which was enacted in 1865.[23] The Italian code, though based on the French codification, differed in various ways—including the inclusion of an introductory portion (the *disposizioni preliminari*) in which, as Zweigert and Kötz note, "for the first time private international law, at the instance of the great Italian lawyer and statesman Mancini, was accorded detailed regulation."[24] The *disposizioni preliminari* also contained a number of provisions that addressed proper application of the rules of law. For instance, the first two articles of the Italian *Codice Civile* of 1865 were virtually identical to the French *Code Civil* of 1804:

> Article 1er—Les lois promulguées par le Roi deviennent obligatoires dans tout le royaume le quinzième jour après la publication, à moins que, dans la loi publiée, il ne soit autrement ordonné.

> La publication consiste dans l'insertion de la loi dans le recueil officiel des lois et décrets, et dans l'avis de cette insertion donné par la Gazette officielle du Royaume.

> Art. 2.—La loi ne dispose que pour l'avenir; elle n'a pas d'effet rétroactif.[25]

The *Codice Civile* of 1865, however, went beyond the French *Code Civil* by including additional guidance such as Article 3, which stated that, "In the application of the law one cannot assign a different meaning than that which is clear from the meaning of the terms according to their combination, and the intention of the legislator."[26] Notably, that same article stated that "[i]f a question cannot be resolved by a specific provision of the law, one may look to the provisions which regulate such cases or analogous matters; If, however, the matter is still questionable, one has recourse to general principles of law."[27] The Italian *Codice Civile* of 1865, therefore, recognized that some matters would not find resolution in specific provisions of the law and expressly directed the judge to seek resolution by parity of reasoning and, as a gap-filler, by consulting general principles of law.

The nineteenth century, however, would see a development in civil law doctrine with the writing of François Gény and the method of "free scientific research" which he articulated.[28] This new approach still recognized the primacy of legislation where it clearly applied to the issue before the court, but sought to free the court to reinterpret legislation in a manner "consistent with the changed conditions which it is now called upon to regulate."[29] Pursuant to this method, the original intention of the legislature ceased to be controlling, and judges were empowered to give the relevant text "that meaning which the legislature would have enacted had it been acting at the present rather than in the past."[30]

> The harbinger of a new era may have been 1899, the year in which Francois Gény published his famous work, *Methode d'Interpretation*. Gény's sharp realist

critique of the mechanical, formalistic judicial practice of his day may be seen as the first coherent attack upon the foundations of a system of legislated equity. He dismissed "the fatuous notion" that the codes provided complete legal coverage and that all legal solutions could be found therein. Rather, he issued the call for "free scientific research" and for recognition of the reality that the texts of the codes inevitably contain gaps, conflicts, and ambiguities sometimes due to their original imperfections, the passage of time, and the evolution of modern society. The judges, he argued, had a fundamental role to play in the establishment and development of legal norms, a striking proposition that French history and the entire constitutional structure seemed to deny.[31]

In his writing, Gény was insistent on custom as a source of law and the need for greater latitude in judicial interpretation. His influence was such that his method is now characteristic of French law and led to a number of breakthroughs in the way modern civil law systems interpret legislation.[32] An example is that of the Swiss Civil Code which came into force in 1912.[33] The Swiss code was notable in many ways, including in its express acceptance of the fact that the judge would need to sometimes look outside the code to find solutions to legal questions. This recognition finds expression in the code's first article, which provides "that judges should decide cases not clearly covered by the text of the code on the basis of customary law or, where no such rule exists, in accordance with the rules that the judge would have established as a legislator."[34]

1. The law applies according to its wording or interpretation to all legal questions for which it contains a provision.
2. In the absence of a provision, the court shall decide in accordance with customary law and, in the absence of customary law, in accordance with the rule that it would make as legislator.
3. In doing so, the court shall follow established doctrine and case law.[35]

Writing in 1916, one commentator lauded this provision as a signal of modernity and even claimed, "[t]his is the most radical statement of its kind in any foreign code known to the writer."[36] Alfred E. von Overbeck has stated, "Swiss legislator was the first modern legislator to recognize that he needs the judge to achieve his own task."[37] Many esteemed jurists have since referred to the provision as the Swiss Code's "famous article 1,"[38] and Benjamin Cardozo even lauded it as being expressive of "the tone and temper in which the modern judge should set about his task."[39] As noted above, codes such as the Italian code also guided the judge to have recourse to analogous matters and, if needed, general principles of law—and did so decades before enactment of the Swiss code.[40] The important difference is that, after the catalyzing influence of Gény and the method of "free scientific research," a Swiss judge was now empowered to interpret the law *in accordance with the rule that it would make as legislator.*

The manner in which civil codes address traditional sources of law may, therefore, vary. Because of their various juridical and philosophical influences, some codes contain more robust provisions defining the sources of law and instructions for interpreting codal provisions. Others, historically, have omitted such provisions.[41] This is even true among civil codes belonging to the same family or tradition. Looking to the Santillana Codes, an initial point of comparison that demonstrates some key similarities and differences among the three codes is the approach of each vis-à-vis sources of law. Each code maintains an approach characteristic of continental civil law, permitting, for instance, the use of custom as a subsidiary source of law. Nevertheless, there are some notable differences.

THE TUNISIAN CODE

As noted, the Tunisian Code of Obligations and Contracts is derived from a plurality of sources, though a study of the manner in which those sources are referenced or incorporated into the code reveals a fascinating array of legislative feats and codal compromises that were necessitated by the political environment in which the Tunisian code was crafted. In contrast to the relatively meticulous and comprehensive approach which characterizes the rest of the Tunisian code, the legal provisions which concern the Tunisian code's sources of law (those which may be called upon in interpreting the code's provisions) tend to be somewhat recondite in that they provide guidance for interpreting the code's provisions but never really articulate or define the sources of law.

The Tunisian code contains its provisions that address sources of law and judicial interpretation in a section entitled *De quelques règles générales de droit*. This section is found in Chapter II (*De l'interprétation des conventions et de quelques règles générales de droit*) of Title VIII (*De la preuve des obligations et de celle de la libération*) of the Tunisian code. In the main, it consists of 31 articles (Articles 532—563) which provide a range of guidance—the judge on how to interpret legislation and the sources that can be used—including sources beyond the text of the code.[42]

In setting forth the sources of law that may be drawn upon for the proper interpretation of codal provisions, the Tunisian code states that, in applying the law, one shall give it no other meaning than that resulting from the ordinary meaning of the law's provisions and the intent of the legislature.[43] In that regard, the Tunisian code specifically states that "[w]hen the law is expressed in general terms, it must be understood in the same sense."[44] Likewise, where the law reserves a particular case, it applies to all other cases which are not expressly excepted. Where a case cannot be decided by a specific provision of the law, a court may look to the provisions governing similar cases.[45] If the solution is still in doubt, the Tunisian code states that a court may decide according to "general rules of law."[46]

Beyond those references to the primacy of legislation and the availability of "general rules of law," the Tunisian code also recognizes custom as a source of law, albeit in a somewhat oblique manner. In Article 543, the Tunisian code states that custom and usage cannot prevail against formal law (*La coutume et l'usage ne sauraient prévaloir contre la loi, lorsqu'elle est formelle.*).[47] Likewise, one wishing to invoke custom or usage must justify its existence—and it must be general and may neither be against public order or immoral.[48] These provisions are notable given how few modern civil codes had expressly recognized custom as a source of law at that time (despite its initial inclusion in the French *projet.*) Santillana saw the use of custom as a critical element of Islamic law that, as Santillana noted in his introduction to the *Avant-Projet,* considered custom to be "like a tacit convention that has the power to create law and modify it."[49] Thus, it is clear that Santillana's approach was not a slavish emulation of the code favored by colonial powers, but a true attempt to synthesize Islamic and continental civil law.

That said, in comparison with more modern codes, the language in the Tunisian code on sources of law seems rather inexact and nebulous. Its phraseology (and the location of the relevant articles of the Tunisian code) is in striking discord with the articles addressing sources of law in civil codes in the Middle East and North Africa. In comparable modern codes, the sources of law are generally set forth in Article 1 of the civil code—an initial article which typically articulates a predictable hierarchy of sources.[50] For example, the Libyan Civil Code, Syrian Civil Code, Egyptian Civil Code, and Algerian Civil Code all contain an initial article (Article 1) which governs the sources of law and, in essence, states that the written provisions of the code govern all matters. In the absence of written provisions, Article 1 of those codes uniformly states that courts may adjudicate matters in accordance with the principles of Islamic law.[51] In the absence of an Islamic rule on a particular matter, the Libyan, Syrian, Egyptian, and Algerian codes permit courts to look to custom and the principles of equity.[52]

But the Tunisian code is different and does not reference Islamic law as a subsidiary source of law, nor any other specific body of law. In that regard, Tunisian courts have held that nothing in the Tunisian code permits recourse to Islamic law as a source of law,[53] and commentators have noted that the very ambiguous reference in Article 535 to the "general rules of law" offers little clarity with regard to other potential sources of law and may have been a purposive ambiguity deemed necessary in this early codification of Tunisian law.[54] Otherwise stated, it has been suggested that this is simple prudence, designed to allow the code to take root and become integrated into Tunisian society.[55]

Interestingly, Professor Haider Ala Hamoudi, in his excellent work on post-conflict constitution drafting in Iraq, posits that when formulating national legislation such as a constitution in a post-conflict environment where key stakeholders may have pronounced "identitarian commitments," it is sometimes advantageous for drafters to permit such legislative lacunae to exist so that long-term solutions can be incrementally achieved.[56]

> [T]he solution well may be to proceed with constitution making, but on par-
> ticularly difficult problems—namely those in which any view to the long term
> is likely to raise the prospect of intractable disputes based on quite inconsistent
> conceptions of statehood—to defer the problem for later, incremental resolu-
> tion. In other words, on such matters of dispute, the solution might well be,
> counterintuitively, to push the problem off in a manner that will reduce the
> stakes.[57]

Santillana may have taken just such an approach with the Tunisian code insofar as it remains ambiguous as to which sources of law may be invoked by Tunisian courts. However, it is also important to remember that, in the early 1900s when Santillana was drafting the Tunisian code, there were few civil codes in force that detailed the sources of law in any remarkable way, and few that provided judges with guidance in interpretation or application of the law. Santillana's provisions on the sources of law, therefore, are not unusual given the legal context in which he was working.

In that regard, a likely reason for the language chosen for the Tunisian code is that Santillana based its language on that of the *disposizioni preliminari* of the Italian *Codice Civile* of 1865. Like the Tunisian code, the *Codice Civile* provided that, if question could not be resolved by a specific provision of the law, a judge could look to analogous matters and, failing that, to general principles of law.[58] A comparison of the portion of the Tunisian code that addresses rules for interpreting the code's provisions with a French trans-lation of the *disposizioni preliminari* of the Italian *Codice Civile* of 1865 reveals that Santillana based much of this section on the Italian code.

The provisions in Santillana's section entitled *De quelques règles générales de droit* are, therefore, certainly in part the product of the legal exegesis of Santillana and the commission drafting the Tunisian code, but are obviously heavily reliant on the language of the *disposizioni preliminari* of the Italian *Codice Civile* of 1865. In fact, when comparing the French translation of the *Codice Civile* and the Tunisian code, one finds that the language and the rule

Table 4.1 Codal Comparison: Sources & Methodology

Codice Civile	*Tunisian Code*
Art. 3—Dans l'application de la loi on ne peut lui attribuer un autre sens que celui qui résulte clairement de la signification propre des termes d'après leur combinaison, et de l'intention du législateur. Si une question ne peut être résolue par une disposition précise de la loi, on aura égard aux dispositions qui règlent les cas semblables ou les matières analogues; si, néanmoins, la question est encore douteuse, on aura recours aux principes généraux du droit.	Art. 532—En appliquant la loi, on ne doit lui donner d'autre sens que celui qui résulte de ses expressions, d'après leur ordre grammatical, leur signification usuelle, et l'intention du législateur. Art. 533—Lorsque la loi s'exprime en termes généraux, il faut l'entendre dans le même sens. Art. 534—Lorsque la loi réserve un cas déterminé, elle s'applique à tous les autres cas qui ne sont pas expressément exceptés. Art. 535—Lorsqu'un cas ne peut être décidé par une disposition précise de la loi, on aura égard aux dispositions qui régissent les cas semblables ou des matières analogues; si la solution est encore douteuse, on décidera d'après les règles générales de droit.
Art. 5—Les lois ne sont abrogées que par des lois postérieures, soit qu'il y ait une déclaration expresse du législateur, soit qu'il y ait incompatibilité entre les nouvelles dispositions et les précédentes, ou que la nouvelle loi règle toute la matière qui était réglée par la loi antérieure.	Art. 542—Les lois ne sont abrogées que par des lois postérieures, lorsque celles-ci l'expriment formellement, ou lorsque la nouvelle loi est incompatible avec la loi antérieure ou qu'elle règle toute la matière réglée par cette dernière.

posited are virtually identical. While the Italian code listed is cited as a source for some of these provisions in the *Avant-Projet*,[59] however, it is not cited nearly as extensively as might seem warranted given the degree of appropriation.[60] Rather, Santillana cites the Digest of Justinian more prominently. This is a glaring oddity given the clear parallels of the language, for instance, between Tunisian Article 532 and the Italian Article 3 or between Tunisian Article 542 and the Italian Article 5. The extent of borrowing from the Italian source appears, to a degree, masked in the *Avant-Projet* among other more obviously indirect sources.

That said, even though those provisions seem to have relied heavily on a European code, it would be inaccurate to dismiss Santillana's citation to Islamic law as an undergirding theory. In the *Avant-Projet*, Santillana also provides numerous citations to Islamic jurists to support the proposed rules, such as Housoul el Mamoul by Bahadour and the works of Ibn Nadjim. It is likely that Santillana sought to find a European model that most closely adhered to what he viewed as the interpretive method utilized by judges in Islamic law. The more rigid model that existed in older codes simply would not have been a fit—and the effort to synthesize the two systems would have failed. It, therefore, makes sense that Santillana would have looked to a more flexible set of rules to accommodate the Islamic juristic approach and found one in a very familiar legal source.

Beyond the interesting issue of the Tunisian code's ultimate sources, two items emerge from these discussions that demonstrate that, whatever the source, Santillana's code represented a development in the approach to sources of law—a break from the French archetype and the strict positivism that defined prevailing legal thought in the civil law world during that era. First, drawn from Santillana's understanding of Islamic law (particularly the Malikite school), custom was expressly given a place in the hierarchy of sources in the Tunisian code by specifying that custom may be a source of law. Santillana doubtlessly also drew from the language of the initial *projet* of the French Civil Code which defined custom and included it as a source of law—though, as discussed, such language was never ultimately implemented in the French code. At the time of its enactment, therefore, the provisions of the Tunisian code addressing custom had no real parallel among the major European codes of that period. While some examples of similar codal language exist—such as the relevant articles of Louisiana code which also broke sharply from French legislative positivism and implemented language similar to that contained in the French *Projet de Code Civil*—the approach was rare. Santillana's inclusion of custom as a source of law must, therefore, be viewed as an innovative use of civil law sources to blend continental civil law and Islamic legal theory.

In addition, it is notable that the Tunisian code directs judges to look to general principles of law when lacunae in the legislation are encountered. Though the language is drawn largely from the Italian code, it is clear that Santillana saw this as a method already in use by judges under the Islamic legal system and, therefore, necessary for implementation in Tunisia. But this was still a rather innovative idea for a civil code at the time. While not as radical as the Swiss code, with its "famous article 1" which was "the most radical statement of its kind in any foreign code,"[61] it did adopt provisions that empowered judges to press against the strictures of the "exegetical" method of judicial interpretation that prevailed at the time. The Tunisian code recognized that not all solutions can be found within the codal text.

While it would be too much to say that these elements of Santillana's work presaged the new method of "free scientific research" that was on the horizon, they do (in the aggregate) represent a subtle stirring within the intellectual ether—a minute but noticeable erosion of the doctrinal status quo. On that score, it is worth noting that, in an article written in 1904 to celebrate the centennial of the French civil code, Gény—the father of the method of "free scientific research"—expressly referred to Santillana and his work as an example for civil law jurists and legislators, referring to Santillana as a "learned and skillful author," and describing the *Avant-Projet* for the Tunisian code as a "complex and highly inspired work."[62] Gény further commended Santillana for the way in which Islamic law was incorporated into his work. This observation by Gény underscores what is perhaps the most significant aspect of the Tunisian code's articles on judicial interpretation and custom as a source of law: the provisions manage to accommodate Islamic legal norms and sources by utilizing a civil law surrogate. Islamic legal requirements find expression through civil law formulations. The voices of Islamic and civil law jurists—Portalis, Bahadour, and Ibn Nadjim—all find a measure of harmony.

THE MOROCCAN CODE

As noted above, the Moroccan *Dahir des obligations et des contrats* (DOC), based largely on Santillana's work in Tunisia, was promulgated in 1913.[63] Like the Tunisian code, the text of the Moroccan code gives little guidance on judicial interpretation, though Moroccan jurists are clearly empowered to interpret the provisions of their code. It is worth, at the outset, briefly comparing the two analogous sections of the Tunisian and Moroccan codes to obtain a better sense of the latter's brevity and truncated style.

The Moroccan code's provisions on sources of law and judicial interpretation are found in the same place as the Tunisian code—in Chapter II (*De l'interprétation des conventions et de quelques règles générales de droit*) of Title VIII (*De la preuve des obligations et de celle de la liberation*). The Moroccan code's section is, however, much shorter. While the analogous Tunisian section contains thirty-one articles, the Moroccan code contains only four. The decision of the Moroccan codifiers, therefore, was to adopt a far less extensive set of rules to guide judges on interpretation of the law. Nonetheless, the main sources of law as applied by Moroccan civil law jurists are familiar to their Tunisian counterparts—and the shortened provisions have done nothing to curb the ability of Moroccan courts to interpret the text of the code. In fact, in a text celebrating the 100th anniversary of the Moroccan code, Professor Radia Bouhlal noted that it was the ability of Moroccan courts to interpret the text of the code that gives the Moroccan code its durability.[64] According to Professor Boulal, when King Hassan II was given the responsibility of reforming the Moroccan code in 1964, he clearly noted that, rather than modify its text, Moroccan courts were to interpret the law and make recourse to other texts when the juridical solution could not be found

within the pages of the Moroccan code.[65] This task, of course, was an easy
one due to the style in which the Moroccan code is drafted.[66]

That said, the Moroccan code reflects the traditional civilian sources of
law. For instance, emphasizing the primacy of custom, Article 474 of the
Moroccan Code states that laws are only abrogated by subsequent legislation
which formally abrogates prior law, when the new law is incompatible with
the former legislation, or when the new law regulates all matters addressed
by the former legislation.[67] In addition, as the discussion below highlights,
Moroccan law clearly recognizes custom as a source of law and, in a manner
more pronounced that we have seen in its Tunisian corollary, the approach
to interpretation taken by Moroccan courts has permitted some recourse to
Islamic law in the interpretation of the code.

As in its Tunisian forbearer, the text of the Moroccan code obliquely
permits the use of custom. The Moroccan code contains an almost verbatim
provision addressing the matter which states simply that custom cannot prevail over formal legislation[68]—such language, *a contrario sensu*, permits the
use of custom as a gap-filler to address matters not clearly addressed by the
law in force. The writing of Moroccan jurists affirms that custom is a source
of law—but only a subsidiary source of law that can never override the text
of a statute or code.[69] Mohammed Jalal Essaid, writing on custom in Moroccan law, defines it as follows: "*La coutume, ou 'orf,' peut être définie comme
étant une règle de droit qui découle d'une pratique ancienne , d'un usage qui
s'était prolongé dans le temps.*"[70] Commentators note that, "[c]ustom is also
a source of law in Morocco," but that it "cannot prevail against a definitive
law," and that it can be invoked "only if it is general or prevailing; and is not
against the public policy or good character."[71]

ISLAMIC LAW AND MOROCCAN CIVIL LAW

This, of course, raises the question of the place of Islamic law as a source of
law in Morocco. The Moroccan code gives no express guidance on that matter. Professor Layachi Messaoudi, a member of the Faculté de droit de Fès in
Morocco, writing in 1995, notes that the place of Islamic law in the Moroccan
legal system is somewhat confusing, enjoying a certain primacy in the rules
governing personal status, the waqf, and estates and non-registered buildings but the role of Islamic law in Moroccan law is largely overwhelmed by
modern law in other areas where its role is more modestly confined (such as
contracts and obligations).[72] Even so, as a survey of opinions from Moroccan
judges makes clear, the Moroccan judiciary has freely made use of Islamic
law as a subsidiary source of law in a wide range of civil matters—including
those which are the subject of the Moroccan code—and as a framework to

inform interpretation of the codal text.[73] Moreover, while the Moroccan jurist may resort to custom as a subsidiary source of law, all custom that is contrary to Islamic law has been declared invalid by virtue of royal decree and Moroccan jurisprudence.[74]

In addition, the burden of proving a custom falls on the person asserting it. The Moroccan text makes clear that the person seeking to invoke a *usage* must prove its existence. In that regard, *usage* cannot be invoked unless it is shown to be in general or dominant use and is not against public order and good morals.[75] Good faith is always presumed, unless the contrary is proven.[76]

THE MAURITANIAN CODE

The Mauritanian code, in turn, largely adopts the Moroccan variations on the Tunisian code, with some interesting differences. For instance, the Mauritanian code maintains the provision stating that laws are only abrogated by subsequent legislation, thus emphasizing the primacy of legislation. Unlike the Tunisian and Moroccan codes, however, the Mauritanian code does not locate this provision in the analogous section of the code. Rather, the Mauritanian code returns this provision to the place it occupies in the French Code Civil—at the very outset of the code in Article 2.[77] Otherwise, the Mauritanian provisions mirror the Moroccan code in that it contains a section entitled *De quelques règles générales de droit* which has some articles addressing judicial interpretation and sources of law, though the Mauritanian code—by moving the article on legislation to Article 2—keeps only three articles in this section.

> Art.486—L'usage et la coutume ne saurait prévaloir contre la loi, lorsqu'elle est formelle.
>
> Art. 487—Celui qui invoque l'usage doit en justifier l'existence.
>
> L'usage ne peut être invoqué que s'il est général ou dominant et s'il n'a rien de contraire à l'ordre public et aux bonnes moeurs.
>
> Art. 488—La bonne foi se présume toujours, tant que, le contraire n'est plus prouvé.

The Mauritanian code states that custom cannot prevail over formal legislation[78] which, as noted, *a contrario sensu*, permits the use of custom as a gap-filler to address matters not clearly addressed by the law in force.[79] As with the Moroccan code, under Mauritanian law the person seeking to invoke a *usage* must prove its existence, and *usage* cannot be invoked unless it is shown to be in general or dominant use and is not against public order and good morals.[80] Good faith is always presumed, unless it is proved otherwise.[81] All of this is generally the same as what is found in its predecessor codes, all of which adopt the civil law model for sources of law: legislation and custom.

There has been some disagreement in the literature regarding the extent to which Islamic law is a source of law in Mauritania.[82] Mohamed Ould Salah has argued that Islamic law "is a compelling source only for the legislator and must be translated into legislation before being applicable in courts."[83] A review of the remainder of the Mauritanian code, however, reveals a final provision that departs from the ambiguity of its Moroccan and Tunisian ancestors. Article 1179 of the Mauritanian code expressly states that "to fill the lacunae of this ordinance, reference may be made to the Malikite rite [of Islamic law]."[84] Accordingly, of the three Santillana Codes, the Mauritanian code is the most expressly permissive of Islamic law—permitting courts to fill the gaps in legislation by reference to the Malikite rite of Islamic law.

CONCLUSION

A review of the Santillana Codes' provisions on sources of law highlights their innovativeness. Enacted in 1906, the Tunisian code—progenitor of the Santillana Codes—elaborated on the proper use of custom in a way few other codes of that period had yet done by specifying that custom may be a source of law and giving guidance as to how it may be used. Drawing from the Italian code, it also directed judges to look to general principles of law when lacunae in the legislation are encountered. The Moroccan code, which came into force shortly after the Swiss code, maintained these innovative provisions as did the Mauritanian code. Through these provisions, a civil law system crystallized in North Africa and the Sahel that very early on recognized custom as a source of law and the fact that legislative texts inevitably contain lacunae, requiring judges to look beyond the codal text for legal solutions.[85] Importantly, these provisions, though formulated using the language of civil codes, accommodate Islamic legal norms and sources.

On that note, while each code permits reference to some outside referent as a gap-filler (such as custom) the legal cultures of each country have given different interpretations to the permissible referent. Tunisia, the birthplace of the Santillana Codes, has been relatively secular for most of its history—a fact which doubtlessly influenced the interpretation of Tunisian courts that discourages reference to Islamic law as a subsidiary source of law. In contrast, the Moroccan judiciary has made use of Islamic law as a subsidiary source of law more freely.[86] Mauritania, in contrast, viewed its adoption of the Santillana model with its modifications as a renewal of Islamic law and includes a provision expressly permitting to fill the gaps in legislation by reference to the Malikite rite of Islamic law. Accordingly, as one proceeds from oldest (Tunisian) to youngest (Mauritanian), one sees an increasingly permissive approach to the judge's use of Islamic law as a subsidiary source of law.

There are, however, other ways that a legal source can find influence in a civil code beyond express references. Even where a code does not expressly permit recourse to a certain body of law—such as Islamic law—elements from a legal tradition may still find relevance by being incorporated into the codal text or through subtler mechanisms that permit those sources to exert influence. This is certainly true for Santillana's work in the Tunisian code, which sought to incorporate Islamic legal principles and to blend those legal rules with European legal norms, effectively fusing two normative orders.[87] Such instances are illuminated in the chapters that follow.

NOTES

1. *See* Lawrence Ponoroff, *The Dubious Role of Precedent in the Quest for First Principles in the Reform of the Bankruptcy Code: Some Lessons from the Civil Law and Realist Traditions*, 74 AM. BANKR. L.J. 173 (2000).

2. *See* JOHN HENRY MERRYMAN ET AL., THE CIVIL LAW TRADITION: EUROPE, LATIN AMERICA, AND EAST ASIA 19 (2d ed., 1994).

3. *Id.*

4. *Id.* at 20.

5. *Louisiana Civil Code* (hereinafter "La. Civ. Code") art. 1, cmt. (b) (citing A.N. Yiannopoulos, *Louisiana Civil Law System* §§ 31, 32 [1977]).

6. La. Civ. Code art. 2.

7. *See* Merryman et al., *supra* note 2, at 22.

8. *Id.* at 22.

9. *See Transcon. Gas Pipe Line Corp. v. Transp. Ins. Co.*, 953 F.2d 985,988 (5th Cir. 1992).

10. *See* M. Kevin Queenan, *Civil Code Article 2324: A Broken Path to Limited Solidary Liability*, 49 LA. L. REV. 1351, 1379 (1989).

11. *Id.*

12. *Id.*

13. *See* Patrick N. Broyles, *Intercontinental Identity: The Right to the Identity in the Louisiana Civil Code*, 65 LA. L. REV. 823, n. 73 (2005).

14. *See* JEAN ETIENNE MARIE PORTALIS, PROJET DE CODE CIVIL PRÉSENTÉ PAR LA COMMISSION NOMMÉE PAR LE GOUVERNEMENT LE 24 THERMIDOR AN VIII 79 (1801), noting in relevant part:

IV. Le droit intérieur ou particulier de chaque peuple se compose en partie du droit universel, en partie des lois qui lui sont propres, et en partie de ses coutumes ou usages, qui sont le supplément des lois.

V. La coutume résulte d'une longue suite d'actes constamment répétés, qui ont acquis la force d'une convention, lâche et commune.

15. *See* Yvon Loussouarn, *The Relative Importance of Legislation, Custom, Doctrine, and Precedent in French Law*, 18 LA. L. REV. 236, 251 (1958), http://digitalcommons.law.lsu.edu/lalrev/vol18/iss2/2.

16. *Id.*

17. *See* Portalis, *supra* note 14, at 82, noting in relevant part:

V. Quand une loi est claire, il ne faut point en éluder la lettre sous prétexte d'en pénétrer l'esprit; et dans l'application d'une loi obscure, on doit préférer le sens le plus naturel et celui qui est le moins défectueux dans l'exécution.

VI. Pour fixer le vrai sens d'une partie de la loi, il faut en combiner et en réunir toutes les dispositions.

VII. La présomption du juge ne doit pas être mise à la place de la présomption de la loi: il n'est pas permis de distinguer lorsque la loi ne distingue pas; et les exceptions qui ne sont point dans la loi ne doivent point être suppléées.

18. *See* Yvon Loussouarn, *supra* note 15, at 240.

19. *Id.*

20. *See* Roscoe Pound, *Sources and Forms of Law*, 21 NOTRE DAME L. REV. 247, 274 (1946), http://scholarship.law.nd.edu/ndlr/vol21/iss4/1

21. Léon Julliot de la Morandière, *The Draft of a New French Civil Code: The Role of the Judge*, 69 HARV. L. REV. 1264, 1266 (1956).

22. Louisiana Digest of 1808, Article 21.

23. KONRAD ZWEIGERT & HEIN KÖTZ, AN INTRODUCTION TO COMPARATIVE LAW 104 (Tony Weir trans., 1998).

24. *Id.* at 104–105.

25. *See* J.B. GADOLFI, CODE CIVIL DE ROYAUME D'ITALIE (1868) (hereinafter "*Codice Civile*"), Arts. 1–2.

26. *Id.*, Art. 3.

27. *Id.*

28. *See* Yvon Loussouarn, *supra* note 15, at 243.

29. *Id.*

30. *Id.*

31. *See* Vernon Valentine Palmer, "May God Protect *Us from the Equity of Parlements*": *Comparative Reflections on English and French Equity Power*, 73 TUL. L. REV. 1287 (1999).

32. Ben Atkinson Wortley, *Jurisprudence* 221(1967).

33. Alfred E. von Overbeck, *Some Observations on the Role of the Judge Under the Swiss Civil Code*, 37 LA. L. REV. 684 (1977), http://digitalcommons.law.lsu.edu/lalrev/vol37/iss3/3.

34. James L. Dennis, *Interpretation and Application of the Civil Code and the Evaluation of Judicial Precedent*, 54 LA. L. REV. 7 (1993), http://digitalcommons.law.lsu.edu/lalrev/vol54/iss1/5

35. *Swiss Civil Code*, Art. 1, https://www.admin.ch/opc/en/classified-compilation/19070042/201604010000/210.pdf.

36. Layton B. Register, *Judicial Powers of Interpretation Under Foreign Codes*, 65 U. PA. L. REV. 39 (1916), http://scholarship.law.upenn.edu/cgi/viewcontent.cgi?article=7600&context=penn_law_review.

37. *See* von Overbeck, *supra* note 33.

38. *See* Dennis, *supra* note 34, at 7.

39. Benjamin N. Cardozo, The Nature Of The Judicial Process 140 (1921).

40. Italian *Codice Civile*, Art. 3.

41. *See* Morandière, *supra* note 21 at 1266; *see also* H. C. Gutteridge, Comparative Law: An Introduction To The Comparative Method Of Legal Study 80–81 (2015).

42. Tunisian Code of Obligations and Contracts, Arts. 532–63.

43. *Id.*, Art. 532.

44. *Id.*, Art. 533.

45. *Id.*, Art. 535.

46. *Id.*

47. *Id.*, Art. 543.

48. *Id.*, Art. 544.

49. *See* M.D. Santillana, Avant-Projet Du Code Civil Et Commercial Tunisien III (1899) [hereinafter AVANT-PROJET].

50. *See, e.g.*, Louisiana Civil Code, Art. 1: "The sources of law are legislation and custom;" Louisiana Civil Code, Art. 4: "When no rule for a particular situation can be derived from legislation or custom, the court is bound to proceed according to equity. To decide equitably, resort is made to justice, reason, and prevailing usages."

51. *See* Libyan Civil Code, Art. 1, para. 2.; Syrian Civil Code, Art. 1.

52. *Id.*

53. *See* Stéphane Papi, L'influence Juridique Islamique Au Maghreb 235 n.1273 (2009).

54. *See* M. Mohamed Kamel Charfeddine, *Esquisse sur la méthode normative retenue dans l'élaboration du Code tunisien des obligations et des contrats*, 48 REV. INT'L De Droit Comparé, 421, 440 (1996) ("Ambiguïté voulue ou ambiguïté dictée par la crainte d'une mise en cause par les juges de l'oeuvre d'unification législative du droit des obligations réalisée pour la première fois en Tunisie? A moins qu'il ne s'agisse que d'une simple prudence pour enraciner le nouveau code et permettre son intégration en imposant le respect strict de ses dispositions.").

55. *Id.*

56. *See* Haider Ala Hamoudi, Negotiating In Civil Conflict: Constitutional Construction And Imperfect Bargaining In Iraq 224 (2013).

57. *Id.*

58. *Codice Civile*, Art. 3.

59. *See* Avant-Projet, *supra* note 49, at Art. 617 *et seq.*

60. *Id.*

61. *See* Register, *supra* note 36.

62. *See* 11 F. Gény, *La Technique Législative dans la Codification Civile Moderne*, *in* Le Code Civil 1804–1904. Livre Du Centenaire (1904).

63. *See* Nicole Souletie, Le Mot De Madame Nicole Souletie In Le Centenaire Du Dahir Formant Code Des Obligations Et Contrats (DOC) 1913–2013 15 (2013).

64. *See* PR. Radia Bouhlal, *Le DOC a L'Epreuve du Temps*, *in* Le Centenaire DU Dahir Formant Code Des Obligations Et Contrats (DOC) 1913–2013 40 (2013).

65. *Id.*

66. *Id.*

67. *See* Dahir du 12/09/1913 (Septembre 12, 1913) formant code des obligations et des contrats (hereinafter *Moroccan Code of Obligations and Contracts*), Art. 474.

68. *Id.*, Art. 475.

69. *See* Mohammed Jalal Essaid, *Introduction a L'Etude du Droit* 255 (5ème ed., 2014).

70. *Id.* at 148.

71. *See* Amin Hajji, *The Commercial Laws of Morocco*, in Digest Of Commercial Laws Of The World, DIGCOMLAWS (Patrick Tinsley & Amin Hajji, eds.) § 35:1 Country Digests and Forms, http://ahlo.ma/wp-content/uploads/2016/06/Chapter-35-The-Commercial-Laws-of-Morocco-2016-2-2.pdf.

72. *See* L. Messaoudi, *Grandeurs et limites du droit musulman au Maroc*, 47 REV. INT'L. DE DROIT COMPARÉ (Janvier–Mars 1995), at 153.

73. Omar Azziman, La Tradition Juridique Islamique Dans L'évolution Du Droit Privé Marocain 251–72 (1992).

74. *See* Essaid, *supra* note 69, citing Dahirs of 1956 and 1957 and Cour Sup., Ch. Civ., 24 Avril 1968, Rec. des arrêts de la Cour Sup., Ch. Civ., 1966—1982, p. 513.

75. *See* Ordonnance n°89—126 du Septembre 14, 1989, In JO du Octobre 25, 1989 (Code des Obligations et des Contrats de Mauritanie), [hereinafter "Mauritanian Code of Obligations and Contracts"] Art. 476.

76. *See id.*, Art. 477.

77. *See* Mauritanian Code of Obligations and Contracts, Art. 2; French Code Civil, Art. 2.

78. *See* Mauritanian Code of Obligations and Contracts, Art. 486.

79. *Id.*

80. *Id.*, Art. 487.

81. *Id.*, Art. 488.

82. *See* Zelezeck Nguimatsa Serge, Researching The Legal System And Laws Of The Islamic Republic Of Mauritania, 1.1 (2009), http://www.nyulawglobal.org/globalex/Mauritania.html.

83. *Id.,* citing M.O. Salah, *Quelques Aspects de la Réception du Droit Français en Mauritanie*, 5 REV. Mauritanienne De Droit Et D'ECON. 25 (1989).

84. *See* Mauritanian Code of Obligations and Contracts, Art. 1179 ("Pour combler les lacunes de cett ordonnance, il est fait référence au rite malékite.").

85. *See* Gény, *supra* note 62.

86. *See* Azziman, *supra* note 73, at 251–72.

87. *See* Maaike Voorhoeve, *Judges in a Web of normative Orders: Judicial Practices at the Court of First Instance Tunis in the Field of Divorce Law* 54 (2011) (Ph.D. dissertation, University of Amsterdam) ("Santillana explicitly referred to the Ottoman Mecelle and Qadri Pasha's works as sources of inspiration, as well as Sahnun's Mudawwana and Khalil's Mukhtasar. When choosing between different solutions from Islamic law, the principle that was closest to French law was chosen.").

Chapter 5

Obligations in General

Continental civil law envisions an obligation as something more expansive than simply a contract (though a contract can certainly form an obligation). Deriving the concept of an obligation from Roman law, civil law theorists have maintained that an obligation is "a legal relationship that compels us to give, to do, or to not do something."[1] This allows for obligations that are bilateral (such as contracts) but also for unilateral obligations by which only a single party is bound.[2]

> In Roman law, according to a text by Gaius, all obligations derive from contract, delict, and several other causes. On that basis, the Corpus Juris asserts the existence of four sources of obligations which, as universally accepted by doctrine with almost no exception, are contracts, quasi-contracts, delicts, and quasi-delicts.[3]

On the other hand, as noted, Islamic law never fully developed a general theory of obligations or contracts in the same way as continental civil law, but did develop specific rules to govern transactions in specific nominate contracts, most of which were modeled on the contract of sale.[4] As a result, most civil codes throughout the Middle East, North Africa, and the Sahel mainly derive their general provisions on obligations derived from continental civil law.[5] The Santillana Codes are, in many ways, no exception to this general rule. On that score, Belknani notes that the general provisions relating to obligations in the Tunisian code are essentially drawn from the continental civil law tradition,[6] and, as the analysis below demonstrates, the civil codes of Morocco and Mauritania largely replicate the Tunisian code's framework for the law of obligations. Each code, therefore, mainly draws the essence of its laws relating to obligations from the European model—though Santillana's synthesis imbues each with qualities familiar to (and important to) Islamic jurists. Santillana's work is informed by Islamic law, which, as in a tapestry, is interwoven with European law to create a unique juridical whole. Moreover, as one might expect, each code was slightly modified and adjusted as it was adopted, creating a natural degree of diversity among them.

OBLIGATIONS IN GENERAL

Each Santillana Code uniformly states that obligations are derived from conventions and other declarations of will, quasi-contracts, delicts, and quasi-delicts.[7] While location of the provision differs in the Mauritanian code (the Mauritanian code places this provision a bit later in the code whereas the others place it at the very beginning)[8] the basic text is the same. Similarly, in each code, the elements necessary for a valid obligation are: (1) the capacity to form an obligation; (2) a valid declaration concerning the essential elements of the obligation; (3) a definite object that can be the object of an obligation; and (4) a lawful cause for the obligation[9]—requirements which echo civil law based on the French model.[10] These rules are also consistent with Islamic law, which requires people entering into contracts to be of sound mind,[11] that the contract have a lawful object,[12] and that the contract have a lawful cause.[13]

It is with regard to the basic issue of capacity to contract that one begins to see the special attention Santillana gave in his codification to the issue of how the law of obligations would apply to persons of different religions. Under each code, all persons have the capacity to form obligations unless declared otherwise by the law.[14] The Tunisian code expressly states that religious differences between Muslims and non-Muslims have no bearing on the capacity to contract, nor do such religious differences impact obligations between Muslims and non-Muslims.[15] This provision may have been a clarification inserted to address any uncertainty that might arise due to the fact that some Islamic legal scholars raised questions regarding the enforceability of contracts between Muslims and non-Muslims.[16] One can see how for a Sephardic Jew from Tunisia, such a provision would have significant importance. The Moroccan and Mauritanian codes, however, in an example of divergence from the Tunisian code, contain no express provision regarding the effect of religious differences on contracts—though each code maintains the rule that all persons have the capacity to form obligations unless declared otherwise by the law.[17]

In his *Avant-Projet*, Santillana mainly cites to the French and Italian civil codes as sources for these provisions on obligations, though he also cites to various Islamic legal sources, notably the writings of Ibn Nadjim, Hamaoui,

Tasouli, and Zarqani.[18] In that regard, Santillana provides some interesting and enlightening glossae. With regard to the elements of a contract, he writes, "It must be that an obligation is for an advantage; an obligation having for its object a grain of wheat would be null and void [citing the Islamic legal commentator Taoudi], as well as that whose object could have no use for man [citing Zarqani]." Interestingly, Santillana had initially included a first article that stated, "An obligation is a legal relationship by virtue of which a person can be bound to another to give, to do, or to not do something in a manner pre-scribed by law."[19] This article was ultimately omitted from the final Tunisian code, though Santillana's glossae on the proposed article notes that, according to the Malikite school, "[t]he idea of obligation as a personal link is clear in the definition of the loan and in the theory of the pledge."[20] This latter glossae gives insight into Santillana's multiplex approach: borrowing from existing civil law models for the construct but extrapolating from nominate contracts under Islamic law to find the general Islamic legal rule that supports it.

UNILATERAL ACTS

Civil law doctrine recognizes, to varying degrees, the concept of a unilateral act.[21] Planiol attributed the more modern approach of permitting a unilat-eral declaration to form a binding obligation to German jurists.[22] While a relatively recent innovation during Planiol's era, unilateral acts are now well-founded in modern civil law doctrine. As Litvinoff noted, "under cer-tain circumstances, the law may attach consequences to a merely unilateral declaration of will which is promissory in nature."[23]

Islamic jurists, on the other hand, have historically been of mixed opinions regarding the enforceability of a unilateral promise. While there is consensus that a promise made to Allah in a form of vow (nadhr) must be enforced, there are different opinions regarding a unilateral promise to do something that is otherwise permissible.[24] Dr. Marjan Muhammad, Hakimah Yaakob, and Shabana Hasan note that classical Islamic jurists had divergent opinions on this matter that can be summarized in three categories:

i. The fulfillment of a promise is recommended, but not obligatory from both religious and legal perspectives (the majority opinion of scholars).
ii. The fulfillment of a promise is religiously and legally obligatory, and thus enforceable in a court of law (the minority view of scholars).
iii. The fulfillment of a promise is legally obligatory if it is contingent upon a condition (according to the Hanafi madhhab), and if the promise is attached to a cause and the promisee has engaged in or acted upon the cause of the promise (the famous view of Maliki scholars).[25]

The majority of classical jurists in Islamic law, including some of the Maliki school, were, therefore, of the opinion that fulfillment of a unilateral promise is recommended (mustahabb) but not obligatory (wajib).[26] Most Maliki scholars, however, believed that "fulfillment of a promise is obligatory and enforceable in court if the promise is attached to a cause/reason and the promisee has acted upon/entered into the cause of the promise."[27] Muhammad, Yaakob, and Hasan give the following example of this view: "When Ahmad says to A: 'Buy a commodity, and I promise to lend you some money,' and A bought the commodity, then it is obligatory for Ahmad to honour his promise."[28]

Under Tunisian law, while a mere promise does not operate to create an obligation,[29] a promise made by posters or other means of advertising which offer a reward to one who finds a lost object or accomplishes a task can create an obligation, and is deemed to be accepted by those who, even without having knowledge of the offer, find the thing or accomplish the task.[30] In such circumstances, the author of the promise is required to provide the promised reward.[31] The Moroccan code replicates these provisions verbatim[32] as does the Mauritanian code.[33] While these provisions comport with the civil law model, they are drawn more from the German model than the French Code Civil and mirror quite closely the 1984 amendments to the Louisiana Civil Code, which "adopted the German-oriented solution, reserving the promise of reward only for the case of performance of a specific fact."[34]

All three codes further state that the promise of reward may not be revoked where the revocation occurs after execution has begun.[35] One who has set a deadline for the completion of the task envisioned by the promise is deemed to have waived the right to revoke the promise until the expiration of the time limit.[36] If several people have accomplished the task at the same time, the promised prize or reward is shared between them.[37] If they have done it at various times, the award belongs to the first to accomplish it. If they each accomplished a portion of the task, then the reward is shared proportionally.[38] If the reward cannot be shared but can be sold, then the price will be shared among the beneficiaries.[39] If this price or reward is an object that has no market value or can only be given to one person, then according to the terms of the promise, the decision is made by drawing lots ("*la décision est remise à la voie du sort*").[40]

All of these provisions are taken directly from the German civil code,[41] thus demonstrating Santillana's reliance on a plurality of European civil law sources when drafting the Tunisian code. Importantly, they also seem consonant with the view of Maliki scholars who maintained that, under Islamic law, a unilateral promise is enforceable "if attached to a cause/reason and the promisee has acted upon/entered into the cause of the promise."[42] Santillana confirms this in the *Avant-Projet*, citing Bennani and Zarqani for the rule that "[t]he offer can no longer be withdrawn by the promisor of the commencement of execution. The reward is due, according to the Malekites, only if the act has been performed in full, in the manner provided for by the one who offered the reward."[43] This exemplifies how Santillana was able to synthesize civil law and Islamic legal precepts.

CONTRACTS (BILATERAL ACTS)

The notion of a bilateral act, of course, dates back to ancient times and was well-developed in Roman law.[44] Modernity and commerce only increased the frequency of this method for forming obligations. Writing in the nineteenth century, civil law jurist A.M. Demante noted that, even during that era, the majority of obligations were formed through the creation of contracts.[45]

The general rule in modern civil law is that a contract is formed by the consent of the parties to the contract.[46] Consistent with this theory, under the Santillana Codes, a bilateral contract is perfected only by agreement of the parties on the essential elements of the obligation, as well as on all other lawful clauses that the parties consider essential to the agreement.[47] Barring a provision to the contrary, changes by the parties by mutual agreement to the contract that occur immediately after its conclusion do not constitute a new contract, but are considered part of the initial agreement.[48] Even so, a contract is not perfected when the parties expressly reserve certain clauses to form the object of a subsequent agreement.[49] The agreement reached under these conditions, on one or more such clauses, does not constitute the conclusion of a contract—even if a preliminary agreement has been drawn up in writing.[50] In any case, reservations or restrictions which are not brought to the attention of the other party are not set aside or restrict the effects of the declaration of intent as provided for in its apparent expression.[51]

In the *Avant-Projet*, Santillana cited to the Roman Digest of Civil Law for support of his proposed articles on bilateral contracts, but also provided Islamic legal authority, citing to *Radd al-Muhtar*, Ibn Abidin's's influential nineteenth-century Hanafite work, and Hamaoui for the proposition that "[t]here is no contract when the will of one of the contracting parties is focused on a different object, or to a part of the object, or to a different agreement from that desired by the other party."[52] Santillana, thus, divined the Islamic legal rule, looked to the civil law model, and designed a rule in his codification that neatly comports with both systems.

THE VICES OF CONSENT

Continental civil law has traditionally allowed that the consent of a party to a contract—a necessary element of contract formation—can be vitiated, and thus dismantling the legal force of the contract or obligation, for three reasons: fraud, error, and duress ("*Le dol, l'erreur et la violence sont les trois causes qui vicient la volonté.*")[53] As civil law jurist Saul Litvinoff noted when explaining this concept:

> Autonomy of the will is the basic idea that underlies the doctrine of juridical acts implicit in the civil codes of France and Louisiana. From the vantage point of that idea, a person's declaration of will produces the intended legal effects when the consent it expresses is informed by a reason, a cause, and is also free from interfering circumstances that frustrate its intention. As clearly stated in the Code Napoleon, consent is invalid when it has been given through error, extorted by duress, or obtained by fraud. When such is the case, though consent has come into existence, it is impaired, defective, it is tainted by a vice that affects its freedom.[54]

Some continental civil law systems, notably those influenced by the French model, posit that there are some vices of consent that prevent formation of a contract at the outset and, accordingly, serve to render the obligation an absolute nullity.[55] "French doctrine sometimes refers to these kinds of vices that prevent formation of a contract as *erreur-obstacle* because the error serves as an obstacle to the creation of a contract."[56] The distinction between an ordinary vice of consent and an *erreur-obstacle* is that the latter negates consent altogether rather than rendering the will of a party defective. Otherwise stated, "[i]t does not concern the validity but the formation of a contract."[57] This means that, as such a contract was never concluded, there might be no need for a judicially declared nullity.[58]

Islamic law, likewise, has long held that fraud,[59] error,[60] and duress[61] are grounds for rescinding contracts. These legal provisions, therefore, form an area of comparative overlap between Islamic law and continental civil law. Indeed, in the *Avant-Projet*, Santillana cited to the Digest of Justinian and the French Code Civil as the inspiration for these articles and divined legal support in Islamic law by citing to the Qur'an, as well as the works of Zarqani, Ibn Nadjim, and Tasouli.[62] Thus, both systems recognize the same vices of consent, permitting the Santillana Codes to incorporate a framework for vitiation of consent that aligns with both systems. Even so, though analysis reveals Santillana principally drew the provisions for his codification from the French model and other European codifications in force at that time. This was a prudent codification decision given the fact that European codes already had language from which Santillana could borrow. Santillana's work, nonetheless, does draw on Islamic legal concepts to devise the legal scheme for vices of consent and also incorporates some cutting-edge civil law innovations. The end result is a common framework for each code in which the consent of a party is annullable when it is given in error, when induced by fraud, and when it is obtained through violence.[63]

ERROR

It is with regard to the vice of consent of error that we are given a glance at Santillana's forward-thinking approach to civil law codification, notably in his approach to the concept of "error of law" but also in incorporation of the notion of "excusability." As a general matter, error has been defined as "a false representation of reality"—something that occurs when a party is ignorant regarding something that exists or when a party wrongly believes in the existence of something that actually does not exist.[64] The civil law doctrine of error is derived from Roman law, which initially recognized only a few specialized categories of mistake. French law expanded upon this legal concept "and brought error into the general analysis of obligations."[65] Early Roman law, however, only permitted mistakes of fact to be a ground for relief and maintained that "a mistake of law would in no circumstances avail one who sought to rely on it[.]"[66] Similarly, while Roman law recognized exclusively error of fact and did not recognize error of law as a vice of consent, French law took a broader view and began to recognize errors of both fact and law as grounds for rescission—and modern civil codes have since developed that concept.

> Though the Code Napoleon deals with error of law only in an incidental manner, the Louisiana Civil Code has dealt expressly with that matter since the Revision of 1825. It is now clear in the law of Louisiana that a party may seek the annulment of a contract when an erroneous understanding of the law was the reason that prompted him to make that contract.[67]

Nevertheless, error of law was slow to emerge in modern civil codes as a singular, coherent concept. By the nineteenth century when Santillana was actively working as a jurist, the idea of "error of law" as a vice of consent existed—but it was at the cutting edge of civil law. French law still only dealt with the matter doctrinally and celebrated French jurist Planiol flatly opined that "[t]he law does not distinguish between errors of law and errors of fact."[68] The Louisiana Civil Code of that era, however, recognized that "[e]rror, as applied to contracts, is of two kinds: 1. Error of fact; 2. Error of law."[69] The Italian *Codice Civile* of 1865 also addressed error of law.[70] But beyond the examples of Louisiana and Italy, at the time Santillana was drafting the Tunisian code, there were few codifications that took error of law into consideration as a separate category.[71]

Santillana, however, made the decision to incorporate the notion of "error of law" into his work rather than simply emulate the language of the French code then in force. Likely drawing again from the Italian *Codice Civile* of 1865, the Tunisian code—and each successive Santillana Code—expressly recognizes legal error and holds that such an error may result in rescission when (1) it is the sole or principal cause for the obligation; and (2) if it is excusable.[72] A review of the applicable language shows Santillana's reliance on the Italian *Codice Civile* of 1865 which, in turn, drew from the French *Code Civil* of 1804.

Santillana's main gloss on the concept imported into his code seems to be the additional requirement that the error also be "excusable." This is notable as the excusability aspect of this provision has no analogue in the French or German codes of that period.[73] Similarly, analogous requirements are not found in the Italian code, nor the other major civil codes of the era. The idea was, however, certainly present in the writings of influential German jurist and historian Friedrich Carl von Savigny, and it was kept alive in the writings of European jurists of Santillana's time.[74] Santillana, instead, seems to have based this requirement on Islamic law.

> Must error be excusable? This theory, accepted by the Hanafites, is controversial among the Malikites; according to Ibn Roched, where the interests of third parties are concerned, error or ignorance is never excusable; when the interest of third parties is not involved, it is necessary to examine whether the error or ignorance qualifies with respect of the person; it is excusable if it does, it is not excusable if the case is the contrary.[75]

Santillana summarizes his synthesis of Islamic and continental law in noting, "In summary, error of law like error of fact can give rise to rescission of a contract; but both must be excusable; they must be such as cannot be attributed to the author either by fault or fraud."[76] This requirement is certainly

Table 5.1   Codal Comparison: Vice of Error

Italian Codice Civile *of 1865*	*Tunisian Code of Obligations and Contracts*	*French* Code Civil *of 1804*
Art. 1109. L'erreur de droit n'est cause de la nullité de la convention que lorsqu'elle en est la cause unique ou principale.	Art. 44. L'erreur de droit donne ouverture à la rescision de l'obligation: 1) lorsqu'elle en est la cause unique ou principale; 2) lorsqu'elle est excusable.	L'erreur n'est une cause de nullité de la convention que lorsqu'elle tombe sur la substance même de la chose qui en est l'objet. Elle n'est point une cause de nullité lorsqu'elle ne tombe que sur la personne avec laquelle on a intention de contracter, à moins que la considération de cette personne ne soit la cause principale de la convention.

consonant with contemporary civil law,[77] though it bears emphasizing that the French *Code Civil* did not incorporate the previously jurisprudential idea of "excusable error" until its 2015 reforms.[78] Santillana's codification was, therefore, among the first to expressly include "error of law" in a codification and to elucidate how such error should be treated—and his code was the first to incorporate the juristic idea of "excusable error."

The Santillana Codes also uniformly state that an error may give rise to rescission when it bears on the identity, type, or quality of the object of the obligation.[79] Error regarding the person or his/her quality does not give rise to rescission, except in the case where the person or his/her quality has been one of the determining factors for the consent given by the other party.[80] These provisions comport with the French model which generally maintains that (a) error is a cause of nullity of a contract when it relates to the substance of the object of the contract and (b) error regarding the essential qualities of the other party is only a cause for nullity in contracts that were concluded in consideration of the person.[81] Parenthetically, this sort of error is referred to as "factual error" in the Tunisian code (*l'erreur de fait*), though the Moroccan and Mauritanian codes do not use this term.[82]

Under the Tunisian and Moroccan codes, simple errors in calculation (*les simples erreurs de calcul*) do not give rise to rescission, but they must be rectified.[83] The Mauritanian code also has this rule but uses a different term, noting that clerical errors (*erreurs matérielles*) when they are manifest are not a cause for rescission but are subject to correction.[84] The Mauritanian code, therefore, differs from its Tunisian and Moroccan brethren by broadening the rule from simple errors in calculation to clerical errors more generally, but adding a requirement that such errors be apparent in order for them to be grounds for rescission.

VIOLENCE (DURESS)

In the civil law tradition, "consent is vitiated when it has been obtained by duress of such a nature as to cause a reasonable fear of unjust and considerable injury to a party's person, property, or reputation."[85] The French word used to describe this vice of consent is *violence*, though it is generally translated in English as "duress."[86] According to this concept, the duress "must be forceful enough as to constrain the will of a person of ordinary firmness."[87]

Roman law utilized a more realistic terminology when it characterized the vice of consent consisting in lack of freedom as *metus*—fear. The same can be said of the Swiss Code of Obligations, which speaks of *crainte*—fear—rather than duress or violence. Duress is actually that which causes the vice rather than the vice itself.[88]

Contemporary civil law models generally hold that "[c]onsent is vitiated when it has been obtained by duress of such a nature as to cause a reasonable fear of unjust and considerable injury to a party's person, property or reputation." Because fear can be subjective, modern civil codes also generally allow that "[a]ge, health, disposition and other personal circumstances of a party must be taken into account in determining reasonableness of the fears."[89] Similarly, civil law systems generally disallow rescission based on "reverential fear" alone unless accompanied by threats of violence.[90]

Islamic law, in turn, also recognizes that duress may vitiate the consent of a contracting party and be grounds for rescission of a contract.[91] Islamic law generally provides that a person exercising duress must be capable of implementing his threats and that the person subject to duress must be sufficiently frightened to agree to execute the obligation under the influence of fear. Islamic law also recognizes that duress can differ according to a person's circumstances and, therefore, "Muslim jurists of all schools have followed the 'subjective' theory in determining the criterion of fear in duress."[92] According to this theory, duress may stem from both physical and verbal threats.[93] The underlying Islamic legal theory of duress is, therefore, quite similar to the continental civil law model.

The vice of consent of duress in the Santillana Codes is defined as "coercion without the authority of the law, and subject to which one brings a person to perform an act to which he or she did not consent."[94] Duress, under each code, gives rise to rescission when the duress was the principal cause for undertaking the obligation and when—having regard to age, gender, status of the person, and their level of impressionability—the duress consists of acts that are of such a nature that they are likely to produce fear of physical suffering, or profound mental disturbance (from fear, exposing that person's honor or possessions to material injury).[95] The fear inspired by the threat of prosecution or other legal channels generally will not give rise to rescission under the framework of the Santillana Codes unless the person making the threat does so in a way that qualifies as legally cognizable duress (the sorts of will-overtaking threats described above) and is done so in a way that abuses the position of the threatened party by seeking to extort excessive or undue benefits from him or her.[96]

Under the Santillana Codes, duress gives rise to rescission of the obligation, even if it was not exercised by one of the parties to the obligation[97] and even if it was exercised upon a person with which the contracting party is closely related by blood.[98] Reverential fear, however, does not give rise to rescission of an obligation unless also accompanied by serious threats or assault.[99] Interestingly, in the *Avant-Projet*, the proposed article on reverential fear was initially more flexible, permitting judges to make decisions on a case-by-case basis, though reverential fear accompanied by serious threats or assault would give rise to rescission as a matter of law.[100] The final article that was implemented only allows for rescission in such cases when that fear is also accompanied by serious threats or assault.[101] This seems to find balance with both Islamic law and continental civil law theory.[102] One sees in the Santillana Codes, therefore, a standard for duress that is consistent with both modern civil law and Islamic law.

FRAUD

Another potential vice of consent recognized in the Santillana Codes is that of fraud. In the civil law tradition, fraud is a vice of consent when it induces "a person into an error by means of a misrepresentation or a suppression of the truth, made with the intention either to obtain an unjust advantage for the inducer or to cause a loss or inconvenience to the one so induced, in the process of making a contract."[103] Fraud can occur when the supposed benefit of a contract of obligation is falsely represented by one party to the other in order to entice the other to enter into the obligation.[104] Similarly, fraud occurs "when the substantial qualities of a thing are falsely represented by one party in order to induce the other to purchase that thing."[105]

Islamic law also recognizes the possibility of rescission when there is fraud involved in an obligation. According to Islamic law, fraud by a contracting party which entices the other party to enter into a contract or obligation is considered an impediment to consent.[106] If the misrepresentation is accomplished by an act, most Islamic legal scholars agree that it is an impediment to consent.[107] "If the misrepresentation is solely verbal, it is not regarded as a cause for voiding the contract unless it is accompanied by undue disproportion between the mutual obligations (*laesio enormis*)."[108] In that regard, the concepts of fraud and *lesion* (discussed below) seem to bleed together under Islamic law. Notably, under Islamic law, fraud can generally also be grounds for rescission of a contract when it is committed by a third party if the third party is in connivance with a contracting party.[109]

Under the Santillana Codes, fraud gives rise to rescission when the tactics or non-disclosures of one of the parties, or a person who represents or is complicit with that party, are of such a nature that without them, the other party would not have contracted.[110] The deceit practiced by a third party has the same effect, when the party that benefits from that fraud had knowledge of it.[111] Fraud with regard to the accessories of the obligation and which was not central to the obligation can give rise only to damages and not rescission.[112] A review of the language of the Italian *Codice Civile* of 1865 and the French *Code Civil* of 1804 demonstrates their influence on the language adopted by Santillana in the Tunisian text.

The Santillana Codes, therefore, mainly adopt the continental civil law concept of fraud as a vice of consent. The main distinction is the express language that states that fraud practiced by a third party gives rise to rescission when the party who profited from it had knowledge of the fraud. This contrasts with the French and Italian civil codes of Santillana's era—neither of which mentioned fraud by a third party. Those European codes instead recognized only the fraud of a contracting party as a vice of consent. Litvinoff explains that the reasons for this are historical.[113]

> At Roman law fraud was considered a delict rather than a vice of consent and gave rise to an action that, because it was criminal in nature, could be brought only against the perpetrator and not against another person even if the latter had benefitted from the fraud.[114]

Although early French and Italian doctrine recognized that fraud by a third person with connivance with one of the parties to a contract could give rise to rescission,[115] it would be 2016 before the French Civil Code expressly addressed fraud by a third person in the text of the civil code.[116] Islamic law, however, in contrast to Roman law and the European systems derived therefrom, historically, has considered fraud as something that vitiated consent and permitted rescission in situations where fraud is perpetrated by a third party.[117] It is, therefore, the Islamic legal solution that one sees in the text Santillana crafted rather than the prevailing European approach of his time. This again highlights a place in which Santillana borrowed from European codes to formulate the text and structure of a legal concept—fraud as a vice of consent—but incorporated an Islamic legal norm which (a) provided greater protection to the victim of fraud; and (b) diverged from the French model. It

Table 5.2   Codal Comparison: Vice of Fraud

Italian Codice Civile of 1865	Tunisian Code of Obligations and Contracts	French Code Civil of 1804
Art. 1115. Le dol est une cause de nullité de la convention lorsque les manoeuvres pratiquées par l'une des parties sont telles, que sans ces manoeuvres, l'autre partie n'aurait pas contracté.	Art. 56. Le dol donne ouverture à la rescision lorsque les manoeuvres ou les réticences de l'une des parties, de celui qui la représente ou qui est de complicité avec elle, sont de telle nature que, sans ces manoeuvres ou ces réticences, l'autre partie n'aurait pas contracté. Le dol pratiqué par un tiers a le même effet, lorsque la partie qui en profite en avait connaissance.	Art. 1116. Le dol est une cause de nullité de la convention lorsque les manoeuvres pratiquées par l'une des parties sont telles, qu'il est évident que, sans ces manoeuvres, l'autre partie n'aurait pas contracté. Il ne se présume pas et doit être prouvé.

also demonstrates, yet again, how Santillana's final product was not an emulation of the French code, but something new and unique inspired as much by Islamic as European legal sources.

LESION

The concept of lesion, which is derived from continental civil law and is of early Roman origin, is one that holds that a sale may be rescinded because the law assumes that, due to the insufficient price being paid for the thing, the consent of the party selling the thing was not truly voluntary.[118] Planiol notes that this cause for rescission of a contract—which the Roman Emperor Justinian attributed to Diocletian[119]—was initially limited to certain situations such as contracts entered into by minors and the sale of immovables.

Article 1674 of the French *Code Civil* of 1804 set a mathematical formula to determine when lesion could be actionable, stating that if the seller had been injured by more than seven-twelfths in the price of an immovable, then he had the right to demand recession of the sale.[120] Thus, lesion depended on whether a formula was met "that measured the relative values of a performance and the return performance[.]"[121] The German civil code, in contrast, allowed such actions in cases where need, inexperience, or indiscretion led a party to undertake an obligation that was "in obvious disproportion to performance."[122]

The version of lesion described in the Santillana Codes, however, is very different from the civil law concept. For each of the Santillana Codes, lesion is defined as any obligation entailing a price differential beyond a third of the given price and the actual value of the thing.[123] Under each code, however, lesion does not give rise to rescission unless it is caused by fraud by the other party, fraud by the other party's representative, or fraud by one who acted for the other party.[124] The only exception to this is when the injured party is a minor or is incompetent, even though he or she would have contracted with the assistance of his guardian or legal counsel in the manner determined by law and although there be no fraud by the other party.[125] Santillana, therefore, blended two legal philosophies in articulating the requirements for lesion. He adopted the French approach of using a mathematic formula to perceive when lesion is actionable, but confined its applicability to cases in which there has been fraud in a manner consistent with Islamic law.

DRUNKENNESS AND SIMILAR IMPAIRMENTS

French law—very early on and at the time Santillana was working on the Tunisian codification—recognized in jurisprudence and doctrine that drunkenness was a potential ground for rescission of a contract because it vitiated the capacity of the affected party,[126] but no provision in the French code addressed intoxication directly. The drafters of the French *Code Civil* considered a proposal that would more directly address the effect of intoxication on obligations but, after some discussion, thought such a revision could be problematic and that the existing provisions were sufficient.[127] Similarly, there is no such provision in the Italian *Codice Civile* of 1865. Even so, the civil law model, as discussed, requires that parties entering into an obligation have the capacity to do so and that "a temporary derangement of intellect, whether arising from disease, accident or other cause, also creates an incapacity pending its duration, provided the situation of the party and his incapacity were apparent."[128]

Under Islamic law, "the validity of contracts concluded by a drunken person was a controversial question."[129] Hanafite jurists took the view that intoxication was not grounds for rescission of a contract because "intoxication is a crime and as such cannot be an excuse for waiving punishments."[130] Other schools, such as the Shafi'i and Maliki schools, posit that "an intoxicated person has no capacity for execution, because his [reason] is completely impaired by the state of intoxication."[131] A split on this question, therefore, exists under Islamic law.[132]

The Santillana Codes, on the surface, also seem have disparate approaches to this issue. The Tunisian code contains an article which expressly states that there is reason to rescind a contract when the party who contracted was in a state of drunkenness which has impaired his faculties (echoing the Shafi'i/ Maliki rule).[133] Although consistent with the civil law model, no such provision appears in either the Moroccan or Mauritanian codes. All of the Santillana Codes, however, note that rescission of a contract based on disease "and other analogous cases" is subject to the discretion of the judges.[134] Accordingly, while the basic rule expressed in all the codes is consistent with the civil law model, the Tunisia code expressly addresses the effect of a party's intoxication on a contract, while, in the Moroccan and Mauritanian codes, the same result would obtain under the more general articles.

TRANSFER OF OBLIGATIONS

Consistent with the continental civil law tradition, the Santillana Codes permit the transfer of obligations. As Litvinoff noted, "[a]s an asset in his patrimony, the creditor or obligee may transfer or assign the obligation to another if he so wishes. In addition, the debtor may substitute another person at his end of the relation. In both instances the obligation remains the same, however."[135] Under the Santillana Codes, the transfer of rights and claims of an original creditor to another person can take place, either pursuant to the provisions of each country's domestic law or pursuant to an agreement between the parties.[136] Rights or claims that are not yet expired may be transferred,[137] though such a transfer may not operate for future rights.[138] Similarly, the transfer is considered null in the following circumstances: where the right or claim may not be transferred by virtue of its constitutive title or by law; where it is intended that the rights or claims are of a purely personal nature; or where the debt cannot be subject to seizure or attachment—though when the right or claim is susceptible of being seized with the concurrence of a party or to have its value determined, the assignment of the right will be valued in the same proportion.[139]

With regard to transfers considered null due to its purely personal character, all of the Santillana Codes initially contained the additional explanatory language, "such as the devolution of a *habous*."[140] A *habous* is a French term used in North Africa to refer to a *waqf*—a property or thing endowed permanently for a charitable or pious purpose.[141] The Tunisian code today has no such language due to later legislation that removed it,[142] though its initial inclusion (thereafter replicated in the Moroccan and Mauritanian codes) was added at the insistence of the shaykh al-Islam Mahammad Bayram and his scholars who thought it best to include some religious-based examples to elucidate the provisions of the code and their applicability.[143]

For all the Santillana Codes, the assignment of a claim includes the accessories that are integral to the claim, such as privileges, with the exception of those that are personal to the assignor.[144] It includes wages, mortgages, and sureties unless there is an express stipulation to the contrary.[145] The Mauritanian code, in variance from its Tunisian and Moroccan cousins, adds that, "[t]he collateral deposit of a bond may not be assigned, without this obligation."[146]

Notably, for the Moroccan and Tunisian codes, an assignment is also assumed to include accrued interest unless there is a stipulation to the contrary. The Moroccan and Tunisian codes state that this latter provision relating to interest, however, is not applicable between Muslims.[147] The Mauritanian code, rather than providing a provision for interest but making it inapplicable to Muslims, removes the provision entirely.[148]

In this article, one finds an example of the impact of the Tunisian 'ulama on the substance of Santillana Codes. This is because such an exception for Muslims did not appear in the Tunisian *Avant-Projet* but was added after the review by shaykh al-Islam Mahammad Bayram and the representatives of the Tunisian 'ulama—a modification to Santillana's draft which imported into the code the concept of "personality of laws" and the traditional Islamic legal approach to accommodating religious plurality.[149]

This exception pertaining to Muslims, of course, is due to the provisions of Islamic law, which disallow the charging of interest in the course of transactions.[150] The authority for this doctrine in Islamic law—which is not interpreted with precise uniformity[151]—is from Qur'anic exhortations against the idea of ribā (or interest)[152] and the hadith in which the Prophet is reported to have said as follows:

> (Sell) gold for gold and silver for silver, wheat for wheat, barley for barley, dates for dates and salt for salt of the same kind for the same kind and the same quantity for the same quantity, from hand to hand and if they differ from each other in quantity sell them as you like but from hand to hand.[153]

In permitting an exception to ordinary civil law for Muslims where interest is involved, the Tunisian code adopted a civil law concept but in a way which permits compatibility with Islamic legal tenets. A religion-based rule of this sort is something not generally seen in civil codes. From the perspective of standard continental civil law, its presence seems almost otherworldly. But it was firmly rooted in a legal tradition well understood by both Santillana and Bayram and, ultimately, was deemed a logical inclusion. It is also utilized in other places in the code to mitigate potential abrasion between civil law and Islamic legal norms. Santillana had incorporated similar provisions in a more limited fashion in the Tunisian *Avant-Projet*, though not specifically with regard to the transfer of obligations, nor in most of the places where

Table 5.3   Codal Comparison: Transfer of Obligations

Language in the Avant-Projet	*Language Adopted*
Article 230	Article 210
La cession d'une créance comprend les acesoires de la créance, telles que cautions, privilèges, gages, hypothèques et droit de rétention, à l'exception des privilèges personnels au cédant; elle comprend également les actions en nullité ou en rescision qui appartenaient au cédant; elle est présumée comprendre aussi les intérêts échus et non payés, sauf stipulation ou usage contraire. La caution ou sûreté ne peut être cédée sans l'obligation, mais celle-ci peut être cédée sans la sûreté ou cautionnement; dans ce dernier cas, la sûreté ou cautionnement s'éteint.	La cession d'une créance comprend les accessoires qui font partie intégrante de la créance, tels que les privilèges, à l'exception de ceux qui sont personnels au cédant. Elle ne comprend les gages, hypothèques et cautions que s'il y a stipulation expresse. Elle comprend également les actions en nullité ou en rescision qui appartenaient au cédant. Elle est présumée comprendre aussi les intérêts échus et non payés, sauf stipulation ou usage contraire: <u>cette dernière disposition n'a pas lieu entre musulmans</u>. La caution ou sûreté ne peut être cédée sans l'obligation.

such language was finally adopted in the codal text (to be discussed *infra*). It is, therefore, fair to say that Santillana included the concept of religious individuation in his draft of the Tunisian code—and that he was clearly comfortable with the concept of religious individuation—but that the Tunisian 'ulama was responsible for its proliferation in the final Tunisian text. This rule of religious individuation was replicated in the Moroccan codification, though not in Mauritania which, as noted, imposes Islamic legal prohibitions more broadly than its antecedent codes.

EXTINCTION OF OBLIGATIONS

The Santillana Codes' articles on the extinction of obligations are drawn from civil law in that they incorporate civil law concepts of remission of debt, novation, compensation, and confusion. Notably, however, these articles also incorporate Islamic legal concepts that provide traditional protections and limit the civil law concepts to the extent their operability could transgress Islamic legal boundaries.

REMISSION OF DEBT

A remission of debt, according to civil law doctrine, is a unilateral act by which a creditor renounces his or her rights against a debtor.[154] Such an act liberates the debtor, extinguishing the debt and all accessory obligations pertaining to the debt.[155] Santillana incorporates this concept in his codification, though alloyed with Islamic legal concepts. Under the Santillana Codes, an obligation is extinguished by the voluntary surrender of the obligation by a creditor that is considered capable of making a donation.[156] The remission takes effect as long as the debtor has not expressly refused it.[157] Each code also notes, however, that the remission granted by an ill person to a third party during his or her last illness is valid up to a maximum of one-third of what remains in the succession after the payment of debts and funeral expenses.[158] This latter provision is derived from Islamic law, which generally places a limit of one-third of the estate on the amount that a person may bequest (preserving the remainder of the decedent's estate for family members)[159] and, therefore, imposes cautionary limits on the ability of an ill person to alienate property and extinguish debts in excess of that limit. For instance, the Mejelle provides as follows:

> If someone in his mortal sickness has given something to one of his heirs and has died, if the other heirs do not allow it, that gift is not good.

But if he has made a gift and delivered it to a person who is not an heir of his, and a third of his estate is sufficient for the whole of the gift, it is good.

If it is not sufficient, and the heirs do not permit the gift, the gift is good up to the amount, for which the third of the estate is sufficient. The rest, the donee is compelled to return.[160]

In addition, special provisions exempt the finality of remissions made by an heir in the case of an inherited debt and where that remission was justified by fraud or deceit on the part of the debtor or other people acting in complicity with the debtor.[161] These protections stand alongside the Islamic legal limitation of "one-third of the estate" which Santillana incorporated into the civil law concept of remission of debt to maintain the integrity of Islamic inheritance law. Otherwise, the provisions of the Santillana Codes are largely consistent with other modern civil codes, holding that the release of any debt in general and without reservation cannot be revoked.[162] It is worth noting here, however, that many continental civil law jurisdictions, likewise, maintain the concept of "forced heirship" (deriving their rules in that regard from Roman law) and similarly prohibit bequests in excess of a certain portion of the decedent's estate.[163] The Tunisian, Moroccan, Mauritanian, Islamic, Roman, and continental civil law rules again tend to bleed into one another at such legal intersections.

NOVATION

The concept of novation is also drawn from Roman law but was adapted by civil law jurists throughout the ages so that it is applicable to modern contracts and obligations.[164] Under the Santillana Codes, novation is the extinction of an obligation due to the creation of a new obligation which is substituted for it.[165] Novation cannot be presumed and, to the contrary, the desire for a novation must be expressed.[166] Both the former obligation and the newly formed obligation must be considered legally valid obligations for novation to have effect.[167]

The Santillana Codes provide that novation occurs in three types of circumstances: (1) when the creditor and debtor agree to substitute a new obligation for the former, which extinguishes or changes the cause of the former obligation; (2) when a new debtor is substituted for the former who is discharged by the creditor (such a substitution may take place without the participation of the first debtor); and/or (3) where, by the effect of a new commitment, a new creditor is substituted for the former creditor, thus discharging the debtor vis-à-vis the former creditor.[168] Such a definition comports with the concept of novation as it appears in modern civil codes based on the French model.[169]

COMPENSATION

Civil law doctrine maintains that when two people owe to one another similar obligations, it is not necessary that each one pay the other. Rather, it is simpler to consider each obligation reciprocally extinguished up to the amount of the lesser debt.[170] Litvinoff notes that, in civil law systems based on the French model, "[c]ompensation takes place by operation of law, that is, independently of the will of the parties. The two obligations extinguish each other reciprocally, to the extent of the lesser object, as soon as they co-exist."[171] In systems based on the German model, in contrast, "compensation does not take place automatically, but must be raised as a defense by the interested party."[172]

The Santillana Codes also recognize this civil law concept, though with a variant on the theme. According to each code, compensation occurs when parties are mutually and personally creditor and debtor of the other. The Tunisian and Moroccan codes further note that compensation "does not take place between Muslims in cases where it would constitute a violation of religious law."[173] The Mauritanian code varies slightly in that regard noting that compensation can occur, "provided that this does not constitute *Riba*."[174] The Santillana Codes, therefore, again adopt a civil law concept but permits an exception to it for Muslims insofar as it might potentially conflict with an important tenet of Islamic law.[175]

After the initial article for compensation was proposed in the *Avant-Projet*, language creating a Muslim-specific prohibition was inserted while permitting compensation to have effect among non-Muslims even when the compensation would otherwise violate religious law. This again demonstrates the impact of shaykh al-Islam Mahammad Bayram and the Tunisian 'ulama on the Tunisian code's final language (language replicated in Morocco)—and the contribution of other Tunisian jurists and religious scholars to the Santillana Codes.

Otherwise, each code permits that compensation may take place between debts that have different causes or are of different portions.[176] When the two debts are not of the same sum, compensation is carried out up to a maximum of the lesser debt.[177] Consistent with civil law doctrine, the Santillana Codes provide that compensation takes place between debts of same kind and quality.[178] The two debts must be liquidated and presently due, but it is not necessary that they be payable at the same place.[179]

CONFUSION

The final device for the extinguishing of an obligation is that of confusion. Planiol defines the civil law concept of confusion as the union of the two

Table 5.4   Codal Comparison: Compensation

Language in the Avant-Projet	Language Adopted
Article 416	Article 369
La compensation s'opère par la volonté des parties out par l'office du juge, lorsque les parties sont réciproquement et personnellement créancières et débitrices l'une de l'autre.	La compensation s'opère, lorsque les parties sont réciproquement et personnellement créancières et débitrices l'une de l'autre. Elle n'a pas lieu entre musulmans dans le cas où elle constituerait une violation de la loi religieuse.

qualities of creditor and debtor in the same person (*"la reunion sur la même tête des deux qualités de créancier et de débiteur"*) and notes that this concept most frequently finds application by the effect of a succession in which a creditor inherits a debt.[180] Under the Santillana Codes, when the qualities of creditor and debtor of an obligation are together in the same person, there is a confusion of rights which eliminates the relationship between creditor and debtor.[181] Consistent with civil law doctrine, each code provides that confusion may be total or partial, depending on whether it occurs for the entire obligation or only a portion.[182] When the cause that produces confusion disappears, the credit right is revived along with its accessories, for all persons, and confusion is deemed to have never occurred.[183] The Santillana Codes' articles on confusion are scant, but generally maintain the civil law concept without modification.

CONCLUSION

The analysis of the way the Santillana Codes address the law of obligations in general highlights Santillana's eclecticism as well as his innovativeness. Santillana's eclecticism is shown by the wide array of sources that were used as resources to develop the law of obligations in Tunisia. These include not only the French, Italian, and German civil codes, but also Islamic legal influences. In the way in which Santillana chose to make fraud by a third-party actionable, one sees the influence of Islamic law creating protections for citizens that were greater than what civil law provided during that era—and adopting a legal rule that, in the context of civil law, was years ahead of its time. Santillana also innovated by giving life to the ideas of civil law jurists of his era. This includes the way in which Santillana was among the first to include "error of law" in a modern code as well as his novel inclusion of the notion of "excusability" as it relates to error. A review of the law of obligations in the Santillana Codes also reveals numerous examples of the pluralistic approach in which religious prohibitions of the majority Muslim population are permitted to have effect within a unitary legal framework. The framework that emerged from this mixture of diverse sources is one that was cosmopolitan, durable, and worthy of emulation.

NOTES

1. A.M. DEMANTE, PROGRAMME DU COURS DE DROIT CIVIL FRANCAIS 246 (1833).
2. *Id.* at 248.
3. SAUL LITVINOFF, LOUISIANA CIVIL LAW TREATISE, THE LAW OF OBLIGATIONS, §1.6, at 10, 12 (2001).
4. J. LIEBESNY, THE LAW OF THE NEAR & MIDDLE EAST 210 (1975).
5. *Id.* at 211.
6. *See* FAOUZI BELKNANI, *Code des Obligations et des Contrats et la Codification*, in LIVRE DU CENTENAIRE DU CODE DES OBLIGATIONS ET DES CONTRATS 1906–2006 21 (2006).
7. Tunisian Code of Obligations and Contracts, Art. 1; Moroccan Code of Obligations and Contracts, Art. 1.; Mauritanian Code of Obligations and Contracts, Art. 22 This article is almost identical in substance to Article 1757 of the Louisiana Civil Code, which states, "Obligations arise from contracts and other declarations of will. They also arise directly from the law, regardless of a declaration of will, in instances such as wrongful acts, the management of the affairs of another, unjust enrichment and other acts or facts." Louisiana Civil Code, Art. 1757.
8. *Id.*
9. Tunisian Code of Obligations and Contracts, Art. 2; Moroccan Code of Obligations and Contracts, Art. 2; Mauritanian Code of Obligations and Contracts, Art. 23.
10. *See* Demante, *supra* note 1, at 252 ("Ces conditions sont au nombre de quatre: le consentement, la capacité, l'objet et la cause.").
11. MAJALLAH EL-AHKAM-I-ADLIYA (THE MEJELLE), TRANSLATED IN THE MEJELLE: AN ENGLISH TRANSLATION OF MAJALLAH EL-AHKAM-I-ADLIYA AND A COMPLETE CODE OF ISLAMIC CIVIL LAW (C.R. Tyser et al. trans. 2001), Art. 957 ("Infants, madmen and people of unsound mind [Ma'tuh] are of themselves prohibited from dealing with their property"), and Art. 966 ("When an infant has not understanding for business [Art. 943] even if his guardian give him permission, his verbal dispositions of property are fundamentally invalid.").
12. Mejelle, Art. 197 ("The existence of the thing sold is necessary") and Art. 199 ("It is necessary that the thing sold should be [permitted by law].").
13. Mejelle, Art. 211.
14. Tunisian Code of Obligations and Contracts, Art. 3; Moroccan Code of Obligations and Contracts, Art. 3; Mauritanian Code of Obligations and Contracts, Art. 24.
15. Tunisian Code of Obligations and Contracts, Art. 4.
16. *See* ABDUR RAHIM, THE PRINCIPLES OF MUHAMMADAN JURISPRUDENCE ACCORDING TO THE HANAFI, MALIKI, SHAFII AND HANBALI SCHOOLS 249. ("Since the application of the Muhammadan system is based on Islam a non-Moslim's legal capacity is regarded as defective[.]".) *See also* GHOLAMALI HADDAD ADEL ET AL., LAW: SELECTED ENTRIES FROM ENCYCLOPAEDIA OF THE WORLD OF ISLAM 128 (2013).

17. Tunisian Code of Obligations and Contracts, Art. 3; Moroccan Code of Obligations and Contracts, Art. 3; Mauritanian Code of Obligations and Contracts, Art. 24.

18. *See* M.D. SANTILLANA, AVANT-PROJET DU CODE CIVIL ET COMMERCIAL TUNISIEN 1–2 (1899) [hereinafter AVANT-PROJET].

19. *Id.* at 1.

20. *Id.* at 2.

21. The degree to which unilateral declarations are considered sources of obligations varies among modern civil codes. *See, e.g.*, Pablo Lerner, *Promises of Rewards in a Comparative Perspective*, 10 ANNU. SURVEY INT'L. COMPARATIVE L. 53, 57 (2004). ("If Puffendorf definitively installed the pactum as the central idea, it was Domat who simplified the problem by putting forth the agreement as the only expression of the autonomy of will. His ideas were adopted by the French legislator, and so the French code does not recognize the unilateral will as a source of obligation.")

22. PLANIOL, TRAITÉ ÉLÉMENTAIRE DE DROIT CIVIL 273 (9th ed., 1923).

23. Linvinoff, *supra* note 3, at 13–14.

24. DR. MARJAN MUHAMMAD, HAKIMAH YAAKOB & SHABANA HASAN, THE BINDINGNESS AND ENFORCEABILITY OF A UNILATERAL PROMISE (Wa'd): ANALYSIS FROM ISLAMIC LAW AND LEGAL PERSPECTIVE, 6 (2011).

25. *Id.,* at 12.

26. *Id.,* at 7.

27. *Id.,* at 8.

28. *Id.*

29. Tunisian Code of Obligations and Contracts, Art. 18.

30. *Id.,* Art. 19.

31. *Id.*

32. Moroccan Code of Obligations and Contracts, Arts. 14–15.

33. Mauritanian Code of Obligations and Contracts, Arts. 35–36.

34. Lerner, *supra* note 21, at 63.

35. Tunisian Code of Obligations and Contracts, Art. 20; Moroccan Code of Obligations and Contracts, Art. 16; Mauritanian Code of Obligations and Contracts, Art. 37.

36. *Id.*

37. Tunisian Code of Obligations and Contracts, Art. 21; Moroccan Code of Obligations and Contracts, Art. 17; Mauritanian Code of Obligations and Contracts, Art. 38.

38. *Id.*

39. *Id.*

40. *Id.*

41. *See* Bürgerliches Gesetzbuch (BGB), Art. 659(2): "If the act has been undertaken simultaneously by more than one person, then each is entitled to an equal portion of the reward. Where the reward cannot be shared due to its quality, or if, according to the terms of the promise of a reward, only one person is to be given the reward, then the matter is decided by drawing lots.". *See also* AVANT-PROJET, *supra* note 18, at 19.

42. *See* Muhammad, Yaakob & Hasan, *supra* note 24, at 8.

43. *See* Avant-Projet, *supra* note 18, at 11.

44. Planiol, *supra* note 22, at 333.

45. *See* Demante, *supra* note 1, at 246.

46. Planiol, *supra* note 22, at 333.

47. Tunisian Code of Obligations and Contracts, Art. 23.

48. *Id.*

49. Tunisian Code of Obligations and Contracts, Art. 24; Moroccan Code of Obligations and Contracts, Arts. 19–21; Mauritanian Code of Obligations and Contracts, Arts. 40–42.

50. *Id.*

51. Tunisian Code of Obligations and Contracts, Art. 25; Moroccan Code of Obligations and Contracts, Arts. 19–21; Mauritanian Code of Obligations and Contracts, Arts. 40–42.

52. *See* Avant-Projet, *supra* note 18, at 19.

53. Planiol, *supra* note 22, at 165.

54. *See* Saul Litvinoff, *Vices of Consent, Error, Fraud, Duress, and an Epilogue on Lesion*, 50 LA. L. REV. 1, 6 (1989).

55. Ronald J. Scalise, Jr., *Rethinking the Doctrine of Nullity*, 74 LA. L. REV. 663, 698 (2014).

56. *Id.*

57. Ignace Claeys, *Reliance as the Key for A Better Understanding of Mistake: A Belgian Law Perspective*, 12 IUS GENTIUM 1, 17 (2006).

58. David P. Doughty, *Error Revisited: The Louisiana Revision of Error as A Vice of Consent in Contracting*, 62 TUL. L. REV. 717, 718 (1988).

59. *See* ABDUR RAHIM, THE PRINCIPLES OF MUHAMMADAN JURISPRUDENCE ACCORDING TO THE HANAFI, MALIKI, SHAFII AND HANBALI SCHOOLS 237 (1911); *see also* Mejelle, Art. 20 and Art. 52.

60. *See* Rahim, *supra* note59, at 237; *see also* Mejelle, Art. 29 and Art. 32.

61. *See* Rahim, *supra* note 59, at 232–37; *see also* Mejelle, Art. 52.

62. *See* Avant-Projet, *supra* note 19, at 21.

63. Tunisian Code of Obligations and Contracts, Art. 43; Moroccan Code of Obligations and Contracts, Art. 39; Mauritanian Code of Obligations and Contracts, Art. 59.

64. *See* Litvinoff, *supra* note 54, at 11.

65. See Doughty, *supra* note 58.

66. Helen Scott, *The Requirement of Excusable Mistake in the Context of the Condictio Indebiti: Scottish and South African Law Compared*, 124 SOUTH AFR. L.J. 827, 828 (2007).

67. *See* Litvinoff, note 54, at 22.

68. *See* Planiol, *supra* note 22, at 104.

69. Louisiana Civil Code of 1870, Art. 1820.

70. *Codice Civile*, Art. 1109.

71. GABRIEL DE LABROUE DE VAREILLES-SOMMIERES, ETUDE SUR L'ERREUR EN DROIT ROMAIN ET EN DROIT FRANCAIS 14 (1871). ("On devine dès à présent que l'erreur de droit, par des raisons d'ordre social, et aussi parce qu'elle est moins excusable, portant sur une objet public et facile à connaître, a été moins souvent prise en considération par le législateur et produit moins d'effets que l'erreur de fait.")

72. Tunisian Code of Obligations and Contracts, Art. 44; Moroccan Code of Obligations and Contracts, Art. 40; Mauritanian Code of Obligations and Contracts, Art. 60.

73. Corry Monlague Stadden, *Error of Law*, 2 COLUMBIA L. REV. 476 (1907).

74. *See* Vareilles-Sommieres, *supra* note 71, at 129.

75. *See* Avant-Projet, *supra* note 18, at Art. 50.

76. *Id.*

77. *See* Litvinoff, *supra* note 54, at 36 ("Since finding that an error, according to the particular circumstances of a case, should be given invalidating force is the sovereign prerogative of the trier of fact, and because in the process of arriving at such finding it is inevitable to delve into the subjectivity of the party alleging error, courts will refuse rescission unless they can conclude that the error, besides meeting the requirements already discussed, is also excusable, that is, that the party in error did not fail to take elementary precautions that would have avoided his failing into error, such as making certain that he was reasonably informed."); *see also,* French Civil Code, Art. 1132. ("Art. 1132.-L'erreur de droit ou de fait, à moins qu'elle ne soit inexcusable, est une cause de nullité du contrat lorsqu'elle porte sur les qualités essentielles de la prestation due ou sur celles du cocontractant.")

78. Julie Klein, *Observations et Propositions de Modifications*, LA SEMAINE JURIDIQUE, EDITION GENERALE, Supp. N. 21 (Mai 25, 2015), at 16.; *See* French Civil Code (2016), Arts. 132 and 1139.

79. Tunisian Code of Obligations and Contracts, Art. 45; Moroccan Code of Obligations and Contracts, Art. 41; Mauritanian Code of Obligations and Contracts, Art. 61.

80. Tunisian Code of Obligations and Contracts, Art. 46.

81. *See* Litvinoff, *supra* note 3, at 16–21; *see also* French Civil Code, Art. 1134.

82. Tunisian Code of Obligations and Contracts, Art. 44 and 45; Moroccan Code of Obligations and Contracts, Art. 40.

83. Tunisian Code of Obligations and Contracts, Art. 47; Moroccan Code of Obligations and Contracts, Art. 43.

84. Mauritanian Code of Obligations and Contracts, Art. 63.

85. *See* Litvinoff, *supra* note 54, at 81.

86. *See* Louisiana Civil Code, Art. 1959, comment (b) (noting that "'duress' is a word of art or technical word in the English language which expresses exactly what is meant by 'violence or threats'").

87. *See* Litvinoff, *supra* note 3, at 9.

88. *See* Litvinoff, *supra* note 54, at 82.

89. La. Civ. Code art. 1959.

90. *See* Litvinoff, *supra* note 54, at 82:Fear of a person in the ascending line, that is, a party's apprehension of incurring the displeasure of such a person if the party fails to make a certain contract—like its counterpart, that is, the willingness to please such a person by making a certain contract—is not operative as duress sufficient to invalidate a party's consent. That kind of fear is called reverential in order to allude to the feelings of respect, or perhaps intimidation, that may warrantedly inspire it. Such fear does not constitute duress by itself since any intimidation a child may feel out of love and

respect for his father, mother, or grandparent is certainly not unlawful, which clearly indicates the absence of a relevant feature of effective duress. That is so whether a party attempts to avail himself of that kind of fear to seek annulment of a contract made with a person other than the feared one, in which case the alleged duress would be one exerted by a third person, or whether a party invokes that fear to seek the nullity of a contract made with the same person that intimidated him through reverential fear.

91. *See* MAJID KHADDURI & HERBERT J. LIEBESNY, ORIGIN AND DEVELOPMENT OF ISLAMIC LAW 193 (1955).

92. *Id.*

93. *Id.*

94. Tunisian Code of Obligations and Contracts, Art. 50; Moroccan Code of Obligations and Contracts, Art. 46; Mauritanian Code of Obligations and Contracts, Art. 66.

95. Tunisian Code of Obligations and Contracts, Art. 51; Moroccan Code of Obligations and Contracts, Art. 47; Mauritanian Code of Obligations and Contracts, Art. 67.

96. Tunisian Code of Obligations and Contracts, Art. 52; Moroccan Code of Obligations and Contracts, Art. 48; Mauritanian Code of Obligations and Contracts, Art. 68.

97. Tunisian Code of Obligations and Contracts, Art. 53; Moroccan Code of Obligations and Contracts, Art. 49; Mauritanian Code of Obligations and Contracts, Art. 69.

98. Tunisian Code of Obligations and Contracts, Art. 54; Moroccan Code of Obligations and Contracts, Art. 50; Mauritanian Code of Obligations and Contracts, Art. 70.

99. Tunisian Code of Obligations and Contracts, Art. 55; Moroccan Code of Obligations and Contracts, Art. 51; Mauritanian Code of Obligations and Contracts, Art. 71.

100. *See* Avant-Projet, *supra* note 19, at 28.

101. Tunisian Code of Obligations and Contracts, Art. 55; Moroccan Code of Obligations and Contracts, Art. 51; Mauritanian Code of Obligations and Contracts, Art. 71.

102. RAJ BHALA, UNDERSTANDING ISLAMIC LAW 543–44 (2011).

103. *See* Litvinoff, *supra* note 54, at 50.

104. *Id.*

105. *Id.*

106. Khadduri & Liebesny, *supra* note 91, at 193.

107. *Id.*

108. *Id.*

109. *See* Mohamed Azam Mohamed Adil et al., *Tadlis in Islamic Transactions*, 9 MALAYSIAN ACC. REV. 2, 43–55 (2010) ("Islamic law permits that fraud issuing from a third party may affect the consent of a party to a contract, so long as the third party is in connivance with the other contracting party.")

110. Tunisian Code of Obligations and Contracts, Art. 56; Moroccan Code of Obligations and Contracts, Art. 52; Mauritanian Code of Obligations and Contracts, Art. 72.

111. *Id.*

112. Tunisian Code of Obligations and Contracts, Art. 57; Moroccan Code of Obligations and Contracts, Art. 53; Mauritanian Code of Obligations and Contracts, Art. 73.

113. *See* Litvinoff, *supra* note 54, at 70.

114. *Id.*

115. M.L. Larombière, 1 *Théorie et pratique des obligations ou Commentaire des titres III et IV livre III du code civil, art. 1101 à 1386*, 42 (1862).

116. John Cartwright, Bénédicte Fauvarque-Cosson, Simon Whittaker, *The Law of Contract, The General Regime of Obligations, and Proof of Obligations, The new provisions of the Code civil created by Ordonnance n° 2016—131 of 10 February 2016*, http://www.textes.justice.gouv.fr/art_pix/THE-LAW-OF-CONTRACT-2-5-16.pdf, providing the following English translation of the new French Article 1138:Art. 1138.—Fraud is equally established where it originates from the other party's representative, a person who manages his affairs, his employee11 or one standing surety for him.It is also established where it originates from a third party in collusion.Note, however, that the Louisiana Civil Code has long recognized that "fraud committed by a third person vitiates the consent of a contracting party if the other party knew or should have known of the fraud." *See* Litvinoff, *supra* note 55, at 72.

117. Khaled Benjelayel, *Islamic Contract Law* (Mar. 10, 2012), https://ssrn.com/abstract=2019550 or http://dx.doi.org/10.2139/ssrn.2019550

118. Planiol, *supra* note 22, at 165.

119. *Id.* at 529.

120. French Code Civil 1804, art. 1674.

121. *See* Litvinoff, *supra* note 54, at 111.

122. Alan Watson, Roman Law & Comparative Law 201 (1991).

123. Tunisian Code of Obligations and Contracts, Art. 61; Moroccan Code of Obligations and Contracts, Art. 56; Mauritanian Code of Obligations and Contracts, Art. 76.

124. Tunisian Code of Obligations and Contracts, Art. 60; Moroccan Code of Obligations and Contracts, Art. 55; Mauritanian Code of Obligations and Contracts, Art. 75.

125. Tunisian Code of Obligations and Contracts, Art. 61; Moroccan Code of Obligations and Contracts, Art. 56; Mauritanian Code of Obligations and Contracts, Art. 76.

126. 2 Gaston Griolet France et al., Nouveau Code Civil: Annoté Et Expliqué D'après La Jurisprudence Et La Doctrine 964 (1905); 2 M.M. Lahaye, Waldeck-Rousseau, Giraudias, De Morineau, Et Faye, Le Code Civil Annoté Des Lois Romaines, Des Lois, Décrets Ordonnances, Avis Du Conseil D'état, Des Circulaires Ministérielles Publiées Depuis Sa Promulgation Jusqu'à Nos Jours, Et Des Opinions Des Auteurs Qui Ont Ecrit Sur Le Code (1843). ("Il est évident que l'ivresse lorsqu'elle va jusqu'au point de faire perdre l'usage de la raison rend la personne qui est en cet état , pendant qu'il dure, incapable de contracter, puisqu'elle la rend incapable de consentement.")

127. *See* Pierre-Antoine Fene, Recueil Complet Des Travaux Préparatoires Du Code Civil 368 (1827).

128. Louisiana Civil Code (1870) Art. 1789.

129. Khadduri & Liebesny, *supra* note 91, at 198.

130. *See* IMRAN AHSAN KHAN NYAZEE, OUTLINES OF ISLAMIC JURISPRUDENCE 145–46 (1998).

131. *Id.*

132. *See* Liebesny, *supra* note 4, at 198.

133. Tunisian Code of Obligations and Contracts, Art. 58.

134. *Id.*, 59; Moroccan Code of Obligations and Contracts, Art. 54; Mauritanian Code of Obligations and Contracts, Art. 74.

135. See Litvinoff, *supra* note 54, at 2.

136. Tunisian Code of Obligations and Contracts, Art. 199; Moroccan Code of Obligations and Contracts, Art. 189; Mauritanian Code of Obligations and Contracts, Art. 206.

137. Tunisian Code of Obligations and Contracts, Art. 200; Moroccan Code of Obligations and Contracts, Art. 190; Mauritanian Code of Obligations and Contracts, Art. 207.

138. *Id.*

139. Tunisian Code of Obligations and Contracts, Art. 201.

140. Moroccan Code of Obligations and Contracts, Art. 191 (par. 2); Mauritanian Code of Obligations and Contracts, Art. 208 (par. 2).

141. *See* MICHAEL E. BONINE, WAQF AND ITS INFLUENCE ON THE BUILT ENVIRONMENT IN THE MEDINA, IN URBAN SPACE IN THE MIDDLE AGES AND THE EARLY MODERN AGE 618 (Albrecht Classen ed., 2009).

142. Loi n° 2005—87 du 15 août 2005, portant approbation de la réorganisation de certaines dispositions du "code des obligations et des contrats tunisien."

143. *See* RAJA SAKRANI, AU CROISEMENT DES CULTURES DE DROIT OCCIDENTALE ET MUSULMANE: LE PLURALISME JURIDIQUE DANS LE CODE TUNISIEN DES OBLIGATIONS ET DES CONTRATS 237 (2009). ALEXANDER MEYRICK BROADLEY, HOW WE DEFENDED ARÁBI AND HIS FRIENDS: A STORY OF EGYPT AND THE EGYPTIANS 77 (1884).

144. Tunisian Code of Obligations and Contracts, Art. 210; Moroccan Code of Obligations and Contracts, Art. 200; Mauritanian Code of Obligations and Contracts, Art. 217.

145. *Id.*

146. Mauritanian Code of Obligations and Contracts, Art. 217.

147. *Id.*

148. *Id.*

149. *See* Avant-Projet, *supra* note 19, at 108.

150. *See* Rahim, *supra* note 59, at 294–95.

151. *Id.* at 294:The Hanafi doctors have interpreted the tradition to mean that whenever an article belonging to the description of similar of capacity or of weight is sold or exchanged for an article of the same species, neither party is allowed to receive anything in excess of the quantity sold by himself, in other words, absolute equality in quantity is insisted upon. The Shafi'is hold that the law of riba only applies to articles of food and such things as constitute price, namely gold and silver.

152. Yasin Dutton, *The Origins of Islamic Law: The Qur'an, The Muwatta, and Madinan 'Amal* 149 (2002):Ribā, like zakat, was another situation where the general

judgment in the Qur'an as clear but the precise details problematic. The main prohibition against ribā comes in Q 2: 278—9 where we read that those who practice ribā
should be aware that they have engaged in "a war with Allah and His Messenger,"
from which the "ulamā" derived the judgement that those who engage in ribā and
refuse to repent are, if they have a power-base [are to be fought as rebels].

153. *See* Rahim, *supra* note 59, at 294.

154. Planiol, *supra* note 22, at 198.

155. *Id.* at 202.

156. Tunisian Code of Obligations and Contracts, Art. 350; Moroccan Code of
Obligations and Contracts, Art. 340; Mauritanian Code of Obligations and Contracts,
Art. 338.

157. *Id.*

158. Tunisian Code of Obligations and Contracts, Art. 355; Moroccan Code of
Obligations and Contracts, Art. 345; Mauritanian Code of Obligations and Contracts,
Art. 342.

159. *See, e.g.*, UN-Habitat, Islam, Land & Property Research Series, *Paper 6:
Islamic Inheritance Laws and Systems*, at 10 (2005). ("[A] Muslim's ability to
bequeath is restricted to only one-third of an individual's estate under certain rules
with the remaining two-thirds devolving according to the compulsory inheritance
rules.")

160. Mejelle, Art. 879.

161. *Id.*

162. Tunisian Code of Obligations and Contracts, Art. 356; Moroccan Code of
Obligations and Contracts, Art. 346; Mauritanian Code of Obligations and Contracts,
Art. 344.

163. Joseph Dainow, *The Early Sources of Forced Heirship: Its History in Texas
and Louisiana*, 4 LA. L. REV. 60 (1941). (Noting that in Louisiana "as in both French
and Spanish law, excessive dispositions are not null, but are reducible to the dispos-
able quantum.")

164. Planiol, *supra* note 22, at 178. ("*La novation est un procédé d'origine
romaine mais qui s'est bien transformé depuis l'antiquité.*")

165. Tunisian Code of Obligations and Contracts, Art. 357; Moroccan Code of
Obligations and Contracts, Art. 347; Mauritanian Code of Obligations and Contracts,
Art. 345.

166. Tunisian Code of Obligations and Contracts, Art. 358; Moroccan Code of
Obligations and Contracts, Art. 347; Mauritanian Code of Obligations and Contracts,
Art. 345.

167. Tunisian Code of Obligations and Contracts, Art. 359; Moroccan Code of
Obligations and Contracts, Art. 348; Mauritanian Code of Obligations and Contracts,
Art. 346.

168. Tunisian Code of Obligations and Contracts, Art. 361; Moroccan Code of
Obligations and Contracts, Art. 350; Mauritanian Code of Obligations and Contracts,
Art. 348.

169. *See, e.g.*, Louisiana Civil Code Art. 1881. ("Novation takes place when, by
agreement of the parties, a new performance is substituted for that previously owed,

or a new cause is substituted for that of the original obligation. If any substantial part of the original performance is still owed, there is no novation.")

170. Planiol, *supra* note 22, at 189; Louisiana Civil Code Art. 1893.

171. *See* Litvinoff, *supra* note 54, at section 19.2.

172. *Id.*

173. Tunisian Code of Obligations and Contracts, Art. 369; Moroccan Code of Obligations and Contracts, Art. 357.

174. Mauritanian Code of Obligations and Contracts, Art. 355.

175. *See* Avant-Project, *supra* note 19, at 175.

176. Tunisian Code of Obligations and Contracts, Art. 377; Moroccan Code of Obligations and Contracts, Art. 364; Mauritanian Code of Obligations and Contracts, Art. 362.

177. *Id.*

178. Tunisian Code of Obligations and Contracts, Art. 373; Moroccan Code of Obligations and Contracts, Art. 361; Mauritanian Code of Obligations and Contracts, Art. 362.

179. Tunisian Code of Obligations and Contracts, Art. 374; Moroccan Code of Obligations and Contracts, Art. 362; Mauritanian Code of Obligations and Contracts, Art. 360.

180. Planiol, *supra* note 22, at 197.

181. Tunisian Code of Obligations and Contracts, Art. 382; Moroccan Code of Obligations and Contracts, Art. 369; Mauritanian Code of Obligations and Contracts, Art. 367.

182. *Id.*

183. Tunisian Code of Obligations and Contracts, Art. 383; Moroccan Code of Obligations and Contracts, Art. 370; Mauritanian Code of Obligations and Contracts, Art. 368.

Chapter 6

Sale and Other Nominate Contracts

A review of the provisions relating to the contract of sale in the Santillana Codes reveals an interesting blending of continental civil law with Islamic legal precepts, both by incorporating requirements that adhere to the Islamic law of sales and, as seen previously, by creating strategic exceptions for those places where Islamic law and continental civil law diverge. In the *Avant-Projet*, Santillana cites numerous civil law sources for the Tunisian articles on sale, including the French, Swiss, and German civil codes.[1] He also cites numerous civil law sources, such as the Mejelle, *Radd al-Muhtar*, and the work of Hamaoui and Ibn Nadjim.[2] One, therefore, again sees the complex mixture of legal traditions that coalesced to create the Santillana Codes.

In the continental civil law system, "a sale is a contract by which a person, who is called the vendor, obliges himself to transfer the ownership of a thing to another, whereas the other person, who is the buyer, obliges himself to pay the value of the thing in money."[3] The necessary elements of such a sale are the consent of the parties, a thing to be sold, and a price to be paid.[4] Modern civil codes around the globe maintain this basic concept of the contract of sale. For instance, under the Louisiana Civil Code, a "[s]ale is a contract whereby a person transfers ownership of a thing to another for a price in money. The thing, the price, and the consent of the parties are requirements for the perfection of a sale."[5]

As Santillana noted in the *Avant-Projet*, Islamic law has a somewhat similar paradigm for a contract of sale (bai').[6] Sale is an important concept in Islamic law as it "was the typical contract on which other contracts were patterned."[7] The Hanafite author Ibrahim al-Halabi defined sale as "the exchange of property against property."[8] This concept of a broader exchange is echoed by Santillana, who writes that "[t]he hanafites define a sale as 'the exchange of a thing having utility for a thing that is equally useful.'"[9] Santillana also notes that the concept of a sale (bai') can apply to a larger group of commutative contracts that includes the exchange of one thing of value for another.[10]

At the outset, the Santillana Codes obviously incorporate classical civil law concepts into their provisions on the contract of sale. The Santillana Codes uniformly define a sale as a contract by which one party transfers ownership of a thing or a right to another contracting party for a price which the latter obligates himself or herself to pay.[11] This paradigm aligns more closely to the civil law idea of sale involving an obligation to "pay the value of the thing in money"[12] rather than something more akin to a contract of exchange (described below). Under each code, a contract of sale is perfected between the parties, as soon as there is consent of the contracting parties (one to sell and the other to buy) and the parties agree on the thing, the price, and the other terms of the contract.[13]

A DETERMINED PRICE

Continental civil law has long permitted the price in a contract of sale to be determined by outside experts or arbiters,[14] and modern civil codes based on the French model have permitted even more laxity with regard to prices set by third parties and even courts.[15] Islamic law, in contrast, has more adamantly required that the price be determined at the time of the formation of the contract.[16] This is due to the prohibition on gharar (the sale of "items whose existence or characteristics is not certain, the risky nature of which makes the transaction akin to gambling").[17] Commentators note that a sale in which the price is deferred is an example of gharar.[18]

A review of the provisions in each Santillana code finds the requirement that the selling price in a contract of sale must be determined—though with differing degrees of laxity. The Tunisian and Moroccan codes, for instance, disallow determination of the selling price by reference to a third party or the price paid by a third party, unless the price is known to the contracting parties.[19] For those codes, the contract may, however, refer to the fixed market price, or a determined rate, or the average of the market prices, when it comes to goods which do not have a variable price.[20] For the Tunisian and Moroccan codes, when the price is variable, contracting parties are presumed to be referring to the average market price.[21]

The Mauritanian code contains a similar regime and states that a sale cannot refer the determination of the selling price to a third party or the price paid by a third party, unless it is to a fixed market price, or a determined rate—and then only when it comes to goods whose price does not undergo change.[22] "When this price is variable, contracting parties are required to specify the sale price."[23]

These requirements are consonant with classical continental civil law insofar as the price must be fixed, but seem to gravitate more toward Islamic law in the rigidity of this requirement—even more so in the case of the Mauritanian code. The Tunisian and Moroccan codes, by expressly disallowing the selling price to be determined by third persons, align more consistently with Islamic law than continental civil law, but still permit a degree of flexibility by permitting a degree of ambiguity regarding the price in the contract, but resolving said ambiguity by stating that the contracting parties are presumed to be referring to the average market price.[24] The Mauritanian code, in another example of its more pronounced inclination toward Islamic law, requires the contracting parties to specify the sale price.[25]

Relatedly, Islamic law's influence on the Tunisian becomes even more pronounced in their articles which hold that a sale is considered null if it is for things that, by nature or circumstances, are unlikely to be delivered to the purchaser; for example: the fish in the water, the bird in the air, the escaped animal.[26] This prohibition also relates directly to the prohibition on gharar sales. Commentators have noted that Islamic law, to varying degrees, has disallowed the sale of fish in the water and escaped things.[27] "Other hadiths, still of contemporary relevance, forbid the sale of a bird in the air, a fish in the water, an escaped animal or slave, or anything else that the vendor might be unable to deliver owing to lack of possession."[28] Neither the Moroccan code nor the Mauritanian code, however, contains such a provision.

NULLITIES OF SALES CONTRA BONOS MORES

Civil law systems have developed doctrines to nullify contracts and obligations that are considered against public order or contra bonos mores.[29] For instance, Article 6 of the French Code Civil states that: "One may not derogate by private agreements from laws which involve public policy and morality." Looking to civil codes more broadly, commentators note that "[t]he reference to both *ordre public* and *contra bonos mores* is ubiquitous in the civil codes and allows for an interesting discussion as to the meaning of public policy under our law, especially as a limitation on party autonomy."[30]

The Santillana Codes adopt a more religious formulation of this requirement. Under each Santillana Code, any contract of sale is considered null if it is between Muslims and for things declared unclean by religious law (for the Tunisian and Moroccan codes "*la loi religieuse*" and for the Mauritanian code "*le charia sauf*") except the objects which "religious law" has authorized for trade, such as animal fertilizer for agricultural purposes.[31] This provision, notably, was present in the proposed article in the *Avant-Projet*[32]—an inclusion which highlights the fact that Santillana was comfortable with the concept of a rule of religious individuation operating within the framework of a civil code. Thus, the Santillana Codes, to differing extents, expressly prohibit contracts that would violate the precepts of Islamic law.

SALE AND THE ACQUISITION OF OWNERSHIP

Continental civil law generally does not require delivery of the thing in order for ownership to transfer to the buyer in a contract of sale,[33] though there is a lack of uniformity with regard to this rule in civil law systems. Under Roman law, while the risk of damage or destruction passed to the buyer at the moment of agreement, ownership passed to the buyer only with physical delivery of the thing.[34] Today, the French and German civil codes diverge on this point. The French *Code Civil* "changed the Roman rule and provided that both ownership and risk get transferred to the buyer at the moment of agreement."[35] Likewise, in Louisiana, the general rule is that "the contract of sale effects an immediate transfer of ownership and risk even if no delivery has been made."[36] German law, in contrast, still requires delivery of the thing before ownership of movable property can be transferred.[37]

Islamic law has generally maintained that ownership transfers with conclusion of the contract of sale and not with delivery.[38] Thus, "[i]f a specific good has not yet been delivered to the buyer, the seller, holding the buyer's property, is obligated to deliver it."[39] As such rules are reflected in the Mejelle, Islamic law is more limiting with regard to what one may do before delivery of the thing. The Mejelle permits a seller to "dispose of the price of a thing sold before he has received it,"[40] and, in the case of immovable property, "the purchaser can sell to another, before delivery, the property sold."[41] Movable property, however, cannot generally be sold to another before delivery.[42] The Mejelle, likewise, gives special significance to delivery in sales involving things sold in quantities that are weighed and do not suffer damage by division (such as corn) in that such a sale becomes final when there is delivery and the amount delivered is correct.[43] Otherwise, the buyer is given a right of option and may annul the sale or purchase for the lesser amount.[44] Under the Mejelle's provisions, if there is excess in such a case, the surplus belongs to the seller.[45]

The Santillana Codes clearly adhere to the French model in this regard as a general matter. Under each of the Santillana Codes, the buyer acquires full ownership of the thing sold, as soon as the contract is perfected by the consent of the parties.[46] As soon as the contract of sale is perfected, the buyer may dispose of the thing sold, even before delivery.[47] Likewise, the seller may assign his or her right to payment, even before the delivery of the thing, unless there is a contrary agreement by the parties.[48]

The Santillana Codes, however, do have exceptions with regard to certain matters expressly regulated by Islamic law. Notably, the Tunisian and Moroccan codes provide that these latter provisions relating to transfer of ownership prior to delivery are inapplicable with regard to the sale of foodstuffs among Muslims[49] and the Mauritanian code, consistent with its more exclusive approach, provides that these latter provisions relating to transfer of ownership prior to delivery are inapplicable with regard to the sale of foodstuffs generally.[50] This exception addresses Islamic legal precept which dictates that "a purchaser of foodstuffs could not re-sell before he had taken physical delivery of them,"[51] a prohibition derived from a sunna which directs Muslims to "[sell] gold for gold and silver for silver, wheat for wheat, barley for barley, dates for dates and salt for salt of the same kind for the same kind and the same quantity for the same quantity, from hand to hand and if they differ from each other in quantity sell them as you like but from hand to hand."[52] Islamic law has, therefore, generally held that when these six specified commodities are involved (gold, silver, wheat, barley, dates, and salt) the law required "equality of offerings and immediate delivery."[53] Divergences of opinion among the schools of jurisprudence caused differing interpretations of this rule. Shafi'i and Hanbali laws applied these requirements to all foodstuffs while Maliki law generally required that this apply only to foodstuffs that can be stored or preserved.[54] Similarly, as noted above, the Mejelle—a compilation of Hanafite rules—required that quantities that are weighed and do not suffer damage by division (such as corn) in that such a sale becomes final when there is delivery and the amount delivered is correct.[55]

Accordingly, with regard to the issue of whether delivery of the thing is necessary in order for ownership to transfer to the buyer in a contract of sale, the Santillana Codes adhere to the French model and state that the buyer acquires full ownership of the thing sold, as soon as the contract is perfected by the consent of the parties.[56] Even so, the codes also include special, specific variances to accommodate religious prohibitions that exist for Muslim citizens. In the Tunisian and Moroccan codes, the variances take the form of individuation of the rule for different religious groups, while in Mauritania that variance takes the form of a general prohibition.

SALE OF A THING BY AN ILL PERSON

Another area of the Santillana Codes that demonstrate their incorporation of Islamic law is the set of rules governing the sale of a thing by an ill person on his or her deathbed.[57] According to that article—which is contained in each code—the sale by an ill person on his or her deathbed ("during his last illness,") where it is made to one of his heirs with the intention to favor that heir (for example, the thing is sold at a price much lower than the real value of the thing) is governed by other provisions of each respective code,[58] all of which, in turn, state that a remission of debt made by an ill person on his or her deathbed to one of his heirs is valid only if the other heirs ratify the act.[59]

In contrast, the sale by an ill person to a non-heir is governed by the provisions of the codes[60] which states that a remission of debt granted by an ill person to a third party is valid up to a maximum of one-third of what remains in the estate after the payment of debts and funeral expenses.[61] Accordingly, such a sale could be limited depending on what debts and expenses remain after the death of the seller. Belknani notes that such a sale would be considered *mawquf* under Islamic law,[62] and a review of Islamic jurisprudence finds this provision of the Santillana Codes to be derived from the Mejelle:

> If a sick person sells something to one of his heirs while he is in his death sickness, it is dependent on the permission of the other heirs, if, after the death of the sick person, they give permission, it takes effect, if they do not give permission, it does not take effect.[63]

Similarly, the Mejelle provides that if a sick person while in his death sickness sells something, for a price less than the value of the thing and a third of his property "is not sufficient to provide for the benefit, the purchaser is compelled to make good the reduction in the price, and if he [does not] make [the reduction], the heirs can annul the sale."[64]

SALE OF THING BELONGING TO ANOTHER

Another area where Islamic influence is clear in the Santillana Codes relates to the sale of a thing belonging to another.[65] According to this article—which repeats itself in each code—the sale of a thing belonging to another is valid: (1) if the true owner of the thing ratifies the sale; or (2) if the seller then acquires ownership of the thing. Where the true owner refuses to ratify the sale, the purchaser may ask for dissolution of the sale. The seller is liable for damages when the purchaser was unaware at the time of the sale that the thing belonged to another. The nullification of the contract, however, can never be opposed by the seller due to the fact that the thing belonged to another.[66] This rule is a departure from continental civil law, which generally maintains that "[t]he sale of a thing belonging to another does not convey ownership."[67] It instead reflects Islamic law—particularly Maliki jurisprudence—which provides avenues for validating the sale of a thing belonging to another. According to Maliki jurisprudence, paying the value of the usurped object permitted the usurper to acquire ownership of the object retroactively from the date of usurpation.[68] If a usurper sold the thing to a third person, the owner could choose to demand its return or could affirm the sale. If the owner chose the latter course of action, the owner could demand that the usurper/seller pay the price of the thing sold.[69]

EXCHANGE

Civil law jurist A.M. Demante, writing in the nineteenth century, noted that the contract of exchange is more ancient than the contact of sale.[70] In that regard, continental civil law has generally regarded the contract of exchange as a distinct nominate contract—a synallagmatic contract in which the parties to the contract agree to exchange anything except money.[71]

> Exchange is a contract whereby each party transfers to the other the ownership of a thing other than money.
>
> Ownership of the things exchanged is transferred between the parties as soon as there is agreement on the things, even though none of the things has been delivered.
>
> If it is the intent of the parties that the transfer of ownership will not take place until a later time, then the contract is a contract to exchange.[72]

In such contracts, each of the parties is individually considered both as vendor and vendee, but the parties create only a single contract rather than two separate contracts.[73]

Islamic law, on the other hand, obviously permits such transactions but envisions a sale (bai') in a sufficiently broad sense to subsume both exchanges of things for currency and for other things.[74] On that score, the Mejelle defined a sale as an exchange of property for property and, among its subdivisions of the concept of sale, expressly envisions a "sale by barter."[75] ("Sale by barter consists of exchanging one specific object for some other specific object, that is to say, of exchanging property for property other than money.")[76] Thus, while continental civil law recognizes the contract of exchange, so does Islamic law—only in a different way.

The Santillana Codes incorporate the concept of this contract in a way that permits it to comport with both legal traditions. In the *Avant-Projet*, Santillana cites to the French code, the Italian code, as well as several Islamic sources as inspiration of the articles he fashioned for the Tunisian code.[77] This includes the Mejelle, the work of the jurist Ibn Salmoun and his articulation of the Malikite formula for a contract of exchange; and the work of Ibn Acem.[78] Drawing from those sources, each code states that a contract of exchange is a contract by which each party gives to another, as property, a movable or immovable thing, or an intangible right, against another thing or right of a similar or of a different nature.[79] This comports with modern civil codes which retain this nominate contract and tend to define it as "a contract whereby each party transfers to the other the ownership of a thing other than money."[80]

Consistent with classical civil law, the Santillana Codes hold that a contract of exchange is perfected by the consent of the parties.[81] When, however, the contract of exchange regards buildings or other objects susceptible to mortgage, the provisions of each code dealing with immovable property are applicable[82] (namely the contract must be made in writing with a date that is certain and will have no effect vis-à-vis third parties unless it is appropriately registered).[83]

For each code, when the exchanged objects are different of values, the parties are permitted to make up the difference through cash payments or other objects, at that time or as a future sale.[84] The Tunisian and Moroccan codes state that this provision has no effect between Muslims when the exchanged objects are commodities.[85] This language does not appear in the *Avant-Projet* and was adopted after the review by shaykh al-Islam Mahammad Bayram and the Tunisian 'ulama, demonstrating again the influence of the Tunisian 'ulama on the final text of the Santillana Codes.[86]

Interestingly, the Mauritanian code states that this provision has no effect if the practice constitutes riba.[87] This is an interesting legislative distinction among the Santillana Codes. While the language of the Mauritanian code obviously is focused on issues related to riba, the Tunisian code and its Moroccan successor (which contain an exception for Muslims rather than a general prohibition) appear to seek to instead accommodate the Islamic rules relating to the sale of commodities and future contracts, which maintain very specific requirements which are occasionally at variance with the continental civil law rules.[88] The Mauritanian legislators, therefore, adjusted the codal

Table 6.1   Codal Comparison: Exchange

Language in Avant-Projet	Language Adopted
Article 837	Article 720
Lorsque les objets échangés sont de valeurs différentes, il est permis aux parties de compenser la différence au moyen de soultes en numéraire ou en autres objets, au comptant ou à terme.	Lorsque les objets échangés sont de valeurs différentes, il est permis aux parties de composer la différence au moyen de soultes en numéraire ou en autres objets, au comptant ou à terme. Cette disposition n'a pas lieu entre musulmans, lorsque les objets de l'échange sont des denrées.

language to address a specific Islamic legal concern, though seemingly one distinct from that which inspired the original language of that provision.

DEPOSIT

The concept of a contract of deposit is derived from Roman law which recognized the contract of *depositum*, or "the gratuitous deposit of a movable."[89] In modern continental civil law, a contract of deposit is "a contract by which a person, the depositor, delivers a movable thing to another person, the depositary, for safekeeping under the obligation of returning it to the depositor upon demand."[90] Under this framework, "[t]he depositary may not use the thing deposited without the express or implied permission of the depositor,"[91] and must "return the precise thing that he received in deposit."[92] Under the civil law model, the depositary is liable for losses sustained as a result of the depositary's failure to exercise diligence and prudence.[93]

While Roman law considered *depositum* to be an essentially gratuitous relationship, French civil law and other civil law jurisdictions have applied the rules relating to a contract of deposit to both gratuitous and onerous contracts.[94] Such contracts are also permissible under Islamic law in the form of the contract of deposit (al-wadi'ah)—which is defined as a contract "to entrust or leave money or any other property in another person's custody to be returned whenever it is requested."[95] This legal regime bears a striking resemblance to its civil law analog and generally provides that "[i]t is impermissible for the keeper to make use of the property kept in his custody in any way except by explicit permission of the depositor."[96] Under the Islamic rules for al-wadi'ah, the keeper is not responsible for any damage to the property unless it is caused by the keeper's acts or negligence.[97] The Mejelle's provisions on this topic, for instance, provide that "if the contract for delivery [for safekeeping] has been made for payment to be made for the safe keeping, in case it is destroyed or wasted by a cause which it is possible to guard against, it becomes a cause of compensation."[98] When, however, the loss is not something that could be guarded against, then the general rule applies that "if it be destroyed or wasted without any [fault] of the person who accepts it and without any fault in the keeping of it, it does not become necessary to make compensation."[99]

In the *Avant-Projet*, Santillana cites to the French, German, Italian, and Swiss codes for his articles the contract of deposit. In addition, he cites numerous Islamic legal sources, principally the Mejelle, the work of Ibn Nadjim, Zarqani, and Ala' al-Din al-Haskafi's work entitled *al-Durr al Mukhtar*.[100] Drawing from those sources, all of the Santillana Codes maintain essentially the same provisions on the contract of deposit, defining it as a contract by which a person surrenders a movable to another person who undertakes to keep the deposited thing and return it in its individuality.[101] A person making or accepting a deposit must have the capacity to form obligations.[102] If, however, a person able to bind himself accepts a deposit made by an incapable person, that person is bound by all obligations arising from the deposit.[103]

For both the Tunisian and Moroccan codes, a contract of deposit must be made in writing if it is of a value exceeding one thousand dinars. This rule does not, however, apply to a necessary deposit which is defined as one that was forced by a fortuitous event or force majeure event, such as a fire, a shipwreck, or another event, the proof of which may be made by any means, regardless of the value of the object of the deposit.[104] No such rule exists in the Mauritanian code, which eschews a writing requirement in this instance.

Under each of the Santillana Codes, the depositary is answerable for any foreseeable loss or damage to the thing when he or she receives a salary for the custody of the deposit; and/or when he or she receives deposits as a result of his or her status or according to his or her functions.[105] The depositary is not answerable for loss or damage caused by nature or problems with the thing deposited or by the negligence of the depositor; or in cases of force majeure or fortuitous events, so long as the depositary has not been already put in default for failure to return the thing deposited—or so long as the force majeure is not the depositary's fault or the fault of persons for which he is responsible.[106] Proof of force majeure or defect of the things is the depositary's burden, when the depositary receives a salary for the filing or when he received the thing by virtue of his status or pursuant to his functions.[107] Otherwise, the depositary shall ensure the custody of the deposit, with the same diligence that one would apply to things that belong to him.[108]

Likewise, under the Santillana Codes, any agreement is void in which the depositary would be held responsible for fortuitous events or force majeure. This is an absolute prohibition under the Mauritanian code.[109] The Tunisian and Moroccan codes provide an exception for those cases in which depositary receives a salary,[110] though that provision only applies between non-Muslims.[111] Otherwise stated, under the provisions of the Tunisian and Moroccan codes, only non-Muslims can have an agreement in which a paid depositary would be held responsible for fortuitous events or force majeure. Under the Mauritanian code, no one may have such an agreement. This rule, placing greater responsibility on the (non-Muslim) depositary who receives a salary, aligns with the provisions of early European civil codes, which provided that a depositary who had received payment and who lost a thing due to force majeure "must restore what he has received."[112] The Tunisian and Moroccan codes, thus, adhere to the civil law model but maintain the Islamic prohibition in matters between Muslims. For Muslims in each country, the rule is the Islamic model for al-wadi'ah, in which the keeper is not responsible for any damage to the property unless it is caused by the keeper's acts or negligence. For non-Muslims in Tunisia and Morocco, a more European rule will apply.

MANDATE

In continental civil law, "[a] mandate is a contract by which a person, the principal, confers authority on another person, the mandatary, to transact one or more affairs for the principal."[113] As with so many civil law concepts, the legal idea of a contract of mandate has its roots in Roman law (the contract of *mandatum*) and has been ramified in the legislation of civil law jurisdictions around the globe.

> In the older codes, as in Roman law, representation was possible within the framework of the contract of mandatum. This contract (and the modern contract of mandate), however, ostensibly granted (and grants) different, and usually more limited, powers to the mandatary than those conferred upon a general representative. Simply put, the mandatary was authorized to act only within the bounds of the authority actually granted him, and only in the name of his principal; acts taken outside the authority actually granted produced no enforceable obligation between the mandator and third parties. In the older codes, as in Roman law, representation was possible within the framework of the contract of mandatum. This contract (and the modern contract of mandate), however, ostensibly granted (and grants) different, and usually more limited, powers to the mandatary than those conferred upon a general representative. Simply put, the mandatary was authorized to act only within the bounds of the authority actually granted him, and only in the name of his principal; acts taken outside the authority actually granted produced no enforceable obligation between the mandator and third parties. Currently, all modern civil codes, with the exception of Quebec's, regulate the broad concept of representation, and treat mandate as a special contract.[114]

Islamic law also recognizes agency contracts (wakalah) which allow for full representation in most contractual arrangements.[115] As Santillana notes in his glossae in the *Avant-Projet*, "according to the Hanafites, the [contract of] mandate always implies *representation*."[116] Citing to the *Radd al-Muhtar*, Santillana also notes that Islamic law considers a mandate "the act of he who substitutes another person in his stead to accomplish an act which is determined and juridically licit."[117] Such contracts can be either gratuitous or onerous and is generally revocable at will by either party.[118] A review of the provisions of the Mejelle reveal similar provisions regarding vekalet—a contract in which a person appoints another to conduct affairs on his or her behalf.[119] Those provisions make clear that the excesses of the person so appointed (the vekyl) do not prejudice third parties but, instead, inure to the detriment of the vekyl.[120]

In the *Avant-Projet*, Santillana cites to fewer civil codes for the contract of mandate, indicating that his principal civil law inspiration for the articles is the Digest of Justinian and the European scholarly texts (such as Aubry and Rau).[121] Santillana also cites to numerous Islamic legal sources, principally the Mejelle, Sheik-el-Haskef's *Eddor el Mokhtar*, Ibn Nadjim, Hamoui, and the *Radd al-Muhtar*.[122] Drawing from those sources, all of the Santillana Codes maintain essentially the same provisions on the contract of mandate, bifurcating the concept of a mandate into two types: special and general.[123] A special mandate is one that is given for one or more specified endeavors, or which confers only specific powers.[124] It gives power to act in specified endeavors and matters necessarily attendant thereto, according to the nature of the matter.[125] A general mandate, in contrast, is one which gives the mandatary the power to manage all the interests of the principal without limit, or which confers broad powers without limit in a particular case.[126] It gives the power to do all that is in the interests of the principal, according to the nature of the case and the usage of trade, and especially to recover what is due, to pay debts, to carry out conservatory acts, to bring possessory actions, and even enter into obligations to the extent necessary to carry out the affairs for which the principal is responsible.[127]

Although this scheme largely parallels the civil law model, the rules governing treatment of revocation of a mandate provide yet another example of the integration of Islamic law into the Santillana Codes.[128] According to that article, the total or partial revocation of the mandate cannot have effect toward third parties of good faith who have contracted with the mandatary before the revocation, except for the principal's recourse against the mandatary.[129] This echoes the Mejelle's provisions stating that the excesses of the vekyl do not prejudice third parties but, instead, inure to the detriment of the vekyl.[130] When the law prescribes a determined form for the establishment of the mandate, the same form is required for revocation.[131]

AGRICULTURAL PARTNERSHIPS: MOUÇAKÂTE AND MOUGHÂRAÇA

In addition, the Tunisian code's inclusion of the Islamic concepts of mouçakâte and moughâraça are examples of how Islamic influences can sometimes become dominant traits within the codal text, especially in the code's treatment of agricultural contracts.[132] With regard to the first of these, the Tunisian civil code incorporates the device of a mouçakâte, defining it as a contract by which the owner of a crop which is ready for cultivation charges another person, referred to as a colon, to do the necessary work of picking or harvesting in exchange for a determined share of the harvest.[133] This sort of arrangement is derived from the Islamic legal arrangement with the same name, also transliterated as musaqah or musāqāt, which is generally defined as a type of contract in which "an owner of trees or crops entrusts his trees or crops to a person to look after and water them until they bear fruit or ripen [in exchange for] a specific portion of such fruit or crops."[134]

The Tunisian code also incorporates the device known as moughâraça, which it defines as a contract which forms an entity which has for its object the fruit trees or other crops with regard to which one of the parties, known as the colon, is responsible for their planting and care in exchange for an undivided share of the land and soil and the trees or crops.[135] This is obviously derived from the Islamic property device of the same name—also transliterated as mugharisah or magharisah—which endows the lessee with real rights and is typically defined as "a contract by virtue of which an owner entrusts land to a person who undertakes to plant it with fruit trees [in exchange for] receiving a portion of the land."[136]

Professor Lisa Anderson provides some context for how such a contract would order society in rural North Africa:

> In both Tunisia and Libya, the Sahil was often home of a contract known as the *magharisah*, in which property was confided to a land-poor farmer for development; upon its harvest, he was to receive half the land as his own. This type of contract was particularly characteristic of the tree-crop regions, where the first harvest of marketable produce was sometimes decades from planting. The *magharsi*—the developer—was tied to the landowner by numerous personal obligations. During the tenure of the contract, he was often obliged to ask for advances in money or in kind from the landowner, much of which he would not be able to return until the expiration of the agreement, and even then, he might find himself better served by a renewal of the contract than under the obligation to repay his debts.[137]

Inclusion of such traditional Islamic legal devices demonstrates the way in which Santillana sought to directly instill certain aspects of Islamic law into the Tunisian code and to preserve both a sense of tradition, historicity, and legal continuity in its text.

Neither the Moroccan nor the Mauritanian code contains such provisions. This is likely due to the fact that the Moroccan Commercial Code, which was enacted in 1913 along with the *Dahir des obligations et des contrats*[138] and broadly provided for all business entities—agricultural or otherwise.[139] These Moroccan codes were enacted in the same timeframe and, therefore, could share the legal universe whereas the Tunisian code, emerging in 1906, would have had less competition. As the Mauritanian code was hewn from the truncated Moroccan version, it did not inherit these Tunisian provisions.

OATHS (LE SERMENT)

Another area where the gravitational pull of Islamic law and Tunisian custom is evident is in the rules governing oaths. Continental civil law recognizes, among other things, the use of oaths as a manner of proving the existence of facts relevant to civil litigation. For instance, Article 1357 of the French Civil Code provides for the use of judicial oaths (*le serment*). This has been described as "a remnant of the formalistic medieval procedure" which is used less frequently today.[140] There are three varieties of such judicial oaths in French civil law: the decisory oath (*serment décisoire*), the supplementary oath (*serment supplétoire*), and the *serment in litem* or *serment in plaids* which deals with damages.

The first of these (the *serment décisoire*) is an oath administered by one party to the other, upon which the result of the action is made to depend.[141] The *serment supplétoire* is the oath administered by the judge to one of the parties in order to determine an issue.[142] The last variety (*serment en plaids*, or *serment in litem*) is a kind of oath in which, under certain exceptional circumstances, the judge may administer to a plaintiff in order to determine the value of the thing forming the object of the action.[143]

Tunisian law also recognizes two types of oaths for purposes of establishing facts in civil litigation: (1) one which a party refers to the other in order to make the case depend upon it (*décisoire*); and (2) one which is brought *ex officio* by the judges to one or the other of parties (*supplétoire*).[144] Although a lengthy discussion of these devices is beyond the scope of this book, it is worth noting that Tunisian civil law incorporates them, but also imbues them with a religious dimension that does not ordinarily exist in continental civil law. Specifically, Article 495 of the Tunisian code notes that "[t]he oath must always be taken in the mosque on Friday or in any other religious place which will be indicated by the party offering the oath and in conformance with the religious sect of the party."[145] If the place where the oath must be taken is further than three miles from the place where the Court sits, the part to which the oath is referred may refuse to go there. Notably, the party who refuses to be sworn in the indicated place is deemed to have refused the oath.[146] Such provisions—requiring an oath to be taken "in the mosque on Friday or in any other religious place"—imbues this procedure with a religious element that gives recognition to the role of religion in civil affairs.

The Moroccan code states that the rules relative to oaths are established by the Moroccan *Dahir* on Civil Procedure, which was established in the French protectorate of Morocco.[147] That document seems to eschew older classifications and states that, to end a dispute, a party may rely on an oath to prove his or her claims. Such an oath must be made before the court in the presence of the other party and must begin with the words "*Je jure devant Dieu*" (I swear to God.)[148] If there is a legitimate impediment that prevents the oath being taken before the other party, the oath may be taken before a judge and the report delivered to the party. Similarly, if the party from whom the oath is required lives in a very remote place, the court may order that it be sworn before the Court of First Instance of his place of residence.[149]

The Mauritanian code also contains provisions governing oaths, though they differ from those found in continental civil and those of its Tunisian progenitor. The Mauritanian code recognizes four kinds of oaths: (1) the *serment d'accusation*—the oath required in case of contention; (2) the *serment de jugement*—the oath required to rebut a virtual contention on the part of one who can plead on its behalf, such as death, absent, or minor; (3) the *serment de dénégation*—the oath used to refute the unproven claim; (4) the *serment complémentaire*—the oath used to support the testimony of one person, or in other similar situations, to establish a property right; and (5) the *serment d'éviction*—an oath for one who has acquired rights, other than funds, to refute a likely claim.[150] Of those oaths, the oaths of *accusation*, *jugement*, and *eviction* can be reversed—but only once.[151] Notably, the Mauritanian code requires an indelibly religious formality for the taking of an oath, noting that, in order to have legal effect, the oath must begin with the phrase, "*Par Allah l'Unique.*"[152]

CONCLUSION

A review of the nominate contracts of sale, exchange, deposit, and mandate—as well as the articles on agricultural partnerships and oaths—demonstrate Santillana's careful blending of Islamic law and continental civil law. With regard to the nominate contracts, Santillana borrowed the forms and concepts from the European legal traditions, but infused them with Islamic legal concepts. The enacted language, influenced by the review of religious authorities in Tunisia, also incorporated within the legal framework devices to maintain Islamic legal prohibitions where applicable in transactions between Muslims—thus bringing the "personality of laws" (and Islamic law's organic pluralism) into the civil code. The Moroccan and Mauritanian codes largely adhere to the Tunisian template, though diverging to accommodate their respective legal cultures and individual polities.

NOTES

1. *See* D. Santillana, Avant-Projet Du Code Civil Et Commercial Tunisien 261–63 (1899) [hereinafter AVANT-PROJET].

2. *Id.*

3. Planiol, Traité Élémentaire De Droit Civil 462 (9th ed., 1923).

4. *Id.* at 464.

5. Louisiana Civil Code, Art. 2439.

6. *See* Avant-Projet, *supra* note 1, at 261.

7. J. Liebesny, The Law Of The Near & Middle East 210 (1975).

8. *Id.* citing Halabi, Multaqa al-Abhur (458, trans. Sauvaire 5–6).

9. *See* Avant-Projet, *supra* note 1, at 261.

10. *Id.*

11. Tunisian Code of Obligations and Contracts, Art. 564; Moroccan Code of Obligations and Contracts, Art. 478; Mauritanian Code of Obligations and Contracts, Art. 489.

12. Planiol, *supra* note 3, at 462.

13. Tunisian Code of Obligations and Contracts, Art. 580.

14. Planiol, *supra* note 3, at 468 ("*La fixation du prix est parfois chose difficile, et les parties conviennent de s'en rapporter pour son chiffre à l'appréciation d'un ou de plusiers arbitres ou experts. Ce procédé est licite*").

15. *See,* for example, Louisiana Civil Code, Art. 2645 ("The price may be left to the determination of a third person. If the parties fail to agree on or to appoint such a person, or if the one appointed is unable or unwilling to make a determination, the price may be determined by the court.").

16. Mejelle, Art. 237 ("It is necessary that the price should be named at the time of the sale [Bey`]. Therefore, if the price of the thing sold is not mentioned at the time of the sale, the sale is bad [Fasid].") *See also* Mejelle, Art. 238 ("It is necessary that the price should be known.").

17. Mahmoud A. El-Gamal, Islamic Finance: Law, Economics, And Practice 58 (2006).

18. Abdul-Rahim Al-Saati, *The Permissible Gharar (Risk) in Classical Islamic Jurisprudence*, 16 J.KAU: ISLAMIC ECON. 3, 3, 8 (1424 A.H/2003 A.D), http://balmeena.kau.edu.sa/Files/320/Researches/50833_20970.pdf (noting that "[d]eferment of the price to an unknown future date" is an example of a *gharar* sale).

19. Tunisian Code of Obligations and Contracts, Art. 579.

20. *Id.*

21. *Id.*

22. Mauritanian Code of Obligations and Contracts, Art. 498.

23. *Id.*

24. *Id.*

25. *Id.*

26. Tunisian Code of Obligations and Contracts, Art. 571.

27. ABDULLAH ALWI HAJI HASSAN, SALES AND CONTRACTS IN EARLY ISLAMIC COMMERCIAL LAW 80 (2007).

28. 2 DAVID EISENBERG, ISLAMIC FINANCE: LAW AND PRACTICE 69 (2012).

29. BGB, art. 138(1) ("A juristic act that is contra bonos mores is void.").

30. Edith Z. Friedler, *Essay: Shakespeare's Contribution to the Teaching of Comparative Law-Some Reflections on the Merchant of Venice*, 60 LA. L. REV. 1087, 1099 (2000).

31. Tunisian Code of Obligations and Contracts, Art. 575. (Note that the widely available Mauritanian translation incorrectly uses the phrase "*haria seuf*" when referencing religious law. This is a mistranslation of "*le charia sauf.*")

32. *See* Avant-Projet, *supra* note 1, at 267.

33. *See* A.M. DEMANTE, PROGRAMME DU COURS DE DROIT CIVIL FRANCAIS 141 (1833) ("La deliverance ou tradition n'est plus aujourd'hui requise pour transférer la propriété[.]").

34. Horacio Spector, *The Future of Legal Science in Civil Law Systems*, 65 LA. L. REV. 255, 265 (2004).

35. *Id.*

36. Robert L. Theriot, *An Examination of the Role of Delivery in the Transfer of Ownership and Risk in Sales Under Louisiana Law*, 60 TUL. L. REV. 1035, 1046 (1986).

37. Ronald J. Scalise Jr., *Why No "Efficient Breach" in the Civil Law?: A Comparative Assessment of the Doctrine of Efficient Breach of Contract*, 55 AM. J. COMP. L. 721, 750 (2007).

38. MAJID KHADDURI & HERBERT J. LIEBESNY, ORIGIN AND DEVELOPMENT OF ISLAMIC LAW 198 (1955).

39. *See* HIROYUKI YANAGIHASHI, *SOCIO-ECONOMIC JUSTICE*, IN THE ASHGATE RESEARCH COMPANION TO ISLAMIC LAW 158 (Rudolph Peters ed., 2014).

40. Mejelle, Art. 252.

41. *Id.* at 253.

42. *Id.*

43. *Id.*

44. *Id.*

45. *Id.*

46. Tunisian Code of Obligations and Contracts, Art. 583; Moroccan Code of Obligations and Contracts, Art. 491; Mauritanian Code of Obligations and Contracts, Art. 502.

47. Tunisian Code of Obligations and Contracts, Art. 584; Moroccan Code of Obligations and Contracts, Art. 491; Mauritanian Code of Obligations and Contracts, Art. 502.

48. Tunisian Code of Obligations and Contracts, Art. 584.

49. *Id.*; Moroccan Code of Obligations and Contracts, Art. 491.

50. Mauritanian Code of Obligations and Contracts, Art. 502.

51. N.J. COULSON, A HISTORY OF ISLAMIC LAW 39 (2011). (Noting, "Although confined to foodstuffs in Medina the rule was extended to Kufa to apply to all moveable goods.")

52. *See* Al-Saati, *supra* note 18, at 294.

53. *See* Coulson, *supra* note 51, at 79.

54. *Id.*

55. Mejelle, Art. 223.

56. Tunisian Code of Obligations and Contracts, Art. 583; Moroccan Code of Obligations and Contracts, Art. 491; Mauritanian Code of Obligations and Contracts, Art. 502.

57. *See* Faouzi Belknani, *Code des Obligations et des Contrats et la Codification*, in Livre Du Centenaire Du Code Des Obligations Et Des Contrats 1906–2006 22 (2006).

58. Tunisian Code of Obligations and Contracts, Art. 565; Moroccan Code of Obligations and Contracts, Art. 479; Mauritanian Code of Obligations and Contracts, Art. 490.

59. Tunisian Code of Obligations and Contracts, Art. 354; Moroccan Code of Obligations and Contracts, Art. 344; Mauritanian Code of Obligations and Contracts, Art. 342.

60. Tunisian Code of Obligations and Contracts, Art. 565; Moroccan Code of Obligations and Contracts, Art. 345; Mauritanian Code of Obligations and Contracts, Art. 343.

61. Tunisian Code of Obligations and Contracts, Art. 355.

62. *See* Belknani, *supra* note 57, at 23.

63. Mejelle, Art. 393.

64. *Id.*, 394.

65. *See* Belknani, *supra* note 57, at 22 n.99.

66. Tunisian Code of Obligations and Contracts, Art. 576; Moroccan Code of Obligations and Contracts, Art. 485; Mauritanian Code of Obligations and Contracts, Art. 496.

67. *See* Louisiana Civil Code Art. 2452 (Sale of the thing of another).

68. Hiroyuki Yanagihashi, A History Of The Early Islamic Law Of Property: Reconstructing The Legal Development, 7th-9th Centuries 117 (2004).

69. *Id.*

70. *See* Demante, *supra* note 33, at 189.

71. *See* Jason P. Bergeron, *Watkins v. Freeway Motors-A Need to Clarify the Principle of Novation*, 58 LA. L. REV. 1241, 1245 (1998).

72. Louisiana Civil Code, Article 2660.

73. *See* Bergeron, *supra* note 71, at 1245.

74. *See* Khadduri & Liebesny, *supra* note 38, at 198.

75. *Id.*

76. *See* Mejelle, Art.122.

77. *See* Avant-Projet, *supra* note 1, at 220–21.

78. *Id.*

79. Tunisian Code of Obligations and Contracts, Art. 718; Moroccan Code of Obligations and Contracts, Art. 619; Mauritanian Code of Obligations and Contracts, Art. 606.

80. *See, e.g.*, Louisiana Civil Code, Art. 2660.

81. Tunisian Code of Obligations and Contracts, Art. 719; Moroccan Code of Obligations and Contracts, Art. 620; Mauritanian Code of Obligations and Contracts,

Art. 607. *See* Demante, *supra* note 513 at 189. ("*Dans les principes de notre Droit français ce contrat est consensuel aussi bien que la vente.*")

82. Tunisian Code of Obligations and Contracts, Art. 719; Moroccan Code of Obligations and Contracts, Art. 620; Mauritanian Code of Obligations and Contracts, Art. 607.

83. Tunisian Code of Obligations and Contracts, Art. 581; Moroccan Code of Obligations and Contracts, Art. 489; Mauritanian Code of Obligations and Contracts, Art. 500.

84. Tunisian Code of Obligations and Contracts, Art. 720; Moroccan Code of Obligations and Contracts, Art. 621; Mauritanian Code of Obligations and Contracts, Art. 608.

85. *Id.*

86. *See* Avant-Projet, *supra* note 1, at 320.

87. Mauritanian Code of Obligations and Contracts, Art. 608.

88. Abu-Muhammad Abdullah Bin Abi-Zayd & Abdur-Rahman Al-Qyrawani, *The Gist of the Treatise on Malikite Jurisprudence* 84 (1994):When grains, legumes, and preserved foodstuffs are bartered in kind, the quantity received should be equal to the quantity given; no delay in delivery is allowed in this exchange. It is forbidden to barter foodstuff delivered immediately for foodstuff to be delivered at a subsequent time, whether the exchange is in kind or not, whether the foodstuff is perishable or not.

89. Michael H. Rubin, *Bailment and Deposit in Louisiana*, 35 LA. L. REV. 825 (1975).

90. Louisiana Civil Code, Art. 2926.

91. *Id.* at 2931.

92. *Id.* at 2933.

93. *Id.* at 2930.

94. *See* Rubin, *supra* note 89, at 828.

95. YUSUF AL HAJJ AHMED, FINANCIAL TRANSACTIONS IN ISLAM: ENCYCLOPAEDIA OF ISLAMIC LAW 52 (2014).

96. *Id.* at 53.

97. *Id.*

98. Mejelle, Art. 777.

99. *Id.*

100. *See* Avant-Projet, *supra* note 1, at 417–19.

101. Tunisian Code of Obligations and Contracts, Art. 995; Moroccan Code of Obligations and Contracts, Art. 781; Mauritanian Code of Obligations and Contracts, Art. 729.

102. Tunisian Code of Obligations and Contracts, Art. 998; Moroccan Code of Obligations and Contracts, Art. 784; Mauritanian Code of Obligations and Contracts, Art. 732.

103. *Id.*

104. Tunisian Code of Obligations and Contracts, Art. 1003; Moroccan Code of Obligations and Contracts, Art. 789.

105. Tunisian Code of Obligations and Contracts, Art. 1021; Moroccan Code of Obligations and Contracts, Art. 807; Mauritanian Code of Obligations and Contracts, Art. 754.

106. Tunisian Code of Obligations and Contracts, Art. 1022; Moroccan Code of Obligations and Contracts, Art. 808; Mauritanian Code of Obligations and Contracts, Art. 755.

107. *Id.*

108. Tunisian Code of Obligations and Contracts, Art. 1005; Moroccan Code of Obligations and Contracts, Art. 791; Mauritanian Code of Obligations and Contracts, Art. 738.

109. Mauritanian Code of Obligations and Contracts, Art. 756.

110. Tunisian Code of Obligations and Contracts, Art. 1023; Moroccan Code of Obligations and Contracts, Art. 809.

111. *Id.*

112. Italian Code art. 1850. *See also* TROPLONG, COMMENTAIRE DU PRÊT, DU DÉPÔT, DU SEQUESTRE ET DES CONTRATS ALÉATOIRES 355 (1845).

113. Louisiana Civil Code 2989.

114. Michael B. North, *Qui Facit Per Alium, Facit Per Se: Representation, Mandate, and Principles of Agency in Louisiana at the Turn of the Twenty-First Century*, 72 TUL. L. REV. 279, 282–83 (1997).

115. Hania Masud, *Takaful: An Innovative Approach to Insurance and Islamic Finance*, 32 U. PA. J. INT'L L. 1133, 1137–38 (2011).

116. *See* Avant-Projet, *supra* note 1, at 450.

117. *Id.*

118. *See* Masud, *supra* note 115.

119. Mejelle, Art. 1449.

120. *See, e.g.*, Mejelle, Arts. 1470–71, 1479.

121. *See* Avant-Projet, *supra* note 1, at 450–52.

122. *Id.*

123. Tunisian Code of Obligations and Contracts, Art. 1116; Moroccan Code of Obligations and Contracts, Art. 890; Mauritanian Code of Obligations and Contracts, Art. 830.

124. Tunisian Code of Obligations and Contracts, Art. 1117; Moroccan Code of Obligations and Contracts, Art. 891; Mauritanian Code of Obligations and Contracts, Art. 831.

125. *Id.*

126. Tunisian Code of Obligations and Contracts, Art. 1119; Moroccan Code of Obligations and Contracts, Art. 893; Mauritanian Code of Obligations and Contracts, Art. 833.

127. *Id.*

128. *See* Belknani, *supra* note 57, at 22 n.100.

129. Tunisian Code of Obligations and Contracts, Art. 1163; Moroccan Code of Obligations and Contracts, Art. 934; Mauritanian Code of Obligations and Contracts, Art. 873.

130. *See, e.g.*, Mejelle, Arts. 1470–71, 1479.

131. Tunisian Code of Obligations and Contracts, Art. 1163; Moroccan Code of Obligations and Contracts, Art. 934; Mauritanian Code of Obligations and Contracts, Art. 873.

132. *See* Belknani, *supra* note 57, at 23.

133. Tunisian Code of Obligations and Contracts, Art. 1395.

134. Farhat J. Ziadeh, Property Law In The Arab World 70–71 (1979).

135. Tunisian Code of Obligations and Contracts, Art. 1416.

136. *Id.*

137. Lisa Anderson, The State And Social Transformation In Tunisia And Libya, 1830–1980 45 (1986).

138. *See* Nicole Souletie, Le Mot De Madame Nicole Souletie In Le Centenaire Du Dahir Formant Code Des Obligations Et Contrats (Doc) 1913–2013 15 (2013).

139. Paul Decroux, Le Droit Des Sociétés Dans Le Maroc Moderne (1961).

140. *See* Peter Emilius Hertzog, Civil Procedure In France 358 (1967).

141. Oliver Eaton Bodington, An Outline of the French Law of Evidence 72–73 (1904). Writing in 1904, Oliver Eaton Bodington noted, "The serment decisoire, or oath administered by one party to the other, may be administered by any party who has proof to make in support of his demand, or of his plea in defence." Importantly, such an oath can be made in a variety of judicial contests but can only be made in regard only to "things done by the person himself, or at the doing of which he was present." Bodington also noted that French courts and commentators have universally held "that the oath can only be administered in regard to facts which are of a decisive character, that is to say, a character which shall determine the issue."

142. *Id.*

143. *Id.*

144. Tunisian Code of Obligations and Contracts, Art. 492.

145. *Id.* 495.

146. *Id.* 496.

147. Moroccan Code of Obligations and Contracts, Art. 460.

148. *Id.* 85.

149. *Id.* 86.

150. Mauritanian Code of Obligations and Contracts, Art. 467.

151. *Id.* 468.

152. *Id.* 469.

Chapter 7

Conclusion

The story of the Santillana Codes takes place in a swirling vortex of political upheaval and cultural confrontation. It is a story that reaches back to Roman times to the earliest origins of continental civil law; develops in nineteenth-century Ottoman Tunisia; culminates as French colonial powers ascended; endured through the destabilizing protests, uprisings, and rebellions of the Arab Spring[1]; and continues today in the arid climates of the contemporary Maghreb and Sahel. As this book has sought to illuminate, these civil codes arose at the convergence of multiple strands of overlapping histories and political currents. French colonial powers may have been the impetus for the undertaking, but it was Maghrebian history and legal culture that dictated the result. The final product was not a slavish emulation of the code favored by colonial powers, but a true attempt—and the first—to synthesize Islamic and continental civil law. The result is a family of civil codes, that is, all at once, uniquely African, relatively European, sufficiently Islamic, and generally pluralistic. Perhaps most significantly, these civil codes have been, for the countries that adopted them, durable legal institutions—bulwarks against the abrading forces of instability and social change.

RETROSPECTUS: THE MAN AND THE CODES

The story of the Santillana Codes is, of course, indissolubly bound with that of the man who was their principal architect. David Santillana was a rather remarkable jurist whose fecund legal mind gave form to a new genre of codification—the first true synthesis of Islamic law and modern, continental civil law based on the European model. Educated in Tunisia, England, and Rome, Santillana grew to become an omilegent comparative law scholar, a skilled

145

practitioner, and an expert in Islamic law who understood the potential for Islamic law's viability in a modern context.[2] Additionally, as a Sephardic Jew, Santillana was also a man born into a community notable for its transnational nature—a community forced to move across frontiers yet able to establish successive enclaves of legal autonomy. It is also a community with a rich tradition of learning that includes legal scholarship and jurists in both the religious[3] and secular[4] traditions. Though rooted in this community, Santillana was still a North African man who was closely connected to Tunisia and even served at senior levels of Tunisian government. A man of many worlds, living in an era that was fulminating with political change and yearning for progress, Santillana was exceptionally well placed to lend his rare talent and international background to the task of crafting a law of obligations and contracts for Tunisia. Moreover, his writing also shows him to be a man of extraordinary perspective. One glimpses his humanity in his *Avant-Propos* in which he notes his view that "[a] true society, a people, is not a bunch of individuals, but a multitude gathered together for a common end, an association whose members help each other and support each other in the interests of all."[5] Interestingly, in the footnote supporting this comment, Santillana cites to Islamic commentary on the Qu'ran for its inspiration.[6] Such a comment—coupled with his source—gives insight into Santillana's wordly outlook and his cosmopolitan approach to law.

The codes that are derived from Santillana's seminal effort are remarkable in both their eclecticism and their syncretism, aspects which derive from his recourse to a vast, impressive spectrum of Islamic legal sources and scholarly writing, and his skillful use of all available civil law models available in that era, including Roman law, civil codes then in force, and the doctrinal writing of generations of civil law luminaries. The result was a legal regime that combined into one system the more desirable traits of many systems—a single code formed from a sprawling constellation of world legal traditions.

With regard to his European influences, Santillana drew from a multiplicity of sources,[7] namely the French civil code,[8] the German civil code,[9] the Italian civil code, French jurisprudence, and the jurisprudence of French courts which were active in Tunisia during its time as a French protectorate.[10] At the same time, Santillana and his fellow jurists delved deeply into the nebula of Islamic law to find analogous legal principles that could be synthesized and harmonized with continental civil law. In his discussion of this effort, Santillana noted the shared traits of European civil law and Islamic law: "[T]he two systems of law, Arabic and our own, both have a common principle, good faith, and proceed, at least in part, from a common root, the Roman Law"[11] This statement is, of course, supported by the many Islamic legal sources painstakingly cited in Santillana's *Avant-Projet* and the analysis in this book which demonstrates the many ways in which Islamic law and continental civil law are in accord. In that regard, the analysis undertaken in this book highlights the presence of numerous Islamic-civil law correlates: the basic parameters of unilateral and bilateral contracts, including nominate contracts such as sale, exchange, and deposit; the elements of a contract, including the need for valid consent; notion of the three vices of consent: fraud, error, and duress; and, more broadly, a general insistence on good faith in carrying out obligations. Santillana saw these commonalities with exceptional clarity and built upon them to bridge two seemingly distant legal worlds.

Undertaking such a synthesis was, as it always is, dangerous alchemy. Adding an incongruous idea into the mix—or a legal concept too alien to be digested or accepted—would have rendered the experiment too volatile and risked the ruination of the entire project. The wrong elements mixed in the wrong proportions could result in a fizzling failure. An unnatural transplant or incorrect addition would have been quickly rejected, and the consequences for the failure of a foundational legal code so early in a state's formation would have been dire. The very undertaking was, therefore, remarkable in many respects—and its continued vitality is a testament to the quality of the product of that endeavor. The right elements mixed in the proper proportions served to create the lasting legal legacy of a "mixed jurisdiction" in which domestic civil law is derived from an array of sources.[12] This synthesis of multiple, disparate legal systems into one unified civil law framework was groundbreaking. The result was, for the first time, a modern civil code that simultaneously embodied the spirit of Islamic law and continental civil law—a code that would then be replicated in other Muslim countries that sought to adopt legal regimes compatible with the larger civil law world.

Though notable as a prototype of this sort of synthesis, Santillana's codal design is also notable for its inclusion of cutting-edge legal ideas. For instance, Santillana's codification elaborated on the proper use of custom in a way few other codes of that period had yet done. Inspired by Islamic legal procedure and drawing from Italian sources, the Tunisian code broke with the rigidity of the French positivist tradition and directed judges to look beyond the text to general principles of law when lacunae in the legislation is encountered—breaking with the view of French colonial powers to adopt a forward-leaning judicial approach and his unique civil law model with a flexibility that many other civil law jurisdictions would not attain for many years (a fact recognized by Gény who referred to Santillana's work as an example of cutting-edge civil law codification.)[13] In addition, Santillana's codification, again drawing on Italian sources, was among the first to include "error of law" in a codification and to elucidate how such error should be treated.[14] And, inspired by Islamic law, Santillana leapt decades ahead of European codes in crafting provisions which allowed rescission of a contract for fraud by a third party. These are examples of ideas that, at the time Santillana was drafting his Tunisian archetype, were either entirely new to civil law or otherwise at the avant-garde of civil law doctrine. Importantly, however, they were also motivated by his desire to find civil law jurisprudential rules that comported with Islamic law and Islamic legal procedure. This demonstrates not only the ingeniousness of Santillana's approach, but the way in which Islamic law acted as a catalyst in the complex mixture of legal sources, sparking brilliant new changes and developments that resulted in a more progressive legal model.

Another remarkable innovation that is present in the Santillana Codes is the unique feature that, in the context of a unified legal framework, permits a degree of individuation based on religious affiliation. This approach—still present in both the Tunisian and Moroccan codes—serves to juridically enshrine pluralism at the same time that it acknowledges the importance of Islamic law. Although not widely incorporated in the *Avant-Projet* (with the exception for the provisions on sale) this device was included in numerous places after a review by the Tunisian 'ulama, demonstrating the importance of the input by the 'ulama to Santillana's work. This feature imports the jurisdictional concept of "personality of laws" that Islamic law had long permitted. While one can only speculate to some degree as to the final discussions surrounding this additional language, it is fair to assume Santillana would have been comfortable with such a method as the idea of a "personality of laws" is one which Santillana's Sephardic Jewish community had long embraced and utilized to their benefit. In any event, its incorporation into the Tunisian code was an innovative and exceedingly pragmatic way of managing the competing needs for a unified national law, the mandates of Islamic law in a majority Muslim country, and the fact of religious diversity. And this mechanism still retains value today. As Paul Schiff Berman notes, such mechanisms "deliberately seek to create or preserve spaces for conflict among multiple, overlapping legal systems. Indeed, developing procedural mechanisms, institutions, and practices along pluralist lines may sometimes be a useful strategy for managing, without eliminating, hybridity."[15] Nevertheless, such legal harmonization is a challenge at every level. As Professor Mireille Delmas-Marty has stated: "Ordering multiplicity without reducing it to sameness, admitting pluralism without giving up on building common law with a common measure for fair and unfair, can ... seem an unattainable goal."[16]

It is in this regard that the Santillana Codes and their natural hybridity are of significant importance to jurists and policymakers. Santillana's model demonstrates how Islamic law can function in a modern context alongside continental civil law as part of a "mixed jurisdiction" in which domestic civil law is derived from a multiplicity of sources—European, African, and Middle Eastern.[17] The result is a codification of civil law which adheres to the modern civil law model inspired by the French civil code, but which is also uniquely well suited to the task of ordering plurality in the Maghreb and Sahel.

PROSPECTUS: THE SANTILLANA CODES AND THE WORLD ORDER

Looking forward to the problems confronting the contemporary world order, an understanding of the Santillana Codes and their functionality remains vital in several respects. Firstly, and perhaps most fundamentally, civil codes are a critical element in the process of formation of a country and the development of the rule of law. In fact, the codification movement was spurred, in part, by the ideas of the French Revolution (which emphasized the freedom and equality of citizens and the need for reconstruction of both whole public and private law) and the "formation of the new modern nations that needed to be reinforced by the territorial unity of the Law."[18] These concepts are closely linked with the basic foundations of a modern state, which must necessarily enshrine certain basic values and govern within a rule of law framework. A review of the modern history of state formation demonstrates the recurring role of civil codes in the quest by sovereigns to consolidate power and authority in their respective realms—mechanisms by which central governments could express sovereignty[19] and, in addition, make government "less arbitrary, more transparent, and more uniform in its treatment of citizens."[20] This is particularly true of the French model on which the Santillana Codes are principally based. Francis Fukuyama notes that this model "was used as model for countless other civil codes outside Europe, from Senegal to Argentina to Egypt to Japan,"[21] and can be considered foundational for the emergence of the modern state and the rule of law in many countries.[22] An understanding of these critical institutions, therefore, is important when considering issues associated with state formation and stability.

Secondly, the study and preservation of civil codes is important to the task of facilitating economic development. This is important for reasons beyond the obvious advantages brought to a country by the development of the market economy. A durable framework that supports the rule of law and enhances economic prosperity can also usher in an increased capacity for democratic governance and a system of government that respects human rights[23]—factors which, in turn, are critical for to the task of providing an enabling environment for sustainable economic and social development.[24]

Legal institutions that govern contracts and their enforcement (such as civil codes) are considered especially significant as they foster "productive investment and arms' length economic transactions."[26] Such development is of enhanced importance in the contemporary Middle East and in regions of Africa—including the Maghreb and Sahel—where economic conditions have led to a degree of disaffection and where terrorist groups actively recruit from among the disaffected. This underscores the importance of understanding and promoting effective civil law frameworks.

Policymakers and academics alike accept the proposition that a country's adherence to law has a multiplicity of economic and democratic benefits. Empirical research indicates that the rule of law is one of the most important components of any institutional explanation of cross-national differences in economic well-being. The rule of law is intricately connected with, if not a causal factor in, the promotion of both democracy and economic development.

> It is clear that strong legal institutions also assure a better human rights record and deepen democracy within countries. Moreover, the efficacy of legal institutions is important internationally as well as within a nation's borders. A country which is able to ensure its citizens physical protection and equal treatment under the law is less likely to be engaged in violent internal conflict and will not be, therefore, the source of potentially destabilizing refugee flows.[25]

Thirdly, and perhaps more broadly, the study of civil codes is an important element of formulating policy and structuring programs for post-conflict states such as those in the contemporary Middle East. In that regard, a major reason for the durability and continued vitality of the Santillana Codes is that Santillana's codal design is one that was eclectic, innovative, and highly functional. The elements infused within their articles combined to make these codes durable legal institutions, standing out in stark relief against a backdrop of political change and volatility. The durability of state institutions—including legal institutions—is a critical aspect of restoring order and government functionality in post-conflict states.[27] In the context of the Middle East and Africa, Chibli Mallat notes that civil codes have served as important institutional "anchors" for many fragile states. In his masterful text on Middle Eastern legal systems, Mallat notes, "civil codes in the Middle East are peculiar in two ways: they have proved more resilient than their public law counterparts, and modern civil codes function as stable institutions offering legal anchors which transcend political changes."[28] Civil codes, thus, are institutions that are at once vital to development of the modern state and notably durable—important points of light in the constellation of institutions that enable statehood.

All of these issues are especially important when undertaking a discussion of North Africa and/or the Sahel. While the focus of this book has been intensely legal (and technical) as it largely pertains to a certain set of civil codes, it would be a mistake to ignore the political realities of the geographic regions and territories where these civil codes are in force. The past decade or so has witnessed a marked increase in the attention paid to legal systems in the Middle East and North Africa.[29] Wars, revolutions, and the increasingly expeditionary foreign policies of Western governments in the twenty-first century (which viewed foreign instability as a threat to domestic national security) have drawn the study of these countries and their institutions into the foreign policy calculus of world powers seeking to promote stability or otherwise assert influence in the region.[30] The challenges faced by countries in the region in the aftermath of the Arab Spring are beginning to draw specific attention to their legal systems.[31] This is, in part, because the deleterious effect of that series of revolutions on the domestic institutions of affected countries has made those countries more prone to "destabilizing ethnic and sectarian rivalries"[32] and "have created opportunities for extremist groups to find ungoverned space from which to destabilize the new governments and prepare attacks against Western interests inside those countries."[33] A major issue of concern for these various regions is the way in which law and legal institutions can effectively address the needs of heterogeneous and pluralistic societies that must co-exist in the context of a unified legal and national framework.[34] This is especially true in those countries that must create new constitutions, adopt new legislation, and confront complex issues associated with the proper role of religion and religious law.[35]

The Santillana model is of particular interest due to the fact that Tunisia—the country of its origin—is emerging as a model for Arab Spring countries seeking a successful transition to democracy. Tunisia, after all, was the genesis and the epicenter of the Arab Spring (which began as the "Jasmine Revolution").[36] While outcomes throughout the region have varied, in the aftermath of those tremorous spasms of discord and political upheaval, commentators have noted Tunisia's relatively successful transition from autocracy.[37] This success is due, in no small part, to the fact that Tunisia experienced a regime change but retained its vital state institutions[38] and has, throughout its process of transition, maintained relative (though imperfect) stability whereas neighboring countries have not.[39] As a result, Tunisia's very real potential for success has redefined it on the world stage as a regional anchor, a lodestar for countries in transition, and "the Arab Spring's last hope."[40]

Even so, Tunisia remains at "a critical intersection of conflict and peace-building," and currently "confronts threats of violent extremism with roots at home and in the surrounding region."[41] Morocco, similarly, has been remarked as exceptionally stable (remarkably so in the aftermath of the Arab Spring)[42] yet still faces the threat of destabilizing transnational forces and "cross-border implications of instability and jihadi terrorism in neighboring Mauritania and nearby Mali, or other countries of the Sahel."[43] In addition, Mauritania, which has suffered great economic deprivation throughout its history as a country, is simultaneously described as, "a rare bright spot amid regional tumult," yet "vulnerable to terrorist destabilization, with the potential return of [militants and jihadists] representing a serious threat."[44] The institutions of each of these countries, therefore, is worthy of study for those seeking to understand the structures that undergird their stability—and to provide assistance to countries in the region in the event that stability should fail. Moreover, a glance at the broader region reveals a number of countries that have suffered near or total collapse in the wake of the Arab Spring (Libya, Syria, etc.) and which will most certainly need to rebuild their basic civil law capacity if order and stability are to be regained and made to endure. In undertaking such tasks, it is essential to heed Professor Christopher L. Blakesley's admonition that knowledge of diverse systems may provide "a chance to see different refractions, a fuller spectrum of possibilities," and "ought to be extremely helpful in solving legal problems facing students, scholars, judges, and practitioners in ... other systems[.]"[45] Knowledge of the Santillana Codes, therefore, can enhance the abilities of policymakers and practitioners seeking solutions relating to civil law and its proper functioning in the Maghreb and Sahel.

This book closes by noting that the Arab Spring—which has changed the physiognomy of the Middle East and North Africa at almost every level—began in the same place as the Santillana Codes: Tunisia. The same small country on the Mediterranean that ignited the revolutions that upended autocrats across the globe, through its history of pluralism, long ago produced a cosmopolitan, Jewish jurist who revolutionized the way civil law could operate in an Islamic legal context. In addition to the manifold reasons articulated above, these codes and their history are also valuable because they challenge popular conceptions about the potential for pluralism in the Muslim world. Their continued force and rich history upend the notion that a Muslim country could not take in a Jewish population and permit them to thrive. They challenge the idea that Islamic law could not help advance continental civil law. They illuminate how much is actually shared between the legal traditions of the Islamic and Western worlds. And they challenge the idea that a Jewish jurist could not make lasting contribution to Islamic law. In fact, the mixed civil law system created by Santillana has persisted for over a century in Tunisia and Morocco, and now is in force in Mauritania. Perhaps aside from the clear value their study provides to scholars and international policymakers, there is a more poignant lesson to be learned from these codes, their history, and their continued vitality. Perhaps Tunisia can be as proud of this aspect of its legal history as it might be about its role in the recent revolutions. And perhaps leaders across the globe—in an era that is seemingly increasingly polarized—might look back over a century to this example of Tunisia and what it has yielded for both civil and Islamic law. It would not be the first time that this small country on the Mediterranean coast illuminated a path for others to follow.

NOTES

1. *See* MARC LYNCH, THE ARAB UPRISING: THE UNFINISHED REVOLUTIONS OF THE NEW MIDDLE EAST 9 (2012). *But see* Asher Susser, *The "Arab Spring": The Origins of a Misnomer*, Foreign Pol'y Res. Inst.: E-Notes (Apr. 2012), http://www.fpri.org/enotes/2012/201204.susser.arabspring.html. ("The tumultuous events that have swept through the Middle East during the last year or so were widely referred to in the West as the 'Arab Spring.'")

2. *See* Donna E. Arzt, *The Application of International Human Rights Law in Islamic States*, 12 HUM. RTS. Q. 202, 213–14 (1990). (quoting Santillana as writing: "There is no doubt that the high ethical standard of certain parts of Arab law acted favourably on the development of our modern concepts and therein has its enduring merit.")

3. *See* JANE S. GERBER, JEWS OF SPAIN: A HISTORY OF THE SEPHARDIC EXPERIENCE 159 (1994). (Discussing the Rabbi Joseph Caro, who, in the fifteenth century, wrote the Shulchan Aruch—a digest of Jewish law that became "the definitive code of Jewish law among Sephardim" and later "emerged as the handy legal manual for all of world Jewry.")

4. Andrew L. Kaufman, *Foreword to the Nature of the Judicial Process*, 1 J.L.: PERIOD. LAB. LEG. SCHOLAR. 317–18 (2011). (Discussing famed U.S. jurist Benjamin Nathan Cardozo, the son of Sephardic Jews whose ancestors had emigrated from Spain and Portugal.)

5. *See* D. SANTILLANA, AVANT-PROJET DU CODE CIVIL ET COMMERCIAL TUNISIEN III (1899) (hereinafter AVANT-PROJET).

6. *Id.*, citing El Kaffal & Razy.

7. *See* Seán Patrick Donlan, *The Mediterranean Hybridity Project: Crossing the Boundaries of Law and Culture*, 4 J. CIV. L. STUD. 355 (2011).

8. *See* FAOUZI BELKNANI, *Code des Obligations et des Contrats et la Codification*, *in* LIVRE DU CENTENAIRE DU CODE DES OBLIGATIONS ET DES CONTRATS 1906–2006 18 (2006).

9. *Id.*

10. *See* Maaike Voorhoeve, *Judges in a Web of normative Orders: Judicial Practices at the Court of First Instance Tunis in the Field of Divorce Law* 54 (2011) (Ph.D. dissertation, University of Amsterdam).

11. *See* Avant-Projet, *supra* note 154.

12. Donlan, *supra* note 7, at 355 (describing "mixed legal systems" as "diverse state laws [that] emerge from different legal traditions," *id.* at 359–60, and noting:

Neither the hybridity nor the diffusion of laws is new. Within Europe, law predated the state and the creation of genuinely national laws; a legal "system" centered on the modern nation-state, and the elimination of competing jurisdictions and marginalization of non-legal norms was a very long historical process. Especially before the nineteenth century, there were multiple contemporaneous legal orders co-existing in the same geographical space and at the same time. Modern national traditions are unique hybrids rooted in diverse customary or folklaws, summary and discretionary jurisdictions, local and particular *iura propria*, the Romano-canonical "learned laws" or *ius commune*, and other trans-territorial *iura communia* (including feudal law and the *lex mercatoria*). *Id.* at 356.

13. *See* 11 F. Gény, *La Technique Législative dans la Codification Civile Moderne*, in Le Code Civil. 1804–1904. Livre Du Centenaire (1904).

14. Tunisian Code of Obligations and Contracts, Art. 44; Moroccan Code of Obligations and Contracts, Art. 40; Mauritanian Code of Obligations and Contracts, Art. 60.

15. *See* Paul Schiff Berman, *Global Legal Pluralism*, 80 S. Cal. L. Rev. 1155 (2007).

16. *See* Mireille Delmas-Marty, Ordering Pluralism: A Conceptual Framework For Understanding The Transnational Legal World 1 (2009).

17. *See* Voorhoeve, *supra* note 10, at 54.

18. *See* Julius Cesar Rivera, *The Scope and Structure of Civil Codes: Relations with Commercial Law, Family Law, Consumer Law and Private International Law*, in The Scope And Structure Of Civil Codes (Julio Cesar Rivera ed., 2013).

19. Henry E. Strakosch, State Absolutism And The Rule Of Law: The Struggle For The Codification Of Civil Law In Australia 1753–1811 50 (1967), 50.

20. Francis Fukuyama, Political Order And Political Decay 16 (2014).

21. *Id.* at 17.

22. *Id.* at 16–18, 74, 342.

23. Leistungsangebot|Advisory Service, *Governance and Democracy, Law and Justice,* https://www.giz.de/de/downloads/giz2011-en-law-justice.pdf

24. Christoph Bail, Future of North-South Relations (Europe and the World Series) 102–15 (1998).

25. Sandra F. Joireman, Colonization And The Rule Of Law: Comparing The Effectiveness Of Common Law And Civil Law Countries 3–4 (2004), http://scholarship.richmond.edu/polisci-faculty-publications/64

26. Matthew C. Stephenson, Judicial Reform In Developing Economies: Constraints And Opportunities, In Annual World Bank Conference On Development Economics: Beyond Transition 311–28 (Francois Bourguignon & Boris Pleskovic, eds., 2007), http://www.law.harvard.edu/faculty/mstephenson/pdfsNEW/JudicialReformABCDE.pdf

27. *See* Jonathan Di John, *Conceptualising the Causes and Consequences of Failed States: A Critical Review of the Literature* 33–34 (Crisis States Res. Ctr., Working Paper No. 25, 2008).

28. *See* Chibli Mallat, Iraq: Guide To Law And Policy 3 (2009).

29. *See* Mallat, *supra* note 28, at xxi (2009) ("A search in American and British law journals yielded 250 entries for articles and notes on Iraq since 2003. There was hardly a tenth that number over the previous 50 years."). *See also* University of London

SOAS, http://www.soas.ac.uk/cimel/ ("The Centre of Islamic and Middle Eastern Law was established in 1990 at the School of Oriental and African Studies in recognition of the growing importance of law in both its Islamic and Middle Eastern dimensions.").

30. For a discussion of the link between comparative law and stability operations carried out by U.S. armed forces, *see* Dan E. Stigall, *Comparative Law and Stability Operations: A Basic Overview and a Few Thoughts on Lésion*, COMPARATIVELAWBLOG (May 21, 2010), http://comparativelawblog.blogspot.com/2010/05/comparative-law-and-stability.html

31. *See Islamic Law in Transitioning Arab Spring Countries Subject of June 4 Program*, http://www.loc.gov/today/pr/2013/13-091.html (noting that the Law Library of Congress and the Library's African and Middle Eastern Division hosted a panel discussion on the role and impact of Islamic law in the developing constitutions and laws of transitioning countries in the Middle East/North Africa region in 2013.).

32. *See* Woodrow Wilson ctr., *U.S. Intelligence: Arab Spring Generated Threats* (Mar. 15, 2013), http://www.wilsoncenter.org/islamists/article/us-intelligence-arab-spring-generated-threats

33. *Id.*

34. *See* Lally Weymouth, *The Arab Spring's Last Hope: An Interview with Rachid Ghannouchi, the Leader of Tunisia's Largest Political Party*, http://www.slate.com/articles/news_and_politics/foreigners/2013/12/rachid_ghannouchi_interview_the_tunisian_leader_of_the_ennahda_party_on.html. (Quoting Rachid Ghannouchi as saying: "I believe that Tunisia will be successful in presenting a successful democratic model because we have a homogenous society, with a small Jewish minority.") *See also* Euro-Mediterranean Network for Human Rights, *The Reform of Judiciaries in the Wake of the Arab Spring*, http://www.refworld.org/pdfid/515009ac2.pdf. ("The 'Arab Spring' is not only 'Arab'. Due regard should be given to the role and contribution of the different ethnic and linguistic minorities in the region, such as Amazigh, Kurds, and many others who equally participated in the democratic uprising.")

35. *See* Clark Lombardi, *Fierce Contest: Constitutional Islam and the Arab Spring*, World Politics Rev. (Oct. 8, 2013), http://www.worldpoliticsreview.com/articles/13280/fierce-contest-constitutional-islam-and-the-arab-spring. ("The struggle between liberals and conservative Islamists often intensifies when constitutions are being drafted or amended. The Arab Spring has thus ushered in an era of fierce contest.")

36. *See Tunisia and Democratic Transition*, Global Brief (March 9, 2011).

37. *See* Judy Woodruff, *Tunisia, Birthplace of the Arab Spring, Struggles to Reset its Democracy*, PBS (Nov. 23, 2013), http://www.pbs.org/newshour/bb/world/july-dec13/tunisia_11-25.html.

38. *See* QUERINE HANLON, THE PROSPECTS FOR SECURITY SECTOR REFORM IN TUNISIA: A YEAR AFTER THE REVOLUTION (2012).

39. *See* AZIZ EL YAAKOUBI, *Tunisia Starts Voting on New Constitution*, REUTERS (Jan. 3, 2014) ("[Tunisia's] final steps to full democracy have been widely watched as a possible model in a region where Egypt, Libya and Yemen, which also ousted their leaders in 2011, are struggling with violence and instability as well as resurgent Islamism.").

40. *See* Lally Weymouth, *supra* note 34.

41. *See* United States Institute for Peace, *USIP Fact Sheet, The Current Situation in Tunisia* (Apr. 27, 2016).

42. David Pollock, *A Moroccan Exception?* J. IN'L. SECURITY AFFAIRS (Fall–Winter 2013), http://www.washingtoninstitute.org/policy-analysis/view/a-moroccan-exception

43. *Id.*

44. Anouar Boukhars, *Mauritania's Precarious Stability and Islamist Undercurrent*, Carnegie Endowment for International Peace (Feb. 11, 2016), http://carnegieendowment.org/2016/02/11/mauritania-s-precarious-stability-and-islamist-undercurrent-pub-62730

45. Christopher L. Blakesley, *Law, Language, Crime, and Culture: The Value and Risks of Comparative Law*, 49 CRIM. L. BULL. 438, 459 (2013).

References

(1881–2011). Socio-histoire d'une profession politique, Tunis/Paris 2013, IGNAZ GOLDZIHER, MUHAMMEDANISCHE STUDIEN (1889).

7 C.C. STEWART, ISLAM, IN THE CAMBRIDGE HISTORY OF AFRICA (J.D. Fage & A.D. Roberts eds., 1986).

A MODERN HISTORY OF THE ISMAILIS: CONTINUITY AND CHANGE IN A MUSLIM COMMUNITY (Farhad Daftary ed., 2010).

A. LAROUI, Moroco from the Beginning of the Nineteenth Century, in AFRICA IN THE NINETEENTH CENTURY UNTIL THE 1880s (J.F. Ade Ajayi ed., 1989).

A. SABATERY, ÉLÉMENTS DE DROIT MUSULMAN, COMPRENANT L'EXPOSÉ DE L'ORGANISATION DE LA JUSTICE DANS LE PACHALIK D'ALGER AVANT 1830, LES PRINCIPES DE DROIT CONTENUS DANS LE KORAN, CLASSÉS DANS L'ORDRE DU CODE NAPOLÉON, LA JURISPRUDENCE EN DROIT MUSULMAN DU TRIBUNAL SUPÉRIEUR ET DE LA COUR IMPÉRIALE D'ALGER DEPUIS LEUR CRÉATION (1866).

A.M. DEMANTE, PROGRAMME DU COURS DE DROIT CIVIL FRANCAIS (1833).

A.N. Yiannopoulos, The Civil Codes of Louisiana, 1 CIV. L. COMMENT. 1 (2008).

ABDUL AZIM ISLAHI, ECONOMIC THINKING OF ARAB MUSLIM WRITERS DURING THE NINETEENTH CENTURY (2016).

Abdulaziz H. Al Fahad, The Prince, the Shaykh—and the Lawyer, 32 CASE W. RES. J. INT'L L. 307, 308 (2000).

Abdulaziz H. Al-Fahad, From Exclusivism to Accommodation: Doctrinal and Legal Evolution of Wahhabism, 79 N.Y.U. L. REV. 485 (2004).

ABDULLAH ALWI HAJI HASSAN, SALES AND CONTRACTS IN EARLY ISLAMIC COMMERCIAL LAW (2007).

ABDULLAHI AHMED AN-NA'IM, TOWARD AN ISLAMIC REFORMATION: CIVIL LIBERTIES, HUMAN RIGHTS, AND INTERNATIONAL LAW (1996).

Abdul-Rahim Al-Saati, The Permissible Gharar (Risk) in Classical Islamic Jurisprudence, 16 J.KAU: ISLAMIC ECON., 3, 3, 8 (1424 A.H/2003 A.D), http://balmeena.kau.edu.sa/Files/320/Researches/50833_20970.pdf

Abdur Rahim, The Principles Of Muhammadan Jurisprudence According To The Hanafi, Maliki, Shafii And Hanbali Schools (1911).

Abū Al-ʿAbbās Ahmad B. Muhammad Ibn Kallikān et al., Ibn Khallikan's Biographical Dictionary (1843).

Abu Umar Faruq Ahmad, Theory And Practice Of Modern Islamic Finance: The Case Analysis From Australia (2010).

Abu-Muhammad Abdullah Bin Abi-Zayd & Abdur-Rahman Al-Qyrawani, The Gist Of The Treatise On Malikite Jurisprudence (1994).

Afif Gaigi, *Tunisia*, in Yearbook Of Islamic And Middle Eastern Law (1994).

Alain A. Levasseur, Louis Casimir Elisabeth Moreau-Lislet, Foster Father Of Louisiana Civil Law (1996).

Alain Levasseur, Deciphering A Civil Code: Sources Of Law And Methods Of Interpretation (2015).

Alan Watson, Roman Law & Comparative Law (1991).

Alexander Meyrick Broadley, How We Defended Arábi And His Friends: A Story Of Egypt And The Egyptians (1884).

Alfred E. von Overbeck, *Some Observations on the Role of the Judge Under the Swiss Civil Code*, 37 LA. L. REV. 684 (1977), http://digitalcommons.law.lsu.edu/lalrev/vol37/iss3/3

Ali Khan, *The Reopening of the Islamic Code: The Second Era of Ijtihad*, 1 U. ST. THOMAS L.J. 341 (2003).

Amin Hajji, *The Commercial Laws Of Morocco*, in Digest Of Commercial Laws Of The World, Digcomlaws (Patrick Tinsley & Amin Hajji eds., 2016).

Amna Arshad, *Ijtihad as a Tool for Islamic Legal Reform: Advancing Women's Rights in Morocco*, KAN. J.L. & PUB. POL'Y 129 (Winter 2006–2007).

Amr Shalakany, *Sanhuri and the Historical Origins of Comparative Law in the Arab World (Or How Sometimes Losing Your Asalah Can be Good for You)*, in Rethinking The Masters Of Comparative Law (Annelise Riles ed., 2001).

Amr. A. Shalakany, *Islamic Legal Histories*, 1 BERKELEY J. MID. E. ISLAMIC L. 1 (2008), http://scholarship.law.berkeley.edu/jmeil/vol1/iss1/1

Andra Nahal Behrouz, *Transforming Islamic Family Law: State Responsibility and the Role of Internal Initiative*, 103 COLUM. L. REV. 1136 (2003).

Andrew L. Kaufman, *Foreword to the Nature of the Judicial Process*, 1 J.L.: PERIOD. LAB. LEG. SCHOLAR. (2011).

Ann Elizabeth Mayer, *Conundrums in Constitutionalism: Islamic Monarchies in an Era of Transition*, 1 UCLA J. ISLAMIC NEAR E. L. 183 (2002).

Anouar Boukhars, *Mauritania's Precarious Stability and Islamist Undercurrent*, Carnegie Endowment for International Peace (Feb. 11, 2016), http://carnegieendowment.org/2016/02/11/mauritania-s-precarious-stability-and-islamist-undercurrent-pub-62730

Anthony G. Pazzanita, Historical Dictionary Of Mauritania (2008).

Arnold H. Green, The Tunisian Ulama 1873–1915 6–7 (1978).

Asher Susser, *The "Arab Spring": The Origins of a Misnomer*, FOREIGN POL'Y RES. INST.: E-NOTES (Apr. 2012), http://www.fpri.org/enotes/2012/201204.susser.arabspring.html

Asifa Quraishi, *On Fallibility and Finality: Why Thinking Like A Qadi Helps Me Understand American Constitutional Law*, 2009 MICH. ST. L. REV. 339 (2009).

Asifa Quraishi-Landes, *Islamic Constitutionalism: Not Secular. Not Theocratic. Not Impossible*, 16 RUTGERS J. L. REL. 553 (2015).

Asma Ghribi, *Role of Islamic Law in Tunisian Constitution Provokes Debate*, Tunisialive (Mar. 4, 2017, 3:42 PM), www.tunisia-live.net/2012/03/22/role-of-islamic-law-in-tunisian-constitution-provokes-debate/#sthash.mgLeAjgP.dpuf

AUGUSTÌN PARISE, PRIVATE LAW IN LOUISIANA: AN ACCOUNT OF CIVIL CODES, HERITAGE, AND LAW REFORM IN THE SCOPE AND STRUCTURE OF CIVIL CODES (Julio Cesar Rivera ed., 2013).

Ayman Daher, *The Shari'a: Roman Law Wearing an Islamic Veil?,* 3 HIRUNDO: MCGILL J. CLASSICAL STUD. 91 (2005).

Ayodeji K. Perrin, *Introduction to the Special Issue on the Arab Spring*, 34 U. PA. J. INT'L L. (2013).

Aziz El Yaakoubi, *Death Threats Disrupt Tunisia Constitution Debate,* REUTERS (Jan. 5, 2014).

Aziz El Yaakoubi, *Tunisia Starts Voting on New Constitution,* REUTERS (Jan. 3, 2014).

Babak Rod Khadem, *The Doctrine of Separation in Classical Islamic Jurisprudence*, 4 UCLA J. ISLAMIC NEAR E. L. 95 (2005).

BEN ATKINSON WORTLEY, JURISPRUDENCE (1967).

BENJAMIN N. CARDOZO, THE NATURE OF THE JUDICIAL PROCESS (1921).

BETTY JANE BAILEY & J. MARTIN BAILEY, WHO ARE THE CHRISTIANS IN THE MIDDLE EAST? (2003).

BOGAC A. ERGENE, QANUN AND SHARIA, IN THE ASHGATE RESEARCH COMPANION TO ISLAMIC LAW (PERI Bearman ed., 2016).

BRIAN MORRIS, RELIGION AND ANTHROPOLOGY: A CRITICAL INTRODUCTION (2006).

Brian Z. Tamanaha, *Understanding Legal Pluralism: Past to Present, Local to Global*, http://www.austlii.edu.au/au/journals/SydLawRw/2008/20.html

C. Snouk Hurgoneje, *Le Droit Musulman*, Revue de l'Histoire des Religions, 19/37 (1898).

CAMRON MICHAEL AMIN ET AL., THE MODERN MIDDLE EAST: A SOURCEBOOK FOR HISTORY (2006).

Chibli Mallat, *From Islamic to Middle Eastern Law: A Restatement of the Field (Part I)*, 51 AM. J. COMP. L. 699 (2003).

CHIBLI MALLAT, INTRODUCTION TO MIDDLE EASTERN LAW (2007).

CHIBLI MALLAT, IRAQ: GUIDE TO LAW AND POLICY (2009).

CHIBLI MALLAT, PHILOSOPHY OF NONVIOLENCE: REVOLUTION, CONSTITUTIONALISM, AND JUSTICE BEYOND THE MIDDLE EAST (2015).

CHRISTOPH BAIL, FUTURE OF NORTH-SOUTH RELATIONS (EUROPE AND THE WORLD SERIES) (1998).

CHRISTOPH MENKE, THE SOVEREIGNTY OF ART (1999).

Christopher A. Ford, *Siyar-Ization and Its Discontents: International Law and Islam's Constitutional Crisis*, 30 TEX. INT'L L.J. 499 (1995).

Christopher L. Blakesley, *Law, Language, Crime, and Culture: The Value and Risks of Comparative Law*, 49 CRIM. L. BULL. 438 (2013).

CIA *World Factbook*, Mauritania, https://www.cia.gov/library/publications/the-world-factbook/geos/mr.html

CIA *World Factbook*, Morocco, https://www.cia.gov/library/publications/the-world-factbook/geos/mo.html

CIA *World Factbook*, Tunisia, https://www.cia.gov/library/publications/the-world-factbook/geos/ts.html

Clark Lombardi, *Fierce Contest: Constitutional Islam and the Arab Spring*, World Politics Review (Oct. 8, 2013), http://www.worldpoliticsreview.com/articles/13280/fierce-contest-constitutional-islam-and-the-arab-spring

Corry Monlague Stadden, *Error of Law*, 2 COLUMBIA L. REV. 476 (1907).

DALE F. EICKELMAN, MOROCCAN ISLAM: TRADITION AND SOCIETY IN A PILGRIMAGE CENTER (2014).

Dan E. Stigall, *Comparative Law and Stability Operations: A Basic Overview and a Few Thoughts on Lésion*, COMPARATIVELAWBLOG (May 21, 2010), http://comparativelawblog.blogspot.com/2010/05/comparative-law-and-stability.html.

Dan E. Stigall, *Iraqi Civil Law: Its Sources, Substance, and Sundering*, 16 J. TRANSNAT'L L. & Pol'y 13 (2006).

DANA ZARTNER, COURTS, CODES, AND CUSTOM: LEGAL TRADITION AND STATE POLICY TOWARD INTERNATIONAL HUMAN RIGHTS AND ENVIRONMENTAL LAW (2014).

DANIEL J. SCHROETER, THE SULTAN'S JEW: MOROCCO AND THE SEPHARDI WORLD (2002).

DAVID EISENBERG, ISLAMIC FINANCE: LAW AND PRACTICE (2012).

DAVID MOTADEL, ISLAM AND THE EUROPEAN EMPIRES (2014).

David P. Doughty, *Error Revisited: The Louisiana Revision of Error as A Vice of Consent in Contracting*, 62 TUL. L. REV. 717 (1988).

David Pollock, *A Moroccan Exception?* J. INT'L. SECURITY AFFAIRS (Fall–Winter 2013), http://www.washingtoninstitute.org/policy-analysis/view/a-moroccan-exception

David Robinson, *Collaboration, Modernity and Colonial Rule: Sidiyya Baba and Mauritania,* http://aodl.org/islamicmodernity/sidiyyababa/essays/64-248-B/

DAVID SANTILLANA, AVANT-PROJET DU CODE CIVIL ET COMMERCIAL TUNISIEN (1899).

DAVID SANTILLANA, ISTITUZIONI DI DIRITTO MUSULMANO MALICHITA CON RIGUARDO ANCHE AL SISTEMA SCIAFIITA (1938).

DAVID SANTILLANA, *Law and Society, in* THE LEGACY OF ISLAM 36 (Thomas Walker Arnold, Sir & Alfred Guillaume eds., 1931).

Donna E. Arzt, *The Application of International Human Rights Law in Islamic States*, 12 Hum. RTS. Q. 202 (1990).

DR. MARJAN MUHAMMAD, HAKIMAH YAAKOB & SHABANA HASAN, THE BINDINGNESS AND ENFORCEABILITY OF A UNILATERAL PROMISE (WA'D): ANALYSIS FROM ISLAMIC LAW AND LEGAL PERSPECTIVE (2011).

DWIGHT L. LING, MOROCCO AND TUNISIA: A COMPARATIVE HISTORY (1979).

E.H. LINDO, THE JEWS OF SPAIN AND PORTUGAL (1848).

Economist, *The Islamic State of Iraq and Greater Syria: Two Arab Countries Fall Apart* (June 14, 2014), http://www.economist.com/news/middle-east-and-africa/21604230-extreme-islamist-group-seeks-create-caliphate-and-spread-jihad-across

Edith Z. Friedler, *Essay: Shakespeare's Contribution to the Teaching of Comparative Law-Some Reflections on the* Merchant of Venice, 60 LA. L. REV. 1087 (2000).

EDMUND BURKE III, THE MOROCCAN ULAMA, 1860–1912: AN INTRODUCTION, IN SCHOLARS, SAINTS, AND SUFIS: MUSLIM RELIGIOUS INSTITUTIONS IN THE MIDDLE EAST SINCE 1500 100 (Nikki R. Keddie ed., 1972).

EDMUND BURKE, III, PRELUDE TO PROTECTORATE IN MOROCCO: PRE-COLONIAL PROTEST AND RESISTANCE, 1860–1912 (2009).

EDWARD GIBBON, THE HISTORY OF THE DECLINE AND FALL OF THE ROMAN EMPIRE (Cambridge University Press, 2013).

Eric Gobe: Les avocats en Tunisie de la colonisation à la revolution (1881–2011). Socio-histoire d'une profession politique, Tunis/Paris (2013).

ERNEST GELLNER, ISLAMIC DILEMMAS: REFORMERS, NATIONALISTS, INDUSTRIALIZATION: THE SOUTHERN SHORE OF THE MEDITERRANEAN (1985).

Euro-Mediterranean Network for Human Rights, *The Reform of Judiciaries in the Wake of the Arab Spring*, http://www.refworld.org/pdfid/515009ac2.pdf

European Parliament, *Briefing: Understanding the branches of Islam: Sunni Islam* (Feb. 2016), http://www.europarl.europa.eu/RegData/etudes/brie/2016/577963/eprs_bri(2016)577963_en.pdf

F. GÉNY, *La Technique Législative dans la Codification Civile Moderne*, in LE CODE CIVIL 1804–1904, LIVRE DU CENTENAIRE (1904).

Fanack, *Chronicle of the Middle East & North Africa, Tunisia*, https://chronicle.fanack.com/tunisia/population/

FAOUZI BELKNANI, *Code Des Obligations Et Des Contrats Et La Codification*, in LIVRE DU CENTENAIRE DU CODE DES OBLIGATIONS ET DES CONTRATS 1906–2006 (2006).

FARHAD DAFTARY, INTELLECTUAL TRADITIONS IN ISLAM (2001).

FARHAT J. ZIADEH, PROPERTY LAW IN THE ARAB WORLD (1979).

FELICITAS OPWIS, *Changes in Modern Islamic Legal Theory: Reform or Reformation?* in AN ISLAMIC REFORMATION? (Michaelle Browers & Charles Kurzman ed., 2004).

Florence Renucci, *David Santillana, Acteur et Penseur des Droits Musulman et Européen*, 7 MONDE(S), May 2015.

FRANCIS FUKUYAMA, POLITICAL ORDER AND POLITICAL DECAY (2014).

FRANZ KOGELMAN, *Maghreb*, in ISLAM IN THE WORLD TODAY: A HANDBOOK OF POLITICS, RELIGION, CULTURE, AND SOCIETY 406 (2010).

French Civil Code (*Code Civil*).

GABRIEL DE LABROUE DE VAREILLES-SOMMIERES, ETUDE SUR L'ERREUR EN DROIT ROMAIN ET EN DROIT FRANCAIS (1871).

GASTON GRIOLET FRANCE ET AL., NOUVEAU CODE CIVIL: ANNOTÉ ET EXPLIQUÉ D'APRÈS LA JURISPRUDENCE ET LA DOCTRINE 964 (1905); 2 M.M. LAHAYE, WALDECK-ROUSSEAU, GIRAUDIAS, DE MORINEAU, ET FAYE, LE CODE CIVIL ANNOTÉ DES LOIS ROMAINES, DES LOIS, DÉCRETS ORDONNANCES, AVIS DU CONSEIL D'ÉTAT, DES CIRCULAIRES MINISTÉRIELLES PUBLIÉES DEPUIS SA PROMULGATION JUSQU'À NOS JOURS, ET DES OPINIONS DES AUTEURS QUI ONT ECRIT SUR LE CODE (1843).

GEORGE N. SFEIR, MODERNIZATION OF THE LAW IN ARAB STATES (1998).

GERHARD BÖWERING ET AL., THE PRINCETON ENCYCLOPEDIA OF ISLAMIC POLITICAL THOUGHT (2013).

German Civil Code (*Allgemeines Bürgerliches Gesetzbuch*).

GHISLAINE LYDON, *Inkwells of the Sahara: Reflections on the Production of Islamic Knowledge in Bilad Shinqit*, in THE TRANSMISSION OF LEARNING IN ISLAMIC AFRICA (Scott Steven Reese ed., 2004).

GHOLAMALI HADDAD ADEL ET AL., LAW: SELECTED ENTRIES FROM ENCYCLOPAEDIA OF THE WORLD OF ISLAM 128 (2013).

GLOBAL BRIEF, TUNISIA AND DEMOCRATIC TRANSITION (March 9, 2011).

GÖTZ NORDBRUCH, TRANSNATIONAL ISLAM IN INTERWAR EUROPE: MUSLIM ACTIVISTS AND THINKERS (2014).

Graziano Krätli, *The Book and the Sand: Restoring and Preserving the Ancient Desert Libraries of Mauritania—Part 1*, World Libraries 14 (Spring 2004).

Great Britain, Parliament, *House of Commons, Reports from Commissioners, Naturalization Commission*, Appendix to the Report (1869).

GUSTAV VON GRUNEBAUM, MEDIEVAL ISLAM: A STUDY IN CULTURAL ORIENTATION (1946).

H. C. GUTTERIDGE, COMPARATIVE LAW: AN INTRODUCTION TO THE COMPARATIVE METHOD OF LEGAL STUDY (2015).

H.H. Wilson, *The Relation of History to the Study and Practice of Law*, Transactions and Reports, Nebraska State Historical Society. Paper 15 (1887) http://digitalcommons.unl.edu/nebhisttrans/15

Haider Ala Hamoudi, *"Lone Wolf" Terrorism and the Classical Jihad: On the Contingencies of Violent Islamic Extremism*, 11 FIU L. REV. 19 (2015).

Haider Ala Hamoudi, *Muhammad's Social Justice or Muslim Cant?: Langdellianism and the Failures of Islamic Finance*, 40 CORNELL INT'L L.J. 89 (2007).

HAIDER ALA HAMOUDI, NEGOTIATING IN CIVIL CONFLICT: CONSTITUTIONAL CONSTRUCTION AND IMPERFECT BARGAINING IN IRAQ (2013).

Haider Ala Hamoudi, *The Death of Islamic Law*, 38 Ga. J. INT'L COMP. L. 293 (2009–2010).

HAÏM ZAFRANI, TWO THOUSAND YEARS OF JEWISH LIFE IN MOROCCO (2005).

HALIM RANE, ISLAM AND CONTEMPORARY CIVILISATION: EVOLVING IDEAS, TRANSFORMING RELATIONS (2010).

Hania Masud, *Takaful: An Innovative Approach to Insurance and Islamic Finance*, 32 U. PA. J. INT'L L. 1133 (2011).

Helen Scott, *The Requirement of Excusable Mistake in the Context of the Condictio Indebiti: Scottish and South African Law Compared*, 124 SOUTH AFR. L.J. 827 (2007).

Helmut Coing, *The Roman Law as ius commune on the Continent*, 89 L.Q.R. 505 (1973).

HENRY E. STRAKOSCH, STATE ABSOLUTISM AND THE RULE OF LAW: THE STRUGGLE FOR THE CODIFICATION OF CIVIL LAW IN AUSTRALIA 1753–1811 (1967).

HIROYUKI YANAGIHASHI, A HISTORY OF THE EARLY ISLAMIC LAW OF PROPERTY: RECONSTRUCTING THE LEGAL DEVELOPMENT, 7TH–9TH CENTURIES 117 (2004).

HIROYUKI YANAGIHASHI, *Socio-Economic Justice*, in THE ASHGATE RESEARCH COMPANION TO ISLAMIC LAW (Rudolph Peters ed., 2014).

HISHAM M. RAMADAN, UNDERSTANDING ISLAMIC LAW: FROM CLASSICAL TO CONTEMPORARY (2006).

Horacio Spector, *The Future of Legal Science in Civil Law Systems*, 65 LA. L. REV. 255 (2004).

Hossein Esmaeili, *The Nature and Development of Law in Islam and the Rule of Law Challenge in the Middle East and the Muslim World*, 26 CONN. J. INT'L L. 329 (2011).

HUGH KENNEDY, THE GREAT ARAB CONQUESTS: HOW THE SPREAD OF ISLAM CHANGED THE WORLD WE LIVE IN (2007).

IBN KHALDUN, THE MUQADDIMAH (1277).

Ignace Claeys, *Reliance as the Key for A Better Understanding of Mistake: A Belgian Law Perspective*, 12 IUS GENTIUM 1 (2006)

IGNAZ GOLDZIHER, VORLESUNGEN UHRER DEN ISLAM (1910).

IMRAN AHSAN KHAN NYAZEE, OUTLINES OF ISLAMIC JURISPRUDENCE (1998).

INDEX MUNDI, MAURITANIA, http://www.indexmundi.com/mauritania/demographics_profile.html

INSTITUT DE CARTHAGE (TUNISIA), 14 REVUE TUNISIENNE (1907).

Intisar A. Rabb, *"Reasonable Doubt" in Islamic Law*, 40 YALE J. INT'L L. 41 (2015).

Irshad Abdal-Haqq, *Islamic Law: An Overview of Its Origin and Elements*, 7 J. ISLAMIC L. CULT. 27 (2002).

Italian Civil Code (*Codice Civile*)

J. LIEBESNY, THE LAW OF THE NEAR & MIDDLE EAST (1975).

J.B. GADOLFI, CODE CIVIL DE ROYAUME D'ITALIE (1868).

J.H. VAN RIEL, THE IBĀḌĪ TRADERS OF BILĀD AL-SŪDĀN (2012).

J.N.D. ANDERSON, LAW AS A SOCIAL FORCE IN ISLAMIC CULTURE AND HISTORY (1957).

JACOB ABADIM, TUNISIA SINCE THE ARAB CONQUEST: THE SAGA OF A WESTERNIZED MUSLIM STATE (2012).

James L. Dennis, *Interpretation and Application of the Civil Code and the Evaluation of Judicial Precedent*, 54 LA. L. REV. 7 (1993), http://digitalcommons.law.lsu.edu/lalrev/vol54/iss1/5

JAMES MILLER, IMLIL: A MOROCCAN, POLITICAL QUARTERLY (MARCH 1, 1984).

JAMIL M. ABUN-NASR, A HISTORY OF THE MAGHRIB IN THE ISLAMIC PERIOD (1987).

JANE S. GERBER, JEWS OF SPAIN: A HISTORY OF THE SEPHARDIC EXPERIENCE (1994).

Jason P. Bergeron, *Watkins v. Freeway Motors-A Need to Clarify the Principle of Novation*, 58 LA. L. REV. 1241 (1998).

JEAN ETIENNE MARIE PORTALIS, PROJET DE CODE CIVIL PRÉSENTÉ PAR LA COMMISSION NOMMÉE PAR LE GOUVERNEMENT LE 24 THERMIDOR AN VIII (1801).

JEAN JOSEPH LÉANDRE BARGÈS, COMPLEMENT DE L'HISTOIRE DES BENI-ZEIYAN: ROIS DE TLEMCEN (1887).

Jean-Louis Halpérin, *The Civil Code* (trans. David Gruning); Olivier Moréteau, *Codes as Straight-Jackets, Safeguards, and Alibis: The Experience of the French Civil Code*, 20 N.C. J. INT'L COM. REG. 273 (1995).

JESWALD SALACUSE, AN INTRODUCTION TO LAW IN FRENCH-SPEAKING AFRICA, VOLUME II, NORTH AFRICA (1975).

JEWISH HISTORY SOURCEBOOK: THE EXPULSION FROM SPAIN, 1492 CE, http://www.fordham.edu/halsall/jewish/1492-jews-spain1.asp

John Cartwright et al., *The Law of Contract, The General Regime of Obligations, and Proof of Obligations, The New Provisions of the Code Civil Created by Ordonnance n° 2016—131 of 10 February 2016*, http://www.textes.justice.gouv.fr/art_pix/the-law-of-contract-2-5-16.pdf

JOHN H. TUCKER, JR., FOREWORD TO THE LOUISIANA CIVIL CODE (2004).

JOHN HENRY MERRYMAN ET AL., THE CIVIL LAW TRADITION: EUROPE, LATIN AMERICA, AND EAST ASIA (2d ed., 1994).

John Makdisi, *A Reality Check on Istihsan as a Method of Islamic Legal Reasoning*, 2 UCLA J. ISLAMIC NEAR E. L. 99 (2003).

John T. Hood, Jr., *The History and Development of the Louisiana Civil Code,* 19 LA. L. REV. (1958), http://digitalcommons.law.lsu.edu/lalrev/vol19/iss1/14

JONATHAN A. C. BROWN, HADITH: OXFORD BIBLIOGRAPHIES ONLINE RESEARCH GUIDE (2010).

Jonathan Di John, *Conceptualising the Causes and Consequences of Failed States: A Critical Review of the Literature* (Crisis States Res. Ctr., Working Paper No. 25, 2008).

JONATHAN KIRSCH, *Foreword* to DOLORES SLOAN, THE SEPHARDIC JEWS OF SPAIN AND PORTUGAL: SURVIVAL OF AN IMPERILED CULTURE IN THE FIFTEENTH AND SIXTEENTH CENTURIES (2009).

Joseph Dainow, *The Early Sources of Forced Heirship: Its History in Texas and Louisiana,* 4 LA. L. REV. 60 (1941).

JOSEPH SCHACHT, AN INTRODUCTION TO ISLAMIC LAW (1982).

JUAN EDUARDO CAMPO, ENCYCLOPEDIA OF ISLAM (2009).

Judy Woodruff, *Tunisia, Birthplace of the Arab Spring, Struggles to Reset its Democracy*, PBS (Nov. 23, 2013), http://www.pbs.org/newshour/bb/world/july-dec13/tunisia_11-25.html

JULIA CLANCY-SMITH, NORTH AFRICA, ISLAM AND THE MEDITERRANEAN WORLD: FROM THE ALMORAVIDS TO THE ALGERIAN WAR (2013).

Julie Klein, *Observations et Propositions de Modifications*, LA SEMAINE JURIDIQUE, EDITION GENERALE, SUPP. N. 21 (Mai 25, 2015).

JULIUS CESAR RIVERA, *The Scope and Structure of Civil Codes: Relations with Commercial Law, Family Law, Consumer Law and Private International Law, in* THE SCOPE AND STRUCTURE OF CIVIL CODES (Julio Cesar Rivera ed., 2013).

Kalidou Gadio, *Codification and Modernization of Law: A Case Study of Mauritania* (April 30, 1987) (unpublished J.D. thesis, Harvard Law School).

KEITH WALTERS, *Education For Jewish Girls In Late Nineteenth And Early Twentieth Century Tunis And The Spread Of French In Tunisia, in* JEWISH CULTURE AND SOCIETY IN NORTH AFRICA (Emily Benichou Gottreich & Daniel J. Schroeter eds., 2011).

Khaled Abou El Fadl, *Muslims and Accessible Jurisprudence in Liberal Democracies: A Response to Edward B. Foley's Jurisprudence and Theology*, 66 FORDHAM L. REV. 1227 (1998).

Khaled Ali Beydoun, *Dar al-Islam Meets "Islam As Civilization": An Alignment of Politico-Theoretical Fundamentalisms and the Geopolitical Realism of This Worldview*, 4 UCLA J. ISLAMIC NEAR E. L. 143 (2005).

Khaled Benjelayel, *Islamic Contract Law* (Mar. 10, 2012), https://ssrn.com/abstract=2019550 or http://dx.doi.org/10.2139/ssrn.2019550

KONRAD ZWEIGERT & HEIN KÖTZ, AN INTRODUCTION TO COMPARATIVE LAW (Tony Weir trans., 1998).

L. Messaoudi, Grandeurs et limites du droit musulman au Maroc, 47 REV. INT'L. DE DROIT COMPARÉ (Janvier–Mars 1995).

L. Messaoudi, *Grandeurs et limites du droit musulman au Maroc*, 47 REV. INT'L. DE DROIT COMPARÉ (Janvier–Mars 1995).

Lally Weymouth, *The Arab Spring's Last Hope: An Interview with Rachid Ghannouchi, the Leader of Tunisia's Largest Political Party*, Slate.com (2013), http://www.slate.com/articles/news_and_politics/foreigners/2013/12/rachid_ghannouchi_interview_the_tunisian_leader_of_the_ennahda_party_on.html

Lama Abu-Odeh, *Modernizing Muslim Family Law: The Case of Egypt*, 37 VAND. J. TRANSNAT'L L. 1043 (2004).

Lawrence Ponoroff, *The Dubious Role of Precedent in the Quest for First Principles in the Reform of the Bankruptcy Code: Some Lessons from the Civil Law and Realist Traditions*, 74 AM. BANKR. L.J. 173 (2000).

Layton B. Register, *Judicial Powers of Interpretation Under Foreign Codes*, 65 U. PA. L. REV. 39 (1916), http://scholarship.law.upenn.edu/cgi/viewcontent.cgi?article=7600&context=penn_law_review

Leistungsangebot | *Advisory Service, Governance and Democracy, Law and Justice*, https://www.giz.de/de/downloads/giz2011-en-law-justice.pdf

LEON CARL BROWN, THE RELIGIOUS ESTABLISHMENT IN HUSSAINID TUNISIA, IN SCHOLARS, SAINTS, AND SUFIS: MUSLIM RELIGIOUS INSTITUTIONS IN THE MIDDLE EAST SINCE 1500 (Nikki R. Keddie ed., 1972).

LEON CARL BROWN, THE TUNISIA OF AHMAD BEY, 1837–1855 (2015).

Léon Julliot de la Morandière, *The Draft of a New French Civil Code: The Role of the Judge*, 69 HARV. L. REV. 1264 (1956).

Liaquat Ali Khan, *Jurodynamics of Islamic Law*, 61 RUTGERS L. REV. 231 (2009).

Library of Congress, *Islamic Law in Transitioning Arab Spring Countries Subject of June 4 Program*, http://www.loc.gov/today/pr/2013/13-091.html

Libyan Civil Code (Jarida al-Rasmiyah, 13 Feb. 1954).

LISA ANDERSON, THE STATE AND SOCIAL TRANSFORMATION IN TUNISIA AND LIBYA, 1830–1980 (1986).

LISBET CHRISTOFFERSEN & JØRGEN S. NIELSEN, SHARI'A AS DISCOURSE: LEGAL TRADITIONS AND THE ENCOUNTER WITH EUROPE (2016).

Loi n° 2005-87 du 15 août 2005, portant approbation de la réorganisation de certaines dispositions du "code des obligations et des contrats tunisien."

Loredana Maccabruni, A Treaty Between the Regency of Tunis and the Grand Duchy of Tuscany, Concerning the Jurisdition Over Tuscan Jews Migrated to Tunisia in "Sharing History", Museum with no Frontiers (2016) http://www.sharinghistory.org/database_item.php?id=object;AWE;it;126;en)

Louisiana Civil Code.

Louisiana Digest of 1808.

M. Cherif Bassiouni & Gamal M. Badr, *The Shari'ah: Sources, Interpretation, and Rule-Making*, 1 UCLA J. ISLAMIC NEAR E. L. 135 (2002).

M. Cherif Bassiouni et al., *Reporter, Islamic Law A Survey of Islamic International Law Contracts and Litigation in Islamic Law the Sources of Islamic Law*, 76 AM. SOC'Y INT'L L. PROC. 55 (1982).

M. Kevin Queenan, *Civil Code Article 2324: A Broken Path to Limited Solidary Liability*, 49 LA. L. REV. 1351 (1989).

M. Mohamed Kamel Charfeddine, *Esquisse sur la méthode normative retenue dans l'élaboration du Code tunisien des obligations et des contrats*, 48 REV. INT'L. DE DROIT COMPARÉ 421 (1996).

M.L. Larombière, *1 Théorie et pratique des obligations ou Commentaire des titres III et IV livre III du code civil, art. 1101 à 1386* (1862).

M.O. Salah, *Quelques Aspects de la Réception du Droit Français en Mauritanie*, 5 REV. MAURITANIENNE DE DROIT ET D'ÉCON. 25 (1989).

Maaike Voorhoeve, *Judges in a Web of normative Orders: Judicial Practices at the Court of First Instance Tunis in the Field of Divorce Law* (2011) (Ph.D. dissertation, University of Amsterdam).

MAHMOUD A. EL-GAMAL, ISLAMIC FINANCE: LAW, ECONOMICS, AND PRACTICE (2006).

MAJALLAH EL-AHKAM-I-ADLIYA (THE MEJELLE), *translated in* THE MEJELLE: AN ENGLISH TRANSLATION OF MAJALLAH EL-AHKAM-I-ADLIYA AND A COMPLETE CODE OF ISLAMIC CIVIL LAW (C.R. Tyser et al. trans., 2001).

MAJID KHADDURI & HERBERT J. LIEBESNY, ORIGIN AND DEVELOPMENT OF ISLAMIC LAW (1955).

MAJID KHADDURI, TRANS., INTRODUCTION TO MUḤAMMAD IBN-AL-ḤASAN AŠ- ŠAIBĀNĪ, THE ISLAMIC LAW OF NATIONS: SHAYBANI'S SIYAR (1966).

MAJID KHADDURI, WAR AND PEACE IN THE LAW OF ISLAM (1966).

MARC LYNCH, THE ARAB UPRISING: THE UNFINISHED REVOLUTIONS OF THE NEW MIDDLE EAST (2012).

Maria Luisa Murilla, *The Evolution of Codification in the Civil Law Legal Systems: Towards Decodification and Recodification*, 11 J. TRANSNAT'L L. POL'Y (2001).

MARK AVRUM EHRLICH, ENCYCLOPEDIA OF THE JEWISH DIASPORA: ORIGINS, EXPERIENCES, AND CULTURE (2009).

Mark L. Movsesian, *Elusive Equality: The Armenian Genocide and the Failure of Ottoman Legal Reform*, 4 U. ST. THOMAS J.L. & PUB. POL'Y 1 (2010).

Mark Wakim, *Public Policy Concerns Regarding Enforcement of Foreign International Arbitral Awards in the Middle East*, 21 N.Y. INT'L L. REV. 1 (2008).

MARY ANN GLENDON, PAOLO G. CAROZZA & COLIN B. PICKER, COMPARATIVE LEGAL TRADITIONS: TEXT, MATERIALS, AND CASES ON WESTERN LAW (3d ed. 2007).

Mathias M. Siems, *Legal Origins: Reconciling Law & Finance and Comparative Law*, 52 MCGILL L.J. 55 (2007).

MATTHEW C. STEPHENSON, JUDICIAL REFORM IN DEVELOPING ECONOMIES: CONSTRAINTS AND OPPORTUNITIES, IN ANNUAL WORLD BANK CONFERENCE ON DEVELOPMENT ECONOMICS: BEYOND TRANSITION 311–28 (Francois Bourguignon & Boris Pleskovic eds., 2007), http://www.law.harvard.edu/faculty/mstephenson/pdfsNEW/Judicial-ReformABCDE.pdf

MATTI BOUABID, PREFACE TO FRANÇOIS PAUL BLANC, CODE ANNOTÉ DES OBLIGATIONS ET DES CONTRATS: LES OBLIGATIONS (1981).

MAURICE SHELDON AMOS & FREDERICK PARKER WALTON, INTRODUCTION TO FRENCH LAW (1963).

Mauritanian Code of Civil, Commercial, and Administrative Procedure, Law No. 62-052 of February 2, 1962, Jorim, Sep. 19, 1962.

Mauritanian Code of Obligations and Contracts (Ordonnance n°89-126 du 14 September 1989).

Melanie D. Reed, *Western Democracy and Islamic Tradition: The Application of Shari'a in A Modern World*, 19 AM. U. INT'L L. REV. 485 (2004).

Michael B. North, *Qui Facit Per Alium, Facit Per Se: Representation, Mandate, and Principles of Agency in Louisiana at the Turn of the Twenty-First Century*, 72 TUL. L. REV. 279 (1997).

MICHAEL E. BONINE, *Waqf And Its Influence On The Built Environment In The Medina*, in URBAN SPACE IN THE MIDDLE AGES AND THE EARLY MODERN AGE (Albrecht Classen ed., 2009).

Michael H. Rubin, *Bailment and Deposit in Louisiana*, 35 LA. L. REV. 825 (1975).

MICHAEL MAAS, READINGS IN LATE ANTIQUITY: A SOURCEBOOK (2012).

MICHAEL WILLIS, POLITICS AND POWER IN THE MAGHREB: ALGERIA, TUNISIA AND MOROCCO FROM INDEPENDENCE TO THE ARAB SPRING (2014).

MIREILLE DELMAS-MARTY, ORDERING PLURALISM: A CONCEPTUAL FRAMEWORK FOR UNDERSTANDING THE TRANSNATIONAL LEGAL WORLD (2009).

Mission scientifique du Maroc, 13 REV. DU MONDE MUSULMAN (1974).

Mohammad Fadel, *Islamic Politics and Secular Politics: Can They Co-Exist?* 25 J.L. REL. 187 (2010).

MOHAMMED JALAL ESSAID, INTRODUCTION A L'ETUDE DU DROIT (5ème ed., 2014).

Moroccan Code of Obligations and Contracts (Sep. 12, 1913) formant code des obligations et des contrats).

Mounira M. Charrad, *Tunisia at the Forefront of the Arab World: Two Waves of Gender Legislation,* 64 WASH. LEE L. REV. 1513 (2007).

MUHAMMAD MUNIR, ISLAMIC INTERNATIONAL LAW (SIYAR): AN INTRODUCTION, HAMDARD ISLAMICUS (2012), http://works.bepress.com/muhammad_munir/21/

MUHAMMAD-BASHEER A. ISMAIL, ISLAMIC LAW AND TRANSNATIONAL DIPLOMATIC LAW: A QUEST FOR COMPLEMENTARITY IN DIVERGENT LEGAL THEORIES 45–46 (2016).

N.J. COULSON, A HISTORY OF ISLAMIC LAW (2011).

Nabil Saleh, *Civil Codes of Arab Countries: The Sanhuri Codes*, 8 ARAB L.Q. 161 (1993).

NADHIR BEN AMMOU, *L'avant Propos De L'avant-Projet De Code Civil Et Commercial Tunisien*, in LIVRE DU CENTENAIRE DU CODE DES OBLIGATIONS ET DES CONTRATS 1906–2006 (Mohamed Kamel Charfeggine ed., 2006).

Nasim M. Soosa, *The Historical Interpretation of the Origin of the Capitulations in the Ottoman Empire*, 4 TEMP. L. Q. 360 (1929–1930).

NICOLE SOULETIE, LE MOT DE MADAME NICOLE SOULETIE IN LE CENTENAIRE DU DAHIR FORMANT CODE DES OBLIGATIONS ET CONTRATS (DOC) 1913–2013 (2013).

NORA LAFI, *Challenging The Ottoman Pax Urbana: Intercommunal Clashes In 1857 Tunis*, in VIOLENCE AND THE CITY IN THE MODERN MIDDLE EAST (Nelida Fuccaro ed., 2016).

Norman Bentwich, *The End of the Capitulatory System*, 14 BRIT. Y.B. INT'L L. 89 (1933).

Office of the Geographer, Bureau of Intelligence and Research, International Boundary Study, No. 78–July 15, 1967, Mauritania–Senegal Boundary (Country Codes: MR-SN).

OLIVER EATON BODINGTON, AN OUTLINE OF THE FRENCH LAW OF EVIDENCE (1904).

OMAR AZZIMAN, LA TRADITION JURIDIQUE ISLAMIQUE DANS L'ÉVOLUTION DU DROIT PRIVÉ MAROCAIN (1992).

OULD MOHAMED SALAH, DROITS DES CONTRATS EN MAURITANIE (1996).

Ousmane Kane, Non-Europhone Intellectuals (2012).

OXFORD ENCYCLOPEDIA OF THE ISLAMIC WORLD (John Esposito ed.) Oxford Islamic Studies Online (2008), http://www.oxfordislamicstudies.com, 2008

Oxford Islamic Studies Online, http://www.oxfordislamicstudies.com/article/opr/t125/e990

Pablo Lerner, *Promises of Rewards in a Comparative Perspective*, 10 ANNU. SURVEY INT'L. COMPARATIVE L. 53 (2004).

Patrick N. Broyles, *Intercontinental Identity: The Right to the Identity in the Louisiana Civil Code*, 65 LA. L. REV. 823 (2005).

PAUL DECROUX, LE DROIT DES SOCIÉTÉS DANS LE MAROC MODERNE (1961).

Paul Schiff Berman, *Global Legal Pluralism*, 80 S. CAL. L. REV. 1155 (2007).

PETER EMILIUS HERTZOG, CIVIL PROCEDURE IN FRANCE (1967).

PIERRE-ANTOINE FENE, RECUEIL COMPLET DES TRAVAUX PRÉPARATOIRES DU CODE CIVIL 368 (1827).

PLANIOL, TRAITÉ ÉLÉMENTAIRE DE DROIT CIVIL (9th ed., 1923).

PR. RADIA BOUHLAL, *Le DOC a L'Epreuve du Temps*, in LE CENTENAIRE DU DAHIR FORMANT CODE DES OBLIGATIONS ET CONTRATS (DOC) 1913–2013 (2013).

Proceedings of the Degree Ceremony: The Honorable John R. Brown, Doctor of Laws, 54 TUL. L. REV. 263 (1980).

QUERINE HANLON, THE PROSPECTS FOR SECURITY SECTOR REFORM IN TUNISIA: A YEAR AFTER THE REVOLUTION (2012).

R. G. Surridge & Rebecca Matthews, Extraterritoriality—A Vanishing Institution, 3 CUM. DIG.

Rahal Boubrik, *Traditional 'Men of Religion' and Political Power in Mauritania,* ISIM NEWSLETTER, Feb. 2, 1999.

RAJ BHALA, UNDERSTANDING ISLAMIC LAW (2011).

RAJA SAKRANI, AU CROISEMENT DES CULTURES DE DROIT OCCIDENTALE ET MUSULMANE: LE PLURALISME JURIDIQUE DANS LE CODE TUNISIEN DES OBLIGATIONS ET DES CONTRATS (2009).

RAKESH KUMAR SINGH, TEXTBOOK ON MUSLIM LAW (2011).

RAPHAEL CHIJIOKE NJOKU, CULTURE AND CUSTOMS OF MOROCCO (2006).

REUTERS, *Tunisia Opts for Civil, not Sharia Law as Assembly Votes on New Constitution* (Jan. 5, 2014), http://rt.com/news/tunisia-rejects-islam-law-196/

ROBERT A. DOWD, CHRISTIANITY, ISLAM, AND LIBERAL DEMOCRACY: LESSONS FROM SUB-SAHARAN AFRICA (2015).

ROBERT EARL HANDLOFF, MAURITANIA, A COUNTRY STUDY (1990).

ROBERT ESTOUBLON, REVUE ALGÉRIENNE, TUNISIENNE ET MAROCAINE DE LÉGISLATION ET DE JURISPRUDENCE (1907).

Robert L. Theriot, *An Examination of the Role of Delivery in the Transfer of Ownership and Risk in Sales Under Louisiana Law*, 60 TUL. L. REV. 1035 (1986).

Ronald J. Scalise Jr., *Why No "Efficient Breach" in the Civil Law?: A Comparative Assessment of the Doctrine of Efficient Breach of Contract*, 55 AM. J. COMP. L. 721 (2007).

Ronald J. Scalise, Jr., *Rethinking the Doctrine of Nullity*, 74 La. L. Rev. 663 (2014).

Roscoe Pound, *Sources and Forms of Law*, 21 NOTRE DAME L. REV. 247 (1946), http://scholarship.law.nd.edu/ndlr/vol21/iss4/1

Roscoe Pound, *The Influence of the Civil Law in America*, 1 LA. L. REV. 4 (1938), http://digitalcommons.law.lsu.edu/lalrev/vol1/iss1/14

SADEK HAMID, SUFIS, SALAFIS AND ISLAMISTS: THE CONTESTED GROUND OF BRITISH ISLAMIC ACTIVISM (2016).

SAHAR BAZZAZ, FORGOTTEN SAINTS: HISTORY, POWER, AND POLITICS IN THE MAKING OF MODERN MOROCCO (2010).

SAMUEL R. THOMAS, SEEKING THE SAINT, FINDING COMMUNITY: CELEBRATING THE HILLULA OF BABA SALI IN RELIGIOUS DIVERSITY TODAY: EXPERIENCING RELIGION IN THE CONTEMPORARY WORLD: EXPERIENCING RELIGION IN THE CONTEMPORARY WORLD (2015).

SANDRA F. JOIREMAN, COLONIZATION AND THE RULE OF LAW: COMPARING THE EFFECTIVENESS OF COMMON LAW AND CIVIL LAW COUNTRIES (2004), http://scholarship.richmond.edu/polisci-faculty-publications/64

SARAH ABREVAYA STEIN, EXTRATERRITORIAL DREAMS: EUROPEAN CITIZENSHIP, SEPHARDI JEWS, AND THE OTTOMAN TWENTIETH CENTURY (2016).

SAUL LITVINOFF, LOUISIANA CIVIL LAW TREATISE, THE LAW OF OBLIGATIONS (2001).

Saul Litvinoff, *Vices of Consent, Error, Fraud, Duress, and an Epilogue on Lesion*, 50 LA. L. REV. 1 (1989).

Sayyid Mohsen Sa'idzadeh, *Fiqh and Fiqahat*, 1 UCLA J. ISLAMIC NEAR E. L. 239 (2002).

Seán Patrick Donlan, *The Mediterranean Hybridity Project: Crossing the Boundaries of Law and Culture*, 4 J. CIV. L. STUD. (2011).

Shameem Akhtar, *An Inquiry into the Nature, Origin and Source of Islamic Law of Nations*, 6 KARACHI L.J. 63 (1970).

SIDY MOHAMED SECK, LES CULTIVATEURS "TRANSFRONTALIERS" DE DÉCRUE A LA QUESTIONS FONCIÈRE IN LA VALLÉE DU FLEUVE SÉNÉGAL: EVALUATIONS ET PERSPECTIVES D'UNE DÉCENNIE D'AMÉNAGEMENTS, 1980–1990 297(1991). See Also JEFFREY WHITE, RURAL TRANSITION: AGRICULTURAL DEVELOPMENT AND TENURE RIGHTS: A CASE STUDY IN THE SENEGAL RIVER VALLEY (2000).

STÉPHANE PAPI, L'INFLUENCE JURIDIQUE ISLAMIQUE AU MAGHREB (2009).

Stephen Cory, *Breaking the Khaldunian Cycle? The Rise of Sharifianism as the Basis for Political Legitimacy in Early Modern Morocco* (2008). History Faculty Publications, http://engagedscholarship.csuohio.edu/clhist_facpub/83

Stephen S. Zimowski, *Consequences of the Arab Spring: How Shari'ah Law and the Egyptian Revolution Will Impact Ip Protection and Enforcement*, 2 PENN ST. J.L. & INT'L AFF. 150 (2013).

SUSAN GILSON MILLER, A HISTORY OF MODERN MOROCCO (2013).

Swiss Civil Code, https://www.admin.ch/opc/en/classified-compilation/19070042/201604010000/210.pdf.

Syrian Civil Code (Decret No. 84 du 15 mai 1949).

The Berkley Center for Religion, Peace, and World Affairs, *Tunisia: From the Roman Empire to Ottoman Rule*, http://berkleycenter.georgetown.edu/essays/tunisia-from-the-roman-empire-to-ottoman-rule

The Qur'an

The Telegraph, *Mauritanian President Overthrown in Bloodless Military Coup* (Aug. 3, 2005), http://www.telegraph.co.uk/news/1495419/Mauritanian-president-overthrown-in-bloodless-military-coup.html

THEODORE MORISON, *Can Islam be Reformed?* in THE NINETEENTH CENTURY AND AFTER (1908).

Timur Kuran, *The Economic Ascent of the Middle East's Religious Minorities: The Role of Islamic Legal Pluralism*, 33 J. LEGAL STUD. 475 (2004).

TIMUR KURAN, THE LONG DIVERGENCE: HOW ISLAMIC LAW HELD BACK THE MIDDLE EAST (2012).

Traité pour L'organisation du Protectorat Français dans L'empire Chérifien (Fès, Mars 30, 1912), http://mjp.univ-perp.fr/constit/ma1912.htm

Transcon. Gas Pipe Line Corp. v. Transp. Ins. Co., 953 F.2d 985,988 (5th Cir. 1992).

TROPLONG, COMMENTAIRE DU PRÊT, DU DÉPÔT, DU SEQUESTRE ET DES CONTRATS ALÉATOIRES (1845).

Tunisian Code of Obligations and Contracts (Code des Obligations et des Contrats [Conformément à la loi n° 2005-87 du 15 août 2005])

UC Berkley School of Law, *Roman Legal Tradition and the Compilation of Justinian.* https://www.law.berkeley.edu/library/robbins/pdf/RomanLegalTradition.pdf

UN-HABITAT, ISLAM, LAND & PROPERTY RESEARCH SERIES, PAPER 6: ISLAMIC INHERITANCE LAWS AND SYSTEMS (2005).

United Nations, Statute of the International Court of Justice, 18 April 1946, Article 38,: http://www.refworld.org/docid/3deb4b9c0.html

United States Institute for Peace, *USIP Fact Sheet, The Current Situation in Tunisia* (Apr. 27, 2016).

University of London SOAS, *Centre of Islamic and Middle Eastern Law (CIMEL)*, http://www.soas.ac.uk/cimel/

VALERIE J. HOFFMAN, THE ESSENTIALS OF IBADI ISLAM (2012).

VANDENHOECK & RUPRECHT, WORLD PEACE THROUGH CHRISTIAN-MUSLIM UNDERSTANDING: THE GENESIS AND FRUITS OF THE OPEN LETTER "A COMMON WORD BETWEEN US AND YOU" (2016).

VELYN BARING, MODERN EGYPT (1911).

Vernon Valentine Palmer, *"May God Protect Us from the Equity of Parlements": Comparative Reflections on English and French Equity Power*, 73 TUL. L. REV. 1287 (1999).

WAEL B. HALLAQ, AN INTRODUCTION TO ISLAMIC LAW 16 (2009).

WAEL B. HALLAQ, THE ORIGINS AND EVOLUTION OF ISLAMIC LAW (2005).

WERNER MINSKI, COMPARATIVE LAW IN GLOBAL CONTEXT: THE LEGAL SYSTEMS OF ASIA AND AFRICA (2006).

WILLIAM BLACKSTONE, COMMENTARIES (1809).

WILLIAM L. BURDICK, THE PRINCIPLES OF ROMAN LAW AND THEIR RELATION TO MODERN LAW (1938).

William Tetley, *Mixed Jurisdictions: Common Law v. Civil Law (Codified and Uncodified)*, 60 LA. L. REV. 677 (2000).

Woodrow Wilson Ctr., *U.S. Intelligence: Arab Spring Generated Threats* (Mar. 15, 2013), http://www.wilsoncenter.org/islamists/article/us-intelligence-arab-spring-generated-threats

YALE STROM, THE EXPULSION OF THE JEWS: FIVE HUNDRED YEARS OF EXODUS 143 (1992).

YASIN DUTTON, THE ORIGINS OF ISLAMIC LAW: THE QUR'AN, THE MUWATTA, AND MADINAN 'AMAL (2002).

Yasir Billoo, *Change and Authority in Islamic Law: The Islamic Law of Inheritance in Modern Muslim States,* 84 U. DET. MERCY L. REV. 637 (2007).

YUSUF AL HAJJ AHMED, FINANCIAL TRANSACTIONS IN ISLAM: ENCYCLOPAEDIA OF ISLAMIC LAW (2014).

YUSUF AL-QARADAWI, APPROACHING THE SUNNAH: COMPREHENSION & CONTROVERSY (2007).

Yvon Loussouarn, *The Relative Importance of Legislation, Custom, Doctrine, and Precedent in French Law*, 18 LA. L. REV. 236 (1958), http://digitalcommons.law. lsu.edu/lalrev/vol18/iss2/2

Zekeria Ould Ahmed Salem, *Les mutations paradoxales de l'islamisme en Mauritanie, Cahiers d'études africaines*, No. 206–207 (2012).

ZELEZECK NGUIMATSA SERGE, RESEARCHING THE LEGAL SYSTEM AND LAWS OF THE ISLAMIC REPUBLIC OF MAURITANIA (2009), http://www.nyulawglobal.org/globalex/Mauritania.html.

Index

About the Author

Dan E. Stigall is an attorney with the National Security Division of the U.S. Department of Justice (DOJ), where he has served as a counterterrorism prosecutor and Counsel for Counterterrorism Policy to the Assistant Attorney General. From 2009–2015, he worked as a Trial Attorney and Coordinator for International Security Affairs with the DOJ Office of International Affairs. In that capacity, he focused on international cooperation with countries in Africa, Asia, and the Middle East (including Tunisia, Morocco, and Mauritania). He previously served on active duty as a U.S. Army Judge Advocate (JAG) from 2001–2009, serving in Europe, the Middle East, and the United States. He has also served as an Adjunct Professor of International Law at The Judge Advocate General's Legal Center and School (U.S. Army) and continues to serve as an officer in the U.S. Army Reserves. In addition, he is a Contributing Fellow for the Louisiana State University Center for Civil Law Studies.